JERRY SEINFELD

The Entire Domain

Kathleen Tracy

A Birch Lane Press Book
Published by Carol Publishing Group

Copyright © 1998 Kathleen Tracy

All rights reserved. No part of this book may be reproduced in any form, except by a newspaper or magazine reviewer who wishes to quote brief passages in connection with a review.

A Birch Lane Press Book
Published by Carol Publishing Group
Birch Lane Press is a registered trademark of Carol Communications, Inc.

Editorial, sales and distribution, rights and permissions inquiries should be addressed to Carol Publishing Group, 120 Enterprise Avenue, Secaucus, N.J. 07094

In Canada: Canadian Manda Group, One Atlantic Avenue, Suite 105, Toronto, Ontario M6K 3E7

Carol Publishing books may be purchased in bulk at special discounts for sales promotion, fund-raising, or educational purposes. Special editions can be created to specifications. For details, contact: Special Sales Department, Carol Publishing Group, 120 Enterprise Avenue, Secaucus, N.J. 07094.

Manufactured in the United States of America
10 9 8 7 6 5 4 3 2 1

Library of Congress Cataloging-in-Publication Data

Tracy, Kathleen.
    Jerry Seinfeld : the entire domain / by Kathleen Tracy.
        p.   cm.
    Includes index.
    ISBN 1-55972-474-9
    1. Seinfeld, Jerry.   2. Comedians—United States—Biography.   3. Television actors and actresses—United States—Biography.   4. Seinfeld.   I. Title.
PN2287.S345T73   1998
791.45′028′3—dc21
    [B]   98-7770
                                                                                   CIP

To Valerie:

For supplying me with press releases, encouragement—
and tequila shots.

—KT

CONTENTS

INTRODUCTION

THERE'S AN INTERESTING PARADOX BETWEEN JERRY SEINFELD THE COMEdian and *Seinfeld* the show. While there is a legion of fans and critics who argue that *Seinfeld* is the best television comedy ever to beam into the living rooms of America, the same has seldom been said about Jerry's place in the pantheon of stand-up history.

Although Seinfeld enjoyed success as a stand-up comedian prior to the debut of his series, he was but one of a number of almost interchangeable comics whose acts were based on observational humor. While Jerry may have had one of the funnier stand-up routines, there was nothing particularly distinguished about him. His observations didn't reflect the social conscience and anger of a Lenny Bruce or Richard Pryor; he didn't seek to offend the sensibilities of women à la Andrew Dice Clay; he wasn't the master of the ethnic, *ba-da-bum*, old-time shtick of Jackie Mason or the king of insults in the tradition of Don Rickles.

Seinfeld's stand-up persona didn't seek to attract attention by pushing any envelope; his only goal was to make people laugh, primarily by obsessing, often with contempt, over the vagaries of the post-Baby Boom, pre–Generation X age group that had become known as yuppies. Seinfeld could create a classic commentary about something as mundane as a parakeet:

> *I had a parakeet when I was a kid. I'd let him out of his cage, he'd fly around the room, and BANG! with his little head, right into the mirror. And I'd always think, "Even if he thinks the mirror is another room, why doesn't he at least try to avoid hitting the other parakeet?"*

However, most of his humor was a mirror reflecting back, well, nothing from his soul. The best stand-up comedy shines a light on deeper, universal truths. Lily Tomlin's one-woman shows not only had people laughing so hard they cried; it was the poignancy of her characters and their place in the world today that stayed firmly etched in the mind and heart when one remembered the show hours, days, or even years later.

Seinfeld the stand-up has never tried to provoke such cerebration. The joke's the thing, and to some critics his style of segueing from one disparate topic to another is simply an excuse to be self-obsessed without ever being self-analytic.

Ironically, the biggest knock on his stand-up approach is precisely what has made *Seinfeld* one of the most popular shows in television history. For while a comedian alone in the spotlight of a club reveling in superficial, self-centered minutiae might leave an audience smiling but unmoved, a well-written, daring sitcom that revolves around a cast of characters who never evolve as people and never advance in life is not only funny; it makes us feel better about ourselves.

The genius of *Seinfeld* is that it allows us to laugh at the worst in ourselves, as exemplified by George's misery, Elaine's self-centeredness, Kramer's idiot-savant childishness, and Jerry's snide irony and emotional distance. They are the kind of people we avoid like the plague in real life and the pretend friends we love to invite into our homes for half an hour a week in order to live vicariously through their "I am the center of my universe" antics.

The genius of Seinfeld the comic was to realize how well his stand-up act would translate to television and the channel-surfing mentality of modern viewers and to be daring enough to create a show with no redeeming social "values" except to be funny, innovative, and willing to fail in the attempt.

Whereas Seinfeld the stand-up never managed to distinguish himself as a bona-fide comic innovator, *Seinfeld* the series has bcome a unique paradigm of 1990s pop culture. While Seinfeld may not be the defining comic voice of his generation, *Seinfeld* will forever typify a certain self-obsessed facet of the premillennium American social character.

Since it is impossible to separate the life of Seinfeld from his series masterwork—exactly who Jerry Seinfeld is determined what *Seinfeld* would be—this book will examine and explore both in detail in an effort to gain insight into the man behind the series and the series itself, which will likely be his most lasting professional legacy. It will be up to the reader to decide the extent to which what we see on-screen reveals the private person, away from the camera, although Julia Louis-Dreyfus offered a telling anecdote about the time the cast gave Jerry a plaque to wear around his neck that said IN CHARACTER on one side and OUT OF CHARACTER on the other: "We're never sure which side should be showing."

JERRY SEINFELD

1

The Kid Who
Collected Cosby

ALTHOUGH BABY BOOMERS TEND TO BE CLUMPED TOGETHER AS ONE ENtity, there's a dramatic difference between the early Boomers and the children born toward the end of America's population growth spurt. Those who were born in the late 1940s and grew up in the 1950s were shaped by a time of unprecedented prosperity in our country and the political conservatism of the era. Those born in the mid- to late 1950s were primarily shaped by television and its ability to transmit pop culture daily into our homes.

These youngsters would be the first generation to replace pretend friends with broadcast playmates. Instead of having to go outside and interact with others in a game of cowboys and Indians, cops and robbers, or angels and devils, children only needed to turn on the television to be transported to another place and time. Among the kids who spent a significant number of hours in front of the television week in and week out was the young Jerry Seinfeld.

Thanks to television, he discovered Abbott and Costello. When he was about five, Channel 11 in New York began airing syndicated reruns of the comedy team's 1952 half-hour show. It's his earliest remembrance of being moved by laughter.

"They were a seminal influence in my life," Jerry recalls. "They made me fall in love with the idea of being funny. I loved them more than anything. I also idolized Jerry Lewis as a child. His name is

Jerry and my name is Jerry, and I think we look a little alike, and he was so funny and I wanted to be funny. In 1997 I appeared on the telethon," Jerry said, referring to Lewis's annual muscular dystrophy telethon. "It was one of the greatest moments of my career."

By the time he was eight, Seinfeld would plan his week around when his favorite comedians were going to be on television, which made *The Ed Sullivan Show* his first personal must-see TV. Jerry would sit mesmerized, studying and absorbing the comedians' timing and stage techniques.

"I thought they were the most amazing people I'd ever seen," he says, thinking back on still-vivid performances. "I remember my parents telling me, 'This man's job is to come out and be funny for people.' I could not believe it. 'That's his whole job? Are you kidding me?' And they said, 'No, he's kidding us.' "

Just as the phenomenon of imprinting operates in animals, causing certain behaviors to be determined by early visual experience, Jerry's destiny in life seemed to be set by the indelible impression the laughter he shared with the comics on television left on his heart and mind.

"I knew I was going to be a comedian at a very young age. It was inevitable," he says. "I remember one time I made a friend laugh so hard that he sprayed a mouthful of cookies and milk all over me. And I *liked* it. That was really the beginning."

JERRY SEINFELD was born in Brooklyn on April 29, 1954, the second child of Kalman and Betty Seinfeld. Just eighteen months earlier, Betty had given birth to their daughter, Carolyn. Compared to the majority of other couples during that time, they had become parents relatively late in life; both were already in their mid-thirties when Carolyn was born. Although raising two children so close in age was often stressful, neither Betty nor Kal minded; they were just thrilled to finally have a family to call their own.

For Kal and Betty, family life was particularly precious because each had grown up in a fractured family that had left them on their own, without the emotional safety net afforded children with strong, loving parental influences. Although Jerry has never divulged many details about his family's private lives, some facts are known.

Jerry's mom was born in Syria, an area where blood ties run deep. However, the depth of those bonds creates a blade that can swing both ways. After Betty's father suffered a severe falling-out with his family, he was so ostracized that he left the country and moved his wife and children to America.

When Betty's mother died, the situation took a dark turn. Her father couldn't cope with raising his children alone; as a result, Jerry's mom was placed in an orphanage, where she would grow up.

Kal Seinfeld also grew up without a mother; she died in childbirth. His father was a cruel and abusive man with little regard for his children. Rather than live under his tyranny, Kal and his siblings left home and moved into a small apartment where they took care of each other. Jerry's dad was only ten years old at the time. He learned to be self-reliant and self-sufficient out of necessity, earning money by taking any job that was available and selling whatever he could on the street.

Despite the difficulties, or maybe because of them, Kal grew into a young man who appreciated laughter and enjoyed seeing people smile. There was so much sadness in the world that he tried to inject a little levity whenever and wherever he could.

When Betty and Kal met, one can assume they recognized their shared measure of loss and found in each other an understanding soulmate. "They hit it off because they realized they had this common background," Jerry muses. "Our family was the first real one my parents ever had."

Child psychologists agree that our personalities are largely set by the time we're toddlers, so it's no surprise to find out that Jerry was a determined, forceful child. His mom recalls her son exercising his strong will when he was little more than a toddler:

"We were at a family gathering in Massapequa, Long Island, and there was this big chocolate cake, and Jerry, who spoke very clearly for his age, told me he wanted a piece. Well, he never wanted just a piece of chocolate cake; it had to be the whole cake, and he always waited until he got what he wanted. I sliced him a good portion, but he said he wanted a bigger piece. When I told him to take what I was giving him, he turned on his little heels and walked away. I remember saying to myself, 'That boy will always get what he wants and never settle for less.'"

"The old Jerry is actually very similar to the young Jerry," says his sister, Carolyn Liebling. "He had a very ordinary childhood, but he was very driven. If he wanted a toy, he'd sit at the table crying or arguing or carrying on. He'd obsess about things like that. He still does, even now that he's gotten to where he is."

"Driven" might not be the term most people would use to describe such a forceful child. Others might say bratty, controlling, or manipulative. Despite his occasional behavioral lapses, caused mostly by his strong will and reluctance to give in, Jerry was not a problem child. However, even back then, he had a unique way of computing information.

"One time when I was seven or eight," he recalls, "I didn't come home; it just slipped my mind. I didn't realize yet I was supposed to come home every day at a certain time."

When describing himself as a child, Jerry often brings up his two obsessions—candy and Superman. According to Jerry, the first ten years of his life were all about a quest for candy. He has incorporated his obsession into his stand-up act.

> *There's nothing else. Family, friends, school . . . they're only obstacles in the way of getting more candy. Kids actually believe they can distinguish between twenty-one different versions of pure sugar. Only a seven-year-old kid can actually taste the difference. When I was a kid, I could taste the difference between different color M&Ms. I thought they were different. For example, I thought the red was heartier, more of a main-course M&M. And the light brown was mellower, kind of an after-dinner M&M.*

Naturally, Halloween became a high point of Jerry's year. In his act, Jerry has included a bit about the intensity of a night's trick-or-treating and his irritation at those home owners who wanted to make small talk about the kids' costumes.

> *Just give me the goddamn candy! I got eighteen houses on this block; I'm not looking to really make friends here.*

Although Jerry was also fond of Spiderman and Batman, Superman was his ideal vision of a superhero. "Everybody wants to look like Clark Kent and turn into Superman," Jerry explains. " 'I may look meek and mild, but inside there's a raging superpower.' Superman, in my mind, was and still is the role I was born to play."

Jerry says he also went through the mandatory animal phase in his preteen years. Of course, he was influenced by one of his favorite television shows. "For a while I also wanted to be an oceanographer because I was really into Flipper," he says. "I thought I might be able to get a job in the Everglades Protection Bureau just like Brian

Kelly's Ranger Ricks. But I wasn't into the science of it; I wanted to communicate with dolphins—you just *know* you can get a laugh from a dolphin."

Although the family was decidedly middle class and not rich, Kal's Signfeld Sign Company was successful enough to allow them to move out of their blue-collar Brooklyn neighborhood to a nicer home in Massapequa, a suburban community of twenty-two thousand on Long Island, when Jerry turned eleven. Kal's business remained based in Brooklyn.

Their new house was located just west of Amityville, the town made infamous in the 1970s by the book and movie *The Amityville Horror*. The story told of alleged supernatural events, later revealed to be a hoax, that had taken place at a house once owned by Ronald DeFeo, who had killed his parents and four siblings nine years earlier, in 1974.

That one bloody episode aside, Massapequa and the surrounding towns were typical suburban areas, filled with shops and mini-malls and working-class families who were determined to ensure that their children would have more than they did. "There's a lot of Irish Catholics and a lot of Jewish families in Massapequa, people with strong work ethics," one resident notes.

Among the better-known citizens of Massapequa is Neil Diamond, who wrote the song "Solitary Man" in his home there. The acting Baldwin brothers grew up not far from the Seinfeld family, as did Ron Kovic, the Vietnam veteran whose life story was the basis for the Tom Cruise film *Born on the Fourth of July,* and political speechwriter Peggy Noonan. Noonan, an Irish Catholic Baby Boomer, describes her lower-middle-class suburb as a world where you are often told, "Not everything is possible. You can't have everything, and that's not bad, that's life. . . . Show respect, love your country, stop complaining!"

It was an area that voted heavily for John Kennedy and mourned his death. Like much of suburbia, Massapequa is isolated just far enough from the troubles of the world that people grow up with a sense of security. Although during his formative years the war in Vietnam was raging and the cultural revolution was in full swing, Jerry was untouched by the tumult that shook so much of our country. Safely nestled in his corner of Long Island, he focused only on the comics he watched on television and the comedy albums he played on the stereo.

Although to Betty and Kal Massapequa represented a step up in life, to the young Jerry it was just another place where not much happened. One of the mainstays in his act is the comment that "Massapequa" is Indian for "near the mall." The family house was located at 311 Riviera Drive South, on a dollop of land looking out on the ocean.

"It was a very ordinary kind of suburban environment—there was nothing there," Jerry says slowly. "Just nothing."

More accurately, there was nothing there that particularly interested him. He had no desire to go outside and play sports all day, nor did he enjoy just hanging out with other kids. What he did enjoy was spending time with his dad, with whom he shared a very warm, close relationship.

Despite his love of all things funny, Jerry was not the comic star of the family. That honor was reserved for Kal. Outgoing and personable, Kal could get along with people from all walks of life, including Mafia boss Carlo Gambino, whom Jerry remembers as an elegant man who played poker with his dad.

"My dad was very funny; quick and very sociable—the kind of guy you'd want at a party," Jerry says. "He was more burlesque than I am. I think I've always been a little on the sly while he was much more out front. He was always making people laugh. I watched the effect he would have on people and I thought, 'That's for me.'

"My father made a big impression on me. He said, 'You can only make a certain amount with your hands, but with your mind, it's unlimited.' That was his one piece of advice in eighteen years. He also turned me on to the secret that it's *fun* to be funny. That's really why I do it."

"His father *was* a real character," according to Jerry's classmate Priscilla Sperling. "He was definitely the life of the party but a bit of an eccentric at the same time. Jerry looked up to him, but at times he also seemed a bit embarrassed by him."

Whatever discomfort Sperling sensed Jerry might have felt about his dad in front of classmates or school friends probably had more to do with Jerry's own lack of ease in social situations than with any negative feelings concerning his dad, whom by all accounts he adored. Kal was not only a parent but a comedy soulmate, someone who appreciated the power of humor in a world where it was often in short supply.

For children raised in the country, treehouses, riverbanks, and the woods out back are often special places where they can commune with a parent privately, getting the one-on-one interaction that can remain vivid for a lifetime. Jerry's special place with Kal was in the cab of the sign truck.

"Somehow, that was our little place," Jerry recalls. "Our relationship had a Zen quality to it. We didn't just have conversations; it was student-teacher dialogues. I'd drive with him in the truck and ask him questions, and he'd answer. He'd explain things to me, like that different people have different brain sizes . . . usually based on the cost of the product they deal in.

"He had this great way of sizing people up and had a great overview of commerce and people. Every business we visited [to sell signs] produced a different mentality—the fruit guy, the pizza guy, the TV guy, the appliance guy, the contractor. He used to tell me how he would intentionally try to make people laugh just so he could see a smiling face instead of stony stares."

Not only was making people laugh fun, it was also a way of exerting a benign but definite power over them; you became a comedic Superman capable of creating roaring laughter in a single bound.

Jerry was also close to his mom, but in a different way. For one thing, with Kal the designated family cut-up, Betty by default got stuck being the unfunny parent, the one who would punish Jerry by taking away his television-watching privileges, which was no insignificant matter.

The young Seinfeld was a couch potato long before the term was coined and only became more entranced by what he saw as he got older. Betty recalls vividly one of her son's favorite shows: "Bill Cosby was his idol, so he watched *I Spy*, with Bill Cosby and Robert Culp, all the time. He even had a full-length poster of Cosby in his room."

When he wasn't watching television, Jerry would memorize Cosby's comedy albums, on which he wove intricate stories about characters like Fat Albert and Weird Harold. Less patient parents might have balked at their son listening to Bill Cosby records over and over and over in order to perfect comic timing, but Kal and Betty never admonished Jerry for his tunnel vision.

"I was proud to be the only kid in my neighborhood with a complete Bill Cosby album collection. When I first listened to his album, it transformed me," Jerry says, still awed by the memory. "I can't say why, but it makes a difference for people to know they can go see somebody or turn on some show and it's well observed, it's respectful of their intelligence, and you laugh. He was my favorite comedian and the first black actor to star in a series. But to me, he was the first adult on TV to wear sneakers on a regular basis. I know that affected me, but I'm not sure in what way."

Although the Seinfeld family was emotionally close-knit, they didn't necessarily spend a lot of time together. Kal worked long hours at the sign company while Betty stayed at home taking care of the house. Both Betty and Kal knew the importance of self-reliance and instilled the quality in their children along with a strong work ethic.

"Both kids grew up very independent and self-reliant," says Betty. "Kal and I had no time to take our kids skating or to ballparks. They earned their own money and learned the value of a dollar."

They also learned how to pass time at home alone. Jerry's generation was among the first to experience a latchkey existence as more families saw both parents working outside the home. In another time, kids might have picked up a book to read or sought the companionship of other neighborhood children, but television changed all that. Now being home alone meant using the television set as the primary diversion—a baby-sitter and playmate all wrapped into a neat, small box. Even though Jerry's mom didn't work outside the home, he was free to watch as much television as he wanted from the time he could remember.

"In a way, my sister and I were raised with a very healthy benign neglect that was great for me because I didn't want to be bothered," Jerry says. "When I was growing up, I felt like I was just rooming in our house. My personality is similar to that of my parents. I'm fiercely independent and self-sufficient.

"My sister and I have talked about how so many other kids, including hers, would get upset if their parents went out and left them behind. They don't like being left with anyone else, because they want *you* to stay with them. But when I was a kid and my parents would go out, I didn't care. They could do whatever they wanted, because I was busy watching TV. We were an independent family and went our own way."

Which is not to say they were distant from one another. "We talked a lot and went on vacations together," Jerry says, "but it wasn't that kind of cloying, got-to-talk-every-day thing. There was plenty of breathing room in the family. We were all just kind of roommates. It was a healthy atmosphere. Even now, my mother doesn't call me every day."

Through the years, Seinfeld has often commented on his aversion to taking vacations, explaining that he would really rather be working. And even as a kid, Jerry found travel less interesting than being able to sit at home listening to Cosby comedy albums or watching stand-ups on television.

"My parents took me to Amish country. As a kid, to see a bunch of people that have no cars, no TV, no phone, you go, 'So what? Neither do I.' Who wants to see a whole community that's been grounded?"

That particular vacation left an indelible imprint on Jerry. Years later he would incorporate it into his stand-up routine.

That's the way they should punish the kids after they've seen Amish country. "All right, son, get up to your room. That's it, I've had it, you are Amish for the rest of this weekend. And don't come down until you've made some noodles and raised a barn."

As a young teen, Jerry began experimenting with different comic bits. But unlike some kids who use their families as a captive audience, Jerry worked on his comedy away from Betty and Kal. Even though his father loved a good laugh, he and his son still saw the world through very different eyes, and they liked different kinds of comedy. Kal liked burlesque, with *ba-dum-bum* one-liners. Jerry, even then, was searching out the idiosyncrasies of everyday life.

"I would never be funny around my parents," Jerry says seriously. "It was a point of view they wouldn't understand."

One of his earliest ventures was to conduct "interviews" with his parakeet, an "every-bird on the street" bit. Just the sheer act of creating something verbally funny was an opiate and reconfirmed his decision to become a comedian.

"When you find something you can do, it helps you do everything else," he explains. "If you feel strength in one area, it gives you strength in all areas. Especially comedy, because it's such a difficult thing to do. When I realized I could do this, I could make people laugh, then I realized I was probably a pretty able person overall. My whole life was about trying to laugh, whether it was me making other people laugh or them making me laugh. I'm obsessed with that moment because when you're laughing, you've left your body; you've left the *planet* for those moments. It's an incredible experience. Even now, it's like sex to me. Everyone's looking for good food and a good laugh because they're little islands of relief in what's often a painful existence."

Although his passion for comedy was deep and genuine, it also served as a safe haven and refuge. When he listened to his comedy albums or watched stand-ups on television, Jerry was part of something wonderful in a place he felt he belonged. Comedy provided Jerry with an escape from the usual angst of adolescence.

"I wasn't the happiest kid in the world," he remembers. "I was small and skinny and was kind of out of it. I wasn't connecting with friends, with sports, with school, with beer or cigarettes or anything everybody else was doing. I got my head in the door of a lot of things but was never really part of anything. When you retreat from contact with other kids, the only playground left is your own mind."

Even an earlier foray in the Cub Scouts had turned out to be a bust. "I didn't fit in anywhere," Jerry confesses. "I'm not a joiner. A lot of it was that I never liked the idea of being part of a big group. I didn't like the way the group would suddenly turn on one guy and just make him a scapegoat and humiliate him. I felt very uncomfortable with the idea that could happen to me. I was too sensitive—if I was in a group that turned on me, I couldn't have dealt with it. So instead, I'd usually find some other disaffected kid and hang out with him. And that was okay because the only thing that interested me was comedy. I haven't changed a lot."

Just because he might have felt distant from most of his peers didn't mean his childhood was completely miserable. In fact, Jerry remembers having quite a bit of fun. "I went swimming and rode my bike a lot. I had a metallic blue Schwinn Sting Ray with the banana seat. The other kids went nuts. I was very proud of that."

Even though he possessed only average athletic skills, Jerry admits he was innately competitive. About everything. Years later, he would include a bit in his routine about how this characteristic came to the fore when physical tests were given in school—for instance, when the school nurse checked your hearing:

> *I wanted to do unbelievable on the hearing test. I wanted them to come over to me after and go, "We think you may have*

*something close to super-hearing. What you heard was a cotton
ball touching a piece of felt."*

In school, it was mandatory to participate in some sport. Jerry
chose the pole vault, because to him it represented challenge. "What
is more dramatic than the pole vault?" he asks. "I had no ability, but
I thought, 'Where is the glory?' The high highs, the low lows—that's
what I like. Was I good at the pole vault? Not really. But I loved it. It
was the glory-boy event."

Even though comedy was his main focus throughout his teenage
years, Jerry's adolescence wasn't completely devoid of early romantic experiences. According to insurance agent Lonnie Seiden, she was
Jerry's first love interest, when they were thirteen-year-old seventh-
graders at Parkside Junior High in Massapequa.

"He was shy with girls but eventually got over it with me," says
Seiden. "He was the first guy I felt serious about. We shared our first
kiss and even did some heavy petting. Once or twice we sort of
wondered whether we should go all the way, but we never did."

Seiden says she first was attracted to Jerry after seeing him blush.
"One day in class, Jerry's fly was open, and my girlfriend was the
one who told him about it. He was so embarrassed he turned bright
red, and I thought that was just the cutest thing. Plus, when he
smiles one side of his mouth turns up. At the time he was tiny and
wore braces, but as he got older he shot up like a string bean and
had these long legs. The first time we kissed was when we were
thirteen, standing in front of my house. I remember thinking his
breath smelled of pepper when he kissed me."

They dated for three years, but their youthful romance drifted
apart after he spent a summer away in Israel, Seiden says. "When he
came back, he brought me a little olive-wood figurine. We couldn't
figure out if it was a swan or a duck, so we called it a *swuck*. I still
have it."

Seiden says she never knew of Jerry having another girlfriend
during high school. "There were five of us who always hung out
together—Michelle, Chris, Cliff, Jerry, and myself," she recalls.
"Michelle dated Chris, and I dated Cliff. Jerry didn't date anyone.
He was kind of the extra wheel. He went everywhere with us, but
alone, not as part of a couple."

After his summer in Israel working on the kibbutz—an experience
his parents believed would be good for their son—Jerry came back

to start his junior year of high school. At Massapequa High, Jerry fell back into his familiar loner pattern. He didn't belong to any clubs, wasn't interested in experimenting with drugs or alcohol, didn't participate in athletics. Although he would later become an active follower of the Mets, in high school he was not apt to be one of the students leading the school victory song, which declared in part:

> Fight on, boys, fight, we'll win this game
> Roll up the score
> Massapequa School
> Beneath the hue of gold and blue
> To victory
> Massapequa School.

Comedy had become such a full-time obsession with Jerry that it often got in the way of his schoolwork. Although he was bright, Jerry seldom studied, preferring to spend his time when at home checking out what was on the tube. "He had lots of friends but few hobbies—besides watching TV," recalls Betty. "Television was his life, and he was constantly glued to the set."

Being an outsider meant that any high school activity that required participation was a potential exercise in humiliation. Most adults tend to glaze over the more difficult aspects of high school with the veneer of nostalgia for a time that never was as good as we'd like to remember it, but Seinfeld recalls the experience vividly. As usual, Jerry shows the pointed truth is much funnier than glossed-over sentimentality.

Any day that you had gym was a weird school day. You had English, Geometry, Social Studies, and then suddenly you're in Lord of the Flies *for forty minutes, hanging from a rope with hardly any clothes, with kids throwing dodge balls at you and snapping towels—you're just trying to survive. And then it's History, Science, Language.*

In the brutal teenage society of high school, popularity is in large part determined by how outgoing and accessible one is. In other words, it's hard for people to be well liked by the majority when they choose to remain enigmatic. But even teenagers who consider themselves above the normal fray of high school life still have a need to be noticed and appreciated. One way that Jerry tried to gain acceptance and ingratiate himself with others was through humor.

"Growing up, I was your typical smart-ass wisenheimer. You know, the one always making the snide comment in the back of the room," he acknowledges.

He had yet to learn the difference between being funny and just annoying. In his younger years, Jerry's attempts at humor in the classroom more often than not fell flat. Although Jerry remembers himself as always being the amusing class clown, others have a different recollection.

"Jerry was a skinny little kid with braces on his teeth," says Linda Hanna, who sat in front of Jerry at Birch Lane Elementary School. "He was a real nuisance. He was always trying to be funny but ended up being just a jerk.

"Jerry wasn't the funniest kid in class. In fact, he wasn't really funny at all," agrees Priscilla Sperling, who also attended Birch Lane with Seinfeld. "He was detached and aloof and a bit of a loner. He didn't belong to any clubs and didn't take part in any school activities. In all honesty, he was considered a nerd."

Being the outsider was a role Jerry seemed to accept readily enough, if for no other reason than that it made the moments when he did get the big laugh that much more satisfying. He had no apparent interest in being part of any clique; his goal was to be the guy who could make anyone laugh, in whatever social circle.

"I remember being on a bus coming home one day and thinking what a great day it had been because I had gotten a huge laugh in class for giving the teacher some smart-aleck answer," Jerry says. "So even early on I responded to the power of laughter. But at the time I didn't realize it was going to *define* my entire life."

Not everybody got the joke.

"The only laugh I ever saw him get in public was on our graduation day from high school," one classmate said. "Jerry stepped on the hem of his robe and tripped as he was going up the steps to get his diploma. Now that was funny."

Seinfeld's former neighbor Anthony Babich remembers Jerry as being a nice enough kid but not someone you would think was particularly special or destined for any kind of greatness. "Speaking for most people who knew Jerry as a teenager," he says, "nobody would have ever guessed that one day he would be a big star."

Nobody except Jerry.

2

The Birth of a Stand-up

HAD HE NOT BEEN ABLE TO GET FINANCIAL ASSISTANCE, JERRY'S OPTIONS for college would have been limited. Fortunately, even though he had not always lived up to his academic potential in high school, Jerry's grades were still good enough to win him a scholarship to Queens College, part of the City University of New York, beginning in the autumn of 1972.

Even though Jerry had already privately decided that comedy was his life calling, his parents had more traditional dreams in mind for their son. They gently prodded Jerry, suggesting that perhaps he might consider studying medicine—something that would guarantee him a secure future. But as far as their son was concerned, his future *was* secure; it never occurred to him that he wouldn't somehow make his living in comedy. He saw college as his chance to start working seriously toward that long-held goal. Although he loved his parents dearly, he was going to college to fulfill his dreams, not theirs. Jerry signed up as a theater arts and communications major.

Although Queens College isn't well known outside the New York area, it's not just some second-rate borough school. Opened in 1937, Queens College was originally built as a city-funded liberal arts commuter school to accommodate the growing local working-class population. As New York grew and Long Island's population became more white collar, the college blossomed into a full-service university. Although locals like Jerry still commuted between school and home, the college was also home to students from over a hundred foreign countries. It was like a little piece of Manhattan in Long Island.

While Jerry had been an underachiever in high school, he found the atmosphere of college more intellectually stimulating. Moreover, the college environment made it easier for Jerry to feel more in control of things. He approached college with a very businesslike attitude. As Jerry walked from class to class along the college's tree-lined seventy-six acres, he was no longer merely some odd-man-out, smart-aleck high school kid. He was now a grown-up taking his future in his own hands.

If he didn't participate in extracurricular activities, it wasn't noticed the way it had been in elementary and high school. As an adult, Jerry would be able to better articulate why so many comics, who onstage would seem to be the life of any party, are really antisocial by nature: "People tend to assume comedians are very uninhibited, with a fearless social energy. But the fact is, being a comedian is really all about being skilled at embarrassment avoidance. They are not extroverts; they are simply people who go to great lengths not to be uncomfortable. I'm the kind of guy you don't want at a party."

Professor Stuart Liebman taught film history and has fond memories of his former student: "He was very bright and had a very appealing personality. And he laughed at my jokes."

Had he chosen to, Jerry could have kept a full social calendar simply by hanging out at the Student Union, which offered organizations for just about any interest, from dance clubs to political groups. The school also presented, through its theater department, a fair amount of plays, both professional and student produced.

However, none of that appealed to Jerry. By day, he was a hard-working, diligent student, living away from home with a fellow student, although he still went to see his parents frequently. But at night, he had started to dip a toe into another world he hoped to call home one day. Rather than spend time getting involved with any of the vast array of social activities afforded by the college, Jerry spent his free evenings combing the smoke-filled comedy clubs of Manhattan.

Life in Long Island is quite removed from the humanity-packed bustle of Manhattan. Although they are only a half hour away from each other, the two are worlds apart in many ways. For one thing, when people talk about Manhattan being the place that never sleeps, it's more than just an advertising slogan.

Tucked down ill-lit side streets or in two-story walk-ups, the city is filled with clubs that keep going well into the quiet hours of the morning, seven days a week. By the mid-1970s, comedy was already a staple at many late-night places, a cheap way to entertain the crowd and keep them there for just one more drink. Or two.

In many ways, Jerry, the nondrinking, nonsmoking, and very young-looking college student, must have looked like a stranger in a strange land wandering through the clubs at night. He watched the people get up onstage and thought about the day he'd finally step up and face the roomful of curious faces. It filled him with a thrilling, tingling dread.

Back home, Jerry would still sit and listen to his ultimate inspiration, Bill Cosby, in even more awe than he had been as a young kid. "I always felt the things I saw him do were very beyond me, beyond my ability."

Cosby's humor was presented not in one-liners but storytelling form, which pulled the listener gently along into another world delineated by Cosby's astute observations. Where Seinfeld would become a master of the isolated microdetail, Cosby would use small, everyday events to say something about the bigger picture of human nature. To Jerry's credit, he did not try to imitate Cosby's style. Instead he studied Cosby to learn timing and other elements of the art of comedy, then applied them to a style that suited his own personality.

For as long as he could remember, Jerry had been fascinated by the small occurrences of everyday life that were insignificant to the overall course of one's life but could so easily ruin your day and make you crazy.

"I see so many details I completely miss the big picture sometimes," he says. "I didn't understand much of Jay Leno's act when I was younger. He used to do this joke about a guy who stops at a 7-Eleven to have his first cup of coffee in the morning and what a wonderful home life he must have. I would think, 'Why would that mean he didn't have a good home life?' Sometimes I don't know the most basic things about everyday living because I'm always preoccupied with some microscopic detail."

He also had a knack for picking up on quirky human behavior or things we're so used to they become invisible, then putting them under a spotlight and dissecting them (I wanna see the guy who buys that horse-bucket-sized popcorn).

That was his strength because that was who he was. With those perceptions, he started putting together ideas for an act. Jerry slowly began to make friends at the comedy clubs and was gearing up emotionally for the night he would finally be ready to take his place on the stage. Until then, he studied diligently and completed his degree in four years. Jerry, then twenty-two, graduated from Queens College in 1976 with honors and on the dean's list with a double major in theater and communication arts.

His parents watched proudly as Jerry was handed his diploma, even if they weren't completely sure what he intended to do with his education. Although he loved his mother and father, he had consciously decided against involving them in his "other life," the one that took him to comedy clubs long after his parents were already sleeping.

Like anyone who has lived with a particular dream or goal since childhood, Jerry was protective of his plans. Even though he was driven to make a life for himself in comedy, he was too busy preparing himself mentally for the next step to invite anyone else in who might not understand why on earth he wanted to be a comedian in the first place. It was one thing to make people laugh while working a regular job; it was another to try to make a living at it.

Rather than open the door for any possible criticism or questioning, Jerry kept his family life completely separate from his would-be club life at this stage, which is why he didn't invite his parents to join him on the night of the day he graduated. In fact, he didn't even tell his parents where he was going.

Jerry had decided that graduation night was as good a time as any to finally get up onstage. So on that July evening in 1976, he headed to amateur night at Catch a Rising Star, one of Manhattan's more famous comedy clubs. Gabe Kaplan, Richard Belzer, and Andy Kaufman were some of the comics who had honed their stand-up skills there.

However, amateur nights were something else. Aspiring comics or people just out for a laugh or on a dare would sign up on a list to get their ten minutes in front of the audience. An amazing assortment of people would come up to the mike, most of whom would be painfully unfunny. As Jerry would soon find out, there was a big difference between being funny at your table or in the car with your friends and standing alone in front of a roomful of strangers who stared back at you with a collective attitude of "Okay, make me laugh."

"I thought comedy was going to be easy because I was always funny as a kid," Jerry says. "All I wanted to do was go out there in a sport coat and tell jokes like Alan King. I had no idea how difficult it was the first time I stood up there."

Jerry had gone over his brief routine several times in his head, but the moment he got the mike in his hand and looked out at the audience, he froze. His debut was well on its way to being a humiliating disaster.

"That first time, I bombed bad," Jerry admits. "I couldn't even speak, I was so paralyzed in total fear. I remember thinking, 'Why should everyone be listening to me? What right do I have to come in and have everyone's attention in this room?' I just felt really out of my place. I had thought I was going to be a hit. It was the usual pie-in-the-sky optimism."

Rather than panic, he concentrated on getting some words to come out of his mouth. "It was supposed to be a fifteen-minute set, but I was only able to remember the subjects I was going to talk about. So I just stood there and said, 'The beach. Driving. Parents. Dogs.' And the people were laughing—they thought that was what I meant to do. I did that for about a minute and a half and then just left. After I was done, some friends came over and congratulated me. They said it was very important the audience liked me, even though I didn't *do* anything."

Hearing the people laugh was like a drug, and from that first night he was addicted. However, his near-choke had taught him that, as Steve Martin once said, comedy wasn't pretty. It was hard work and an unforgiving taskmaster. If you didn't put in the time and dedication, you'd be left dangling surrounded by a painfully uncomfortable silence.

Far from scaring Jerry off, that realization energized him. He took what he had learned and spent the next three months developing a new act. The next time out, he would be better prepared and not leave anything to chance. "When I went back a month later with a whole new act, this time I had memorized it. The first time I hadn't."

Even though his act was raw and unpolished, Jerry was still able to strike a chord with the audience. His early routines included observations on a Tide commercial (If you get a T-shirt with bloodstains, maybe laundry is not your problem now) and the sport of luge (It's the only sport where people could be competing against their will and you wouldn't know it).

Jerry performed his first paid professional gig at the Golden Lion Pub. Within a few months he was a regular at Catch a Rising Star's amateur night and would haunt other clubs as well, looking for any opportunity to ply his craft. He felt more than just comfortable on the small stage, he felt at home.

Jerry's family wasn't oblivious to his late nights out, and it didn't take them long to realize just how serious he was about comedy. While Jerry's mother might have been more of the wait-and-see type, his father had absolute faith that his son would make it. According to old acquaintances, Kal used to tell virtually everybody he met, "Hey, you should meet my son. He's a pretty funny guy."

"My dad was extremely encouraging about it," Jerry says. "He was a salesman, and that's a similar type of life. You're not really doing any legitimate kind of work, you're just making a living talking people into things. That isn't much different from what a comic does."

Although Kal might have originally envisioned his son taking a different path in life, he was ultimately supportive of whatever Jerry endeavored to do. He might not have understood what drove Jerry, but he understood how to be a good dad.

"There were many times I'd drive into Manhattan at midnight and hang out until three in the morning waiting to get onstage and then not get on," Jerry recalls. "I'd get home at four-thirty depressed, and my dad would wake up and come into the kitchen, sit there and talk to me about it."

Jerry's act became long enough and polished enough to take him past the amateurs and into the ranks of the professionals, insofar as he started getting paid for his stand-up sets. However, getting paid didn't necessarily mean making a living. Although he began performing regularly, the money was negligible. There were many nights when Jerry made only twenty dollars.

He was facing a quandary that most struggling young performers confront at some point: how to make enough money to survive without committing to a job that will interfere with what you're trying to accomplish. Unlike actors, who need to keep their daytime hours free for auditions, stand-ups are creatures of the night, so Jerry looked for afternoon work. Since he wanted to keep his ties loose, he drifted toward menial jobs that could be left at a moment's notice without creating problems for himself or his employer. Also, having to show up at an awful job was a daily reminder of where Jerry really wanted to be.

"That was by conscious design," he says. "To have your back to a cliff, to not have anything to fall back on, that's the best way to accomplish something."

His less than memorable jobs included working as a telephone salesman, cold-calling people to pitch long-life lightbulbs. Later, he would frequently joke that "there aren't a lot of people sitting home in the dark saying, 'I can't hold out much longer.' "

Never one to pass up a comic opportunity, Seinfeld would later use his nine-to-five job experiences as fodder for his act.

Frankly, I don't believe people think of their office as a workplace anyway. I think they think of it as a stationery store with Danish. You want to get your pastries, your envelopes, your supplies, your toilet paper, six cups of coffee, and you go home.

As he has said, maybe Jerry was drawn to sales jobs because, in a certain sense, selling merchandise isn't that different from selling a joke. However, stand-ups don't usually have to worry about being arrested for being illegal vendors—as Jerry did while he was selling cheap costume jewelry on the sidewalk in front of Bloomingdale's in Manhattan. His cart had wheels to facilitate a quick getaway. More than once, Jerry was unable to pack up quickly enough and was caught by unamused police officers, although he was never charged.

"Here I was," he says, "a former dean's list student two months out of college running from the police on the streets of Manhattan— a parent's dream come true."

Actually, his parents had no idea that their son was becoming a familiar face to the NYPD. "I really wasn't aware," Betty claims. "You don't worry about your kids after they leave home. You assume they're doing okay unless you hear otherwise."

While in retrospect those youthful adventures sound exciting and thrilling, they are much funnier now than they were at the time. For someone who likes to control his environment as much as Jerry does, being at the mercy of the police and low-rent employers was not so much demoralizing as it was insulting. Jerry knew he was better than that. He also knew he would never be happy living a typical nine-to-five existence.

"I remember the day when I truly knew I *had* to make it as a comic," Jerry asserts. "I was working at a film-editing studio sweeping the floors, and one day I went out to lunch. I was sitting on a ledge at Chase Manhattan Bank, watching people going to their jobs. Right then, I decided I never wanted to have a job. I wanted to do something I was really in love with, and that was more important than a job. Even if I wasn't any good at it."

He tried his hand at being a waiter at a popular lunch spot, but taking orders from occasionally surly customers didn't mesh with Seinfeld's personality. Worse, he would often run into customers who had seen him perform. That, he says, "was embarrassing. You'd go over to a table and they'd say, 'Didn't I see you onstage last night? What kind of crummy show was that? We go to a show and the next day we go to lunch and the comedian's a waiter? They were charging us five dollars to get into that place. We thought they were supposed to be professionals.'

"To me, the most exciting part of my whole career was when I handed back my waiter's apron in September of 1976. I was working the ten-to-two lunch shift at Brew and Burger on Third and 53rd when I got a gig emceeing at the Comic Strip. I already had one night, then got another night and was making thirty-five dollars a night. I thought I could make it on seventy dollars a week, so I turned in the apron.

"I went out to visit my parents. I remember standing on the platform of the Long Island Rail Road in Massapequa. That was the highest moment of my career. I was a comedian. I had made it. That was the biggest moment of my life."

For the next four years, Catch a Rising Star became Jerry's second home and comedy graduate school; it gave him an opportunity to experiment and mature as a performer and to share and exchange ideas and good times with other up-and-coming comics. His goal was to fashion a killer set that would take him out of the safety net of Manhattan and onto the testing ground of the road. During his time there, he also formed extended-family ties. Among the other young guns of Manhattan's stand-up clubs between 1976 and 1980 was Paul Reiser, who would become one of Jerry's lifelong friends. Another early acquaintance to whom Seinfeld would grow extremely close was Mario Joyner. Unlike so many others in entertainment, who lose track of people as their careers advance, Jerry would consistently maintain his early ties.

Although Seinfeld still thought Cosby was a comic god, he also

found inspiration in the intelligent humor of Robert Klein. A comic
who mixed political and observational humor, Klein would go down
in stand-up history for his 1975 HBO special, which was the first
uncensored stand-up performance to be aired on national TV.
HBO's decision to allow comics complete artistic freedom on its
cable network would eventually be one of the major forces that
shaped the future of stand-up in America.

Klein, an alumnus of the revered Second City improvisational
comedy troupe, is sometimes referred to as the dean of stand-ups
and was idolized by those coming up behind him. "Robert had a big
influence on all of us," Reiser says. "He just brought stand-up to a
very accessible level. His act wasn't like the old lounge acts: 'Take
my wife—please.' It was hip and new. He created a language that
wasn't there before."

In 1978, Seinfeld, Reiser, and some other young comics started a
club they dubbed the Funniest Men in the World. "A group of us—
Paul, Larry Miller, Mark Schiff, and a guy named Michael Cane—
decided to get together every New Year's Day because New Year's
Eve is so brutal for a stand-up," Jerry explains. "We called it the
Funniest Men in the World because at the time we were some of the
better comedians working in New York."

His stand-up friends continue to form the core of Seinfeld's social
and emotional life: "Having comedians as friends is one of the greatest things about being a comedian because they are so funny and
unusual, and their minds are so active and irritable. The reason I like
funny people is that we share the same mind-set. Just the slightest
little thing pisses them off—'Why does that have to be like that?'
That's how we have fun.

"Most of my friends are outgoing. I'm not, so they draw me out.
Take my friend Mario Joyner, for instance. He loves going out to
dance clubs. He knows all the doormen, where the VIP room is, and
who *not* to talk to. I would never go by myself. Ever. But I'll go
along with Mario. I'm like the sidecar. I climb in the sidecar, they
ride the motorcycle, and we both get there at the same time."

Although you wouldn't know it by their group's name, there were
also quite a few successful female comics working stand-up then too.
Lest he be accused of being sexist, Jerry denies that he thinks men
are generally funnier than women. "Not at all. The average woman
is funnier than the average man," he says, then adds a qualifier. "But

it's kind of like chefs. The average woman is a better cook than the average man, but the best chefs are men."

As Seinfeld, Miller, Reiser, and Joyner became more successful, their careers took them in different directions away from New York, but they still make the effort to share their one special day. They were together again on January 1, 1998. "We usually have brunch at the River Café and walk across the Brooklyn Bridge, and that somehow was our transition from the old year to the new," Jerry explains. "That was the kind of thing we would do when we used to get together a lot, but now we've splintered off and only have that one day a year. I have just a few close friends, and I've kept them close. When some people become famous, they enter another social orbit, but I stay with my old friends. I return their calls promptly so they won't feel, 'Oh, he can't be bothered now.' "

The fact that the group is still meeting twenty years later is indicative of how important Jerry considers his friendships with other comics, who provide him with an environment where he doesn't have to worry about offending anyone. Seinfeld admits he encounters that problem with "civilians":

> *My sense of humor offstage is usually kind of raw and antisocial. I'm often thought of as rude because I say things as they occur to me. That's why I like to hang out with other comedians. They have a similar head. It's like people who are cops, or hookers. The only people who know what that kind of life is like are the people who do the same thing you do. The same is true with being a comedian. Those who don't do it don't know what my life is like, and it's hard to be close friends with someone who lacks that understanding.*

Besides similar backgrounds—Reiser grew up in New York City and began hanging out in comedy clubs in college—there was another shared trait that brought the Funniest Men in the World together. They were all stand-ups because they truly believed it was their destiny.

"Becoming a comedian is like becoming a murderer," Jerry says. "No matter what people tell you, you're going to do it."

Just as most actors will tell you they knew from childhood or adolescence that they had to act or that being in the high school play was an epiphany that changed their life, this group of stand-ups felt they were fated to pursue comedy. Their lifelong calling made them embrace comedy and approach it differently than stand-ups who more or less fell into it.

Although he had dabbled with performing, the smell of the greasepaint and the roar of the crowd didn't particularly hit Drew Carey with a bolt of lightning; it was just a fun thing to have done. Drew didn't burn with an innate desire to get up in front of a bunch of strangers and make them laugh and only got into it after getting fired from yet another waiter job.

Ellen DeGeneres was drifting through a series of clerical jobs in New Orleans when a coworker suggested she should try her hand at a stand-up amateur night since she was always so funny in the office. Some friends put together a local benefit and asked her to do something onstage; she agreed but was so unsure of herself that she only prepared one bit. It was enough to bring down the house and jumpstart a career.

Brett Butler was a single mother in Texas working as a waitress when some of her diner customers encouraged her to sign up for a local comedy amateur night. She wrote some material and won the contest; four thousand performances later, she landed her own sitcom.

But stand-up to Seinfeld wasn't a fallback profession or an accident. It was his frame of reference for life and for self-discovery. "That's what stand-up is. That's what life is. You have to discover yourself. It means nothing what everyone else is doing. They're just like big guideposts."

"When I was a little kid, I always wanted to be a comedian but didn't know you could," says Reiser. "Then when I was in high school and college, I started to see people actually doing it, and those people, like Gabe Kaplan and David Brenner, started going from clubs onto television. I think most of the guys in my generation of comics did stand-up solely because that was what they felt called and compelled to do. There was just no other choice. It wasn't like, 'Gee, should I be a dental hygienist or a comic?' And you stay in it because there is nowhere else you want to be."

Although it sometimes seemed like it, not all the up-and-coming comics were young East Coast white guys. Stand-up is an equal opportunity profession, and one of Jerry's first and more enduring friendships was with George Wallace, an amiable black man who in those days called himself "the Reverend." Unlike Jerry, George had lived another life prior to turning to comedy.

Wallace had grown up in Atlanta and went to work selling disposable rags for an Ohio company. Later, he moved to New York and eventually became vice president of an advertising agency that specialized in billboard accounts. But George tired of the nine-to-five grind and decided to trade his three-piece suit for a shot at a career in stand-up and a new set of threads.

"I came onstage with my gold cape and carrying the yellow pages," Wallace laughs. "Jerry thought I was crazy. But we became really good friends one night when he showed up at the club sick. He had a cold, and I had a car, so I drove him to an all-night drugstore and bought him some NyQuil."

"George is the host of life," says Jerry with affection. "We share a worldview that life is good and to hell with the bull. George makes you feel good."

They say comedy makes strange bedfellows, and Wallace and Seinfeld were certainly an odd couple. Jerry was thin and already a strict adherent of the "my body is a temple" lifestyle: no alcohol, no smoking, no junk food. George, short and balding, was more of an earthy soul, fond of the tasty fried foods that would make Jerry's stomach shiver and not averse to enjoying a drink now and then.

"He's so perfect that I told him when they lower him into his grave, I'm going to say, 'He tried everything,' " George says dryly.

Although Jerry may not have been the most personally adventurous guy playing the clubs, he was unquestionably one of the most dedicated and hardworking. While he loved hanging out and getting into comedy riffs with his friends, he never let his fun get in the way of his comedy.

"He is just so disciplined in whatever he does," says Wallace. "Back then he would sit down *every* day with his pad and pen and write, working on his act. Nothing would make him miss a day."

To Jerry, that was simply part of the job. Being funny didn't just happen. It wasn't just a knack. It was an art and a craft that required constant care and attention.

"A good act takes years to develop," Seinfeld explains. "You can put an actor in the movies, shoot him the right way, and suddenly he's a star. But you can't do that in comedy. There's no 'Oh, he's got a smoldering quality that women just love' in comedy; nobody can 'create' you or push you beyond your ability because of the way you look or who you know. It's either there or it isn't, and that's what makes it pure."

3

The Hair on the Bathroom Tile

THE ONLY WAY TO MOVE PAST TWENTY DOLLARS A NIGHT AND INTO THE stand-up big time is to develop a routine that keeps the audience laughing and in their seats drinking. And the only way to improve your act is to keep doing it night after night, wherever someone will allow you to. Jerry remembers performing in small cities around the country in venues that tested his comic commitment.

"They weren't clubs," he says. "I played in places that were just restaurants with a table missing. I'd be standing in the middle of the room at two in the morning telling jokes to three people who were putting on their coats."

Stand-ups working the circuit become very familiar with one another, which can create deep bonds of friendship or cause long-lasting ill will. For example, Jerry often found himself working the same places with George Wallace, and the experience of sharing the often less than glamorous adventures of being a young stand-up on the road contributed to their still-close friendship.

Rather than complain about the tedium of traveling from one city to another, staying in cheap hotels or apartments supplied by the clubs, Seinfeld mined his road days for material.

The worst way of flying, I think, is standby. You ever fly standby? It never works. That's why they call it standby. You end up standing there going, "Bye."

28

I'm on the plane, we left late, and the pilot says, "We're going to be making up some time in the air." I thought, "Isn't that interesting. They just make up time." Of course, when they say they're making up time, obviously they're increasing the speed of the aircraft. Now my question is, if you can go faster, why don't you just go as fast as you can all the time? Come on, there are no cops up here. Give it some gas. We're flying.

Even though comedy acts have been a mainstay of the American entertainment scene since the days of vaudeville, stand-up was enjoying a particularly golden moment in the early days of Jerry's career. Between 1980 and 1985 hundreds of comedy clubs sprang up across the country, catering to upwardly mobile yuppies who liked to see the foibles and peccadilloes of their own lives satirized onstage. This reality was not lost on Seinfeld.

I would say the concept behind the car phone, and the phone machine, the speakerphone, the airline phone, the portable phone, the pay phone, the cordless phone, the multiline phone, the phone pager, the call waiting, the call forwarding, call conferencing, speed dialing, direct dialing, and the redialing is that we all have absolutely nothing to say, and we've got to talk to someone about it right now!

Jerry's style of observational humor fit in with the times. America was moving full speed into the Information Age, where every iota of data suddenly seemed potentially important and significant, whether it was or not. Faxes and cellular phones were becoming commonplace, and people drowning in the flood of information craved the immediate relief stand-up comedy offered. Bert Haas, who was the general manager of the comedy club chain Zanies, once suggested that comics like Seinfeld and Leno were simply products of their time. "If you go to a comedy play, a certain amount of time is lost setting up the plot of characters. But in stand-up comedy, you get three or four laughs in one minute. It's like a shot of adrenaline."

Like a lot of his peers, Jerry was a clean comic with a traditional presentation. Earlier in the 1970s, stand-ups like Steve Martin, Albert Brooks, Robin Williams, and Andy Kaufman had exploded on the stand-up scene and knocked it a bit off balance with their onstage antics. Experimental and willing to take risks, these comics often added a significant amount of physicality to their routines;

sometimes they literally flung themselves about the stage, frequently veering into barely controlled mania. These were not observational stand-ups; they were part comics, part modern vaudeville performers, with a little slapstick occasionally thrown in.

But the stand-ups who came later—like Seinfeld, Dennis Miller, Larry Miller, and Paul Reiser—were more traditional and reflected the more conservative attitudes of the 1980s. They were uniformly clean-cut types who projected a levelheaded sensibility through their humor. They offered a more conversational style, worked without props, and avoided any excessive expenditure of energy. You would never seen Seinfeld do pratfalls in his act or mud-wrestle women from the audience the way Williams and Kaufman, respectively, did.

"The best comedians are the ones who stay the closest to their own personalities," Jerry says. "When you affect a persona, it's very tiring for the comedian, and ultimately for the audience, to sustain the illusion."

This is why, in the case of Seinfeld and others like him, to know the stand-up was in many cases a way to know the man. Their routines reflected not only what they saw around them but who they were as people.

Overall, as a group, Jerry and the other observational comics were far more slick than earlier stand-up generations, no doubt because they had all been weaned on television and were aware that eventually they would be beaming into people's homes. On the other hand, for all the professionalism they exuded, their uniformly polished acts had a tendency to make them indistinguishable from one another, since none at that time had yet developed a particular television identity.

However, their clean-cut wholesomeness also meant they were far more likely to live to enjoy their success than some of their less-disciplined peers. Although not to the degree of rock music, stand-up too had suffered its share of shocking losses and untimely, scandalous deaths. Lenny Bruce, whose real name was Leonard Schneider, was one of the original angry young comics who reached his peak of popularity and controversy in the early 1960s. By today's standards his act would be considered mild, but at the time his routines, laden with four-letter-words and references to sex, resulted in his arrest and criminal conviction, in 1964, for giving an obscene performance. But his real demons were internal, and he died in 1966 of a drug overdose.

Freddie Prinze was one of the brightest lights on the stand-up scene in 1973. A year later the former high school dropout was starring in his own NBC series, *Chico and the Man*. Ironically, Prinze emulated Lenny Bruce in his club act and was even briefly engaged to the late stand-up's daughter, Kitty. Unfortunately, he was another comic whose offstage life was troubled with the all-too-familiar problem of too much money and too many drugs, as well as an unhealthy appetite for guns. On January 27, 1977, he shot himself in the head; he died two days later.

Even though he proved to be a survivor, Richard Pryor seemed a man with a death wish who played Russian roulette with drugs and wound up setting himself on fire while trying to freebase cocaine in bed.

For these men, their inner pain helped fuel their stage personas and humor. They siphoned off their raw emotion and let it spill over onto the audience. This was not the case with Jerry and the others of his ilk. They were more coolly intellectual, which made for more comfortable but less passionate comedy.

Other than Dennis Miller, the stand-ups of this group were not particularly political either. And most notably, because of the increasing importance of television to a comic's career, most were decidedly less "blue" than their predecessors. The purposefully offensive sexual humor of Andrew Dice Clay, the obscenity-laden railings of Eddie Murphy, the rawness of Sam Kinison's rage-filled act: these were exceptions to a new, cleaner rule.

Richard Fields, the owner of Catch a Rising Star, said the change was not so much cultural as practical and based on business considerations: "The networks want comedians to work clean."

Television, both network and cable, had become a major influence on the direction of stand-up in America. The lure of starring in a TV special or series had caused a growing number of young performers to throw their hats into the live comedy performance ring merely as a way to get onto the small screen.

Some within the stand-up community bemoaned that the avalanche of stand-ups was diluting the talent pool, Seinfeld believed the quantity was irrelevant as long as the level of quality was maintained. "The number of stand-ups in the world doesn't affect what makes people laugh. They generally laugh at funny things," he noted, although *what* they find funny sometimes amazed him. "I once did a joke about horse racing and horses not knowing they're racing. I couldn't believe people were laughing."

But every audience is different, and one of the skills he developed early was to read the room. "I adjust my act every night in front of every audience," he asserts. "In fact, I can tell what type of people they are and what their sense of humor is. That said, though, I don't think, 'Here's something that people will like.' I start with what I like."

Maybe that was true for Jerry and others dedicated to the artistry of live comedy performance, but whereas the goal was once to cut an album or headline in Las Vegas, being a comic in the 1980s became less an art form for many young comics playing the circuit than a stepping-stone. It seemed as if the single best way to get on a series was to develop a stand-up routine and use it as a personal showcase. Their acts were geared toward the casting agents in the audience.

Of course, the synergy between televisions and comedy is as old as the medium itself. Television's first stars were all comedians. *Your Show of Shows* with Sid Caesar, Milton Berle's *Texaco Star Theater, The Red Skelton Show,* and *I Love Lucy* all helped make television a cultural phenomenon.

Because life as a stand-up comedian is so hard, given the travel, the competition, and the need to constantly come up with material, "there are very few people who are cut out to be stand-up comedians over an entire career," notes Seinfeld. "It's a truly difficult career, so I think it will always be that most people in it come to a time to move on to something that is not quite so brutal on them."

The sheer volume of comics now saturating the market made the really good ones stand out even more. So it wasn't much of a surprise when Jerry was approached one night in Los Angeles by a Hollywood casting agent. It seemed that his moment of television destiny had finally arrived.

AFTER spending four years perfecting a solid routine, which meant honing and defining existing material, weeding out weak jokes, and blending in new bits, Seinfeld finally felt he was ready to graduate to the next comedy tier. In 1980, when he was twenty-six, he packed a few belongings and relocated to California.

"That's what you do as a stand-up," says one longtime comic. "You come to Los Angeles to get showcased and get an agent so you can go out on the road for six weeks to earn enough money to come back and live while going out on auditions and doing more showcase work."

At the time, the two top venues for stand-ups were the Improv and the Comedy Store, each of which has a history of—or at least takes credit for—helping launch dozens of careers. Jay Leno, Robin Williams, and David Letterman are among the alumni of these two L.A. establishments. The Improv is a sister club of the original in New York, which was started by Bud Friedman and his partner, Mark Lonow, a sometime actor who appeared in the disco flick *Thank God It's Friday*. The club is located on a stretch of Melrose Avenue dotted with art galleries and expensive furniture stores. Inside, the club has a Manhattan feel to it, with a bar in back that attracts a regular flow of actors, agents, casting directors, and other comics.

Because of its association with the New York club scene, the Improv is a beacon for East Coast stand-ups new to town. It's also a kind of comic halfway house. Young comics working at the Improv get meals at half price and are allowed to run tabs. The club is truly a haven for hungry comics, literally and figuratively.

The Comedy Store is located at the eastern end of the Sunset Strip. It's a large club, with three different showrooms that each charges separate admission. Owner Mitzi Shore (the mother of Pauly Shore, the former MTV veejay who went on to star in a string of films such as *The Son-in-Law* and *Encino Man*) presides over the club like a benevolent den mother. Most young performers work both clubs, picking up whatever sets are available.

"The clubs are more than just places to work," says comic Thomas Tully. "They also become the center of your social life when you're first starting out. It's a place to meet up with other comics, watch everyone's routines, and just sit and absorb the atmosphere. There's just something so seductive about the club atmosphere, especially when everyone's on a roll and the laughs are coming fast and loud.

"Jerry was always in the middle of things when he was around. Unlike some comics who prefer to stay to themselves or feel like outsiders—Drew Carey comes to mind—Jerry enjoyed schmoozing and hanging out. He was always very personable in those kinds of situations, especially when his buddies were there, like Larry Miller and George Wallace. He was also good friends with Jay Leno, but

. . . even then Jay was constantly on the road somewhere. But when he was in town, you'd see Leno and Seinfeld hanging out together, laughing."

One thing Seinfeld and Leno shared was their love of performing, anywhere, anytime. "Some people run every morning," said Jay. "I go onstage every night. It's my job."

The one glaring drawback of working at the Improv and Comedy Store circa 1980 was that neither club paid the struggling stand-ups any money for their sets. The headliners would get paid, but the unknowns worked for free. The comics were little more than interns, their compensation being the privilege of performing at a club teeming with agents, casting directors, and television and film executives.

That cushy arrangement changed shortly after Jerry arrived in town with the notorious Comedy Strike. "Nobody expected to get rich performing at either club, but considering how much money the clubs made while these unknown guys were doing sets, it was really scandalous," recalls one strike participant, who requested anonymity. "So the regulars all got together and staged a strike against the Improv and Comedy Store. There was a picket line with signs, and it was very organized.

"The way the clubs saw it, they were providing the stand-ups a priceless opportunity; the performers felt they were being treated like indentured servants for the local comic aristocracy. It was really a serious matter, and although nobody will admit it, the few guys who crossed the picket line were never forgiven—and their careers never recovered. Other than working for Mitzi, they went nowhere."

The comics were passionate about their cause, and emotions were running high. Both sides had dug in, and the strike could have gone on a very long time had not a tragedy put everyone's differences in perspective.

"The holdout was really hard on the young guys because their lives were being completely disrupted," the comic recalls. "One guy, who was obviously unstable to begin with, decided to become a martyr for the cause. He told some friends that he was going to shame Bud and Mitzi into ending the strike. So he killed himself by jumping off the roof of the hotel next to the Comedy Store. That was when Bud put an end to the strike by agreeing to pay the stand-ups a nominal fee per set and Mitzi agreed to pay whatever Bud did."

Once the strike was settled, the audience could enjoy the shows guilt-free, and the comics went back to doing their nightly sets in hopes of catching the eye of that right person who they hoped would change their lives. But not every opportunity was golden.

One night after watching Jerry perform at the Comedy Store, a casting scout in the audience was impressed enough to search Seinfeld out and ask him to come in for a meeting. This eventually led to Jerry's being hired on the series *Benson*, a spinoff from *Soap*, which was a farcical takeoff on the never-ending drama of daytime serials. *Soap* created controversy through its depiction of transsexuality, male impotence, organized crime, and any other sensational topic creator and writer Susan Harris could think of.

Benson starred Robert Guillaume as the majordomo for the governor of an unnamed southern state. It had premiered in 1979 but underwent some cast additions for the second season, including the role of Frankie, the governor's joke writer. Jerry was hired for the part and was signed to a $4,000-per-episode contract.

Joining a television series had become an expected career move for any halfway popular stand-up whose goal was to star in his or her own. In 1975, Gabe Kaplan was everyone's favorite high school teacher in *Welcome Back, Kotter*. Three years later Andy Kaufman, as Latka Gravas, became of the original cast members in *Taxi,* and Robin Williams was signed to star in *Mork and Mindy* after producers saw Williams's maniacal, and genius, ad-libbing with an improvisational group at the Comedy Store.

But Seinfeld's first foray into prime time wasn't the breakthrough he had anticipated it would be. After years of being a stand-up and therefore, in essence, his own boss with complete control over his stage material, Jerry was suddenly plopped into a world where he was little more than comic cattle. Up until now, Jerry had spent his days writing new material and tinkering with his act. When in Los Angeles, he would perform at either the Improv or the Comedy Store if there were any available sets. On the road, his routine was the same. He developed material during the day and at night performed in whatever club had hired him. Through it all, the words he spoke were his own.

However, bit players in sitcoms are at the mercy of the writers. Although *Soap* had been one of the best-written series on television, *Benson* was middle-of-the-road sitcom fare. Rewrites were done on the run, and the humor was often mediocre, at best.

Robert Guillaume, an experienced actor whose character had already been fleshed out on *Soap* as the educated but exasperated cook, did not fare badly, but the rest of the cast were more or less cartoons and caricatures. Even though Jerry had majored in theater in college, he wasn't really comfortable just acting. Unlike his friend Paul Reiser, who had just been cast in *Diner* and would further prove his capabilities as a film actor in *Beverly Hills Cop* and *Aliens*, Jerry was most comfortable just playing Jerry. Not surprisingly, his character of Frankie fell flat, and Seinfeld was let go after only four episodes.

"It happened so fast it was like a car accident" is how Jerry described his brief employment and unexpected firing. "I flew in from New York the day the show was supposed to start shooting again after the break. I showed up at the studio and went to sit down at the table to read the script, but there was no script and no chair for me. Then the assistant director called me aside to tell me they forgot to tell me I wasn't on the show anymore." Later, he would bitterly comment that he was "fired for telling someone else's crummy jokes."

The experience proved humiliating. He felt a complete victim of circumstances and others' lack of talent. In some ways, he felt he had been set up by the system that tolerated, and even encouraged, the inane and mundane. It wasn't television itself that was the enemy, it was the fact that those involved so often were willing to settle for less than the best they could do. He vowed that the only way he would ever do television again was if he ran his own show. Next time—if there ever was a next time—he would succeed or fail on his own talents, not the lack of talent of others.

More than anything, the *Benson* experience left Jerry angry at Jerry. In a self-flagellating way, he almost felt that the miserable result was his punishment for having been too quick to abandon stand-up. Jerry was angry at himself for having compromised himself by taking the job in the first place and for betraying the purity of his comedy by not devoting himself solely to it. Since arriving in Hollywood, he had somewhat mindlessly followed the lead of others and split his energies between stand-up and auditioning for television and movie roles.

Reiser wasn't the only comic in Jerry's peer group to break into the movies. Jay Leno, still considered a fast-rising stand-up, had already appeared in several movies, including a major role in *Ameri-*

can Hot Wax; Robin Williams had crossed over to films as a leading man in *Popeye* but still showed up at the Comedy Store, hilarious as ever; even Jerry's old friend Larry Miller had appeared in the film *Take Down* without missing a beat in his stand-up routine.

But for Jerry, anything other than total devotion and time meant he wasn't giving his stand-up act its just due. He had to decide whether he was a stand-up or a comic actor and then go for it. In his heart, he was first and foremost a stand-up performer. That's what gave him the greatest thrill and joy. It was also where he could truly be the master of his domain.

"As a stand-up comic, nobody can fire me like that," he pointed out. "Being a stand-up is my mission in life; it's my passion. My ongoing goal is to simply be funny, on my own, in front of a roomful of strangers. By comparison, television shows are no big deal."

Making a decision to rededicate himself to stand-up helped Jerry put the firing behind him. As he had always done, and would continue to do, he turned a setback into something positive. He made sure the people around him, especially his manger, George Shapiro, understood his focus and supported him in it.

George Shapiro and his partner, Howard West, were former William Morris agents who left the talent agency to be managers and producers. "We were established agents who had a bit of a following who broke off to do what we wanted to do," Howard says. "We wanted to do a little bit of everything but not be in meetings the rest of our lives."

In addition to producing several television and film projects, including *The 2,000-Year-Old Man* with Carl Reiner and Mel Brooks, Shapiro and West managed directors, writers, and stand-ups, including Andy Kaufman. In addition to Jerry, they also represented Seinfeld's close friend George Wallace. They were business-savvy men who weren't "suits" who looked for clients with whom they thought they could both have fun and success. When they saw Jerry perform shortly after he moved to Los Angeles, they wasted no time asking if he'd be interested in having them represent him. Seinfeld agreed, and their partnership is still going strong.

Jerry's recommitment to stand-up was cathartic and took on an almost mystical resolve that was as much physical as it was mental and emotional. Jerry was like an athlete in training, approaching his goal with unwavering focus. He worked daily on developing new routines and improving existing ones. He strengthened both his mind and body with yoga and health foods and studied Zen.

"Zen," explains Seinfeld, "is just looking at something from a different perspective, which is exactly what a lot of comedy is."

During the early 1980s, Seinfeld also sought to find a personal edge in the controversial quasi-religion Scientology. Founded by former science-fiction writer turned philosopher-entrepreneur L. Ron Hubbard, Scientology emphasizes self-realization and personal advancement as opposed to devotion to a particular deity.

"Jerry acted like he had just discovered the sun," says an associate. "He came into the Comedy Store all excited about this wonderful new thing he had found and was anxious to tell his friends about it and suggest they should look into it too. Not that he was trying to convert anybody—Jerry doesn't believe in preaching, and, quite frankly, he wasn't that concerned about others. He just thought it was something really great and worthwhile and that it could help him out. He respected it because it was all about the self."

Because the entertainment business can take such an emotional toll on struggling, would-be performers, many actors and comics in Hollywood have been drawn to Scientology, which, in simplistic terms, promotes personal achievement. Seinfeld had been introduced to Scientology by a girlfriend and was very involved for a while, reading the literature and attending some of the meetings. But just as quickly as he became enamored of the teachings, Jerry cooled on it. Whereas some accept the philosophy as a kind of religion, Seinfeld approached the group's teachings like a consumer. He listened to the pitch, picked out the concepts and ideas he thought were useful, then moved on.

In later years he would downplay his association with Scientology. "I took a few courses in Scientology a long time ago, and it helped me straighten out a few things," he would say. "But I'm not really a part of the Church."

"First of all," notes the associate, "Jerry isn't big on joining in big groups. If Jerry's the only member of Jerry's church, then Jerry's happy. But I don't think it was so much that he became disenchanted with Scientology as it was he found out what interested him, took what it had to offer him, and then moved on to something else, as is typical of Jerry."

As mentioned earlier, Jerry and his peers were similar-looking and -sounding clean comics, which made establishing a distinct identity difficult. To Jerry, it simply meant he would have to stand out on the strength of his material. There were some who thought he could hasten the process if he added a little spice to his act.

"His act was so clean, they suggested he put a little more sex into it," says his mother, Betty. "But Jerry didn't want that. He gets his material from everyday life and likes being the Mr. Clean of comedy."

To Jerry it wasn't so much a matter of aesthetics as of staying true to the old masters of comedy, like Laurel and Hardy. "Maybe it just reflects me in some way, but that's always been one of the challenges for me in comedy—to do something positive. Comedy often puts people or things down. 'Isn't this stupid, aren't they stupid?' But that's too easy."

In other words, Jerry didn't believe in using ridicule to get a laugh. Nor was Jerry interested in adding any edgy political observations to his act, as Leno and Dennis Miller did.

"I don't mix politics and comedy," Jerry says firmly. "To me the stage is not a pulpit. It's not funny to say, '*I'm upset.*' It may be provocative or interesting, but that's not what comedy is about. To me, comedy is about getting upset at the wrong things."

Once back on track, Jerry's stand-up evolved quickly, and it wasn't long before *The Tonight Show* came calling. Once the date was set, he called and told his parents the good news. His mother took it in her usual stride. "She's never impressed by anything that happens to me, or anything I do or any amount of money I could make," he says matter-of-factly.

His father, however, turned Jerry's appearance into a neighborhood event and made sure as many people as possible knew his son was going to be on national television. Using his craftsman's skill, he created a sign for his van that blared JERRY'S ON CARSON TONIGHT.

Seinfeld, twenty-seven, made his debut appearance on *The Tonight Show* May 7, 1981. On that broadcast, Jerry did some classic Seinfeldian bits, including one where he's a hair on a bathroom tile. He also showed his Zen-influenced way of looking at ordinary things when he mused about renting a tuxedo.

There's a thrill wearing a suit that's already been worn by eighty high school seniors on the most exciting night their glands have ever known.

Although funny, polished, and a crowd pleaser, Jerry's first *Tonight Show* appearance wasn't a complete success because he didn't get the ultimate Carson compliment, to be invited over to sit down and chat with the host—an accomplishment both Ellen DeGeneres and Drew Carey achieved on their initial visits.

But that was a minor ego setback. Jerry would be invited back to *The Tonight Show* regularly and eventually got to have his one-on-one moments with Johnny. The most important thing was the national exposure of appearing on Carson's show, which almost guaranteed an immediate boost in bookings, which in turn would increase both the stand-up's professional profile and personal pocketbook.

Always an astute businessman, Jerry made sure he parlayed his *Tonight Show* appearance into a significant career boost, which translated into more road dates and an appearance on HBO's *Sixth Annual Young Comedians Special*. And with each return appearance on *The Tonight Show,* his name recognition increased and his bookings improved from smaller, lower-paying clubs to the well-paying, larger A-list venues.

The more dates his representatives booked, the happier Jerry became. Peggy Mulloy, a former publicist for Atlanta's Punch Club, remembers Jerry when he was still early enough in his career to be staying at a condominium supplied by the comedy club instead of a hotel he could pay for himself.

"He was a hot young comic with lots of *Tonight Show* appearances to his credit," recalled Mulloy. "As I drove to pick him up for a local interview I wondered if he'd be one of those guys with an attitude, but he was so unpretentious that when I stopped for gas, he hopped out to fill the tank."

About the only thing that annoyed Jerry at this point in his career was the people's tendency to mispronounce his name. The most glaring misnomer was when Don Rickles once introduced him as George Stanberry, but more often than not he was mistakenly introduced as Jerry *Ste*infeld. Even though he preferred that people get the name right, he believed the aggravation would prove to be temporary. If he kept them laughing, they'd eventually know his name.

4

Turning Nothing Into Something

IN 1987, JERRY'S FATHER DIED OF CANCER AT SIXTY-FIVE. ALTHOUGH HE wouldn't live to see his son become a part of television history, Kal at least had the peace of mind that came from knowing that Jerry was making a comfortable living working at a profession he was passionate about.

Jerry dealt with his dad's passing by delving back into work. "It wasn't just a way of dealing with the grief of losing his dad," says a friend. "It was also a way of honoring Kal."

In August of that year, *Time* named Seinfeld, along with Steven Wright and Judy Tenuta, as its stand-up stars of the future. It touted Jay Leno as the hottest comic in America at that time; he had just been named the once-a-week substitute host for Johnny Carson and landed a primetime special for NBC.

In the article, writer Richard Zoglin describes the three comics' styles, deeming Wright an absurdist (I was once arrested for walking in someone else's sleep) and Tenuta a nutty, accordion-playing existentialist (You know what scares me? When you have to be nice to some paranoid schizophrenic just because she lives in your body).

Compared to those two, Seinfeld seemed tame and in fact is referred to as Leno's "suburban-preppy cousin." Both found their material in the commonplace concerns and shared memories of the

Baby Boom generation, especially TV, and perfected a lithe, fast-paced style.

"They are similar in style and subject matter, although Seinfeld has a softer edge," wrote Zoglin. "When talking about movie refreshment stands, he complains about popcorn that comes in huge buckets" (I don't need that much roofing insulation).

While it's true Seinfeld presents a softer comic edge onstage, it doesn't necessarily carry over offstage. Although Leno can be cutting—once, when describing a *Cagney and Lacy* reunion movie, he commented on Tyne Daly's and Sharon Gless's marked weight increase by noting that "pound for pound, it was the best TV movie of the year"—Jay worries more about the consequences of his humor. Jerry believes in letting the comedy chips fall where they may.

"If someone writes a letter to Jay and says a joke he did offended them or was offensive to whatever group they belong to, he'll either write back or call them up and arrange to have dinner with them," Seinfeld notes. "That's Jay. But I think you almost always have to offend in some way just to do comedy. I mean, if people don't have a sense of humor about themselves and they are the subject of the comic observation, they are going to be offended. To me it's like, 'Get away from me. This is comedy and somebody's got to get hurt.' Somebody's got to get hurt—and somebody's got to make the money."

Still, even though Jerry doesn't worry about offending with his humor, he is careful not to ridicule specific individuals or groups. Ridicule has elements of cruelty and meanness, lines Jerry doesn't cross.

Jerry is amazed at how happy Leno is to commune with his fans. "Jay's open to anyone. He'll sit in an airport just signing autographs for people. I really like *not* dealing with people," Seinfeld admits. "I'll go to unbelievable lengths to avoid minimal contact with another human being. Like, when I'm on a plane, I always make sure to do everything the stewardess wants me to before it needs to be done just so she doesn't have to come over and say anything.

"I've never had much interest in being liked, and I think people appreciate that. It's a relief because so many people want to be liked. I'm not a great conversationalist. I usually don't have much to say or much interest in what anyone else is saying. I could do a talk show with perhaps four people I'm really interested in. But I would not be able to take asking some actress about her next movie.

"The funny thing about being a comedian is, you have to have this great love for humanity on a mass level—because that's why you work so hard to do something good for people you don't even know—and yet still manage to absolutely hate every single individual you come in contact with."

Seinfeld says in his routine:

I believe the closest thing that we have to royalty in America are the people that get to ride in those little carts through the airport. If you're too fat, slow, and disoriented to get to your gate in time, you're not ready for air travel. The other people I hate are the people that get onto the moving walkway and then just stand there like it's a ride. Excuse me, there's no animated pirates here—do your legs work at all?

Misanthropy never sounded so good or so funny, and Jerry was getting both big laughs and big money for it. The years of worrying about having to get a day job were long past. Although Seinfeld knew he had reached a certain level of professional success, he was working so many club dates and spending so much time on the road that the extent of his accomplishments, and how it translated financially, occasionally sneaked up on him.

"I was supposed to do a performance in Boston once, and when I landed at the airport, nobody came to pick me up," he recalls. "I must have waited for about three hours, and I was really pissed off. So I thought, 'The hell with this. I'm just going to get back on the next plane. Screw them if they think I'm going to pay for a rental car.' Then I looked in my book and saw I was being paid $17,000 for this particular job. I had gone from being a $1,500 comic to a $15,000 comic without even noticing. And I realized I *could* afford a rental car."

In September 1987, Jerry appeared on his first HBO special, *Jerry Seinfeld's Stand-up Confidential.* Although television was already an important showcasing tool for comics, led by *The Tonight Show* and *The Late Show With David Letterman,* by the late 1980s any stand-up with even a modicum of appeal could also expect an opportunity to showcase his or her act with a cable special. Under the direction of Michael Fuchs, Home Box Office had embraced the concept of presenting uncensored stand-up comedy acts to its subscribers via a regular series of later-evening specials.

For "blue" comics—stand-ups who used a lot of sexual references or swearing—the HBO comedy specials were particularly important. These shows enabled them to do their real acts rather than the highly edited versions that Carson or Letterman required because of network broadcast standards. Subscription cable is not bound by the same rules, so comics got to present their acts as originally developed.

Since Seinfeld was already a clean comic, the uncensored aspect of the special wasn't nearly as important as simply being able to reach a wider audience as the star of his own showcase. An important segment of that audience was other members of Hollywood's creative community. Among those who paid closer attention to Seinfeld after his HBO show was Carl Reiner.

"He's not just a comedian," says the legendary comedy writer and producer. "He's different. When he talks about a young child not having bones in his body, that's brilliant. When you watch Jerry, you're seeing things you've never seen or heard before."

Such as his amazement with Swiss army knives:

Here's a weapon that has kept a nation at peace for centuries. Back off, I have the toenail-clipper right here.

With each appearance, Seinfeld's reputation grew, and he was regularly approached about projects. In the spring of 1988 executives from Castle Rock Entertainment called to see if he was interested in auditioning for the lead in a series pilot titled *Past Imperfect*. Although the *Benson* experience still reverberated within Jerry's psyche, Castle Rock had a solid comedy pedigree, so when it wanted to talk, Jerry agreed to listen. This brief flirtation with the company would play a pivotal role in his life a few years down the road.

Castle Rock Entertainment had been formed by Rob Reiner and several other veteran sitcom writers and producers who had all been associated in one way or another with Norman Lear, the man behind *All in the Family* and *Maude*. Reiner and his compatriots' mandate for television was simple. "Our goal from the beginning was to create successful sitcoms," says Glenn Padnick, who was Castle Rock's president of television. "That's all we wanted to do."

Castle Rock was in a bind. The pilot for *Past Imperfect*, which had originally been ordered by ABC, had been just days away from filming when production was abruptly curtailed because of a glaring casting problem. It was obvious to all involved that the lead actor, a comedian who was just coming off a successful run on a very popular hospital drama, was not working out.

ABC liked the pilot well enough that they were willing to proceed with another actor. Castle Rock went after Jerry as their first replacement choice.

"In our eyes he was terrific," recalls Padnick. "He even added jokes to the material."

Jerry felt comfortable enough with the Castle Rock executives, and confident enough in himself, to agree to give television another chance. As it turned out, though, ABC got cold feet. Even though Seinfeld was a nationally recognized stand-up with impeccable comedy credentials, he had no meaningful primetime television track record other than *Benson,* which had been an ABC series. Whether it was simply Seinfeld's lack of experience, or whether some at the network remembered his performance on *Benson,* ABC had second thoughts, and the project was dropped.

This time, however, Jerry suffered no emotional fallout and was able to walk away feeling pretty good about everything. Instead of seeing television as an albatross around his neck, Seinfeld began to consider it a comedic challenge. How could one maintain comic purity while working within the parameters of the very unfunny network hierarchy? How could a stand-up, such as himself, do a television comedy that remained true to his overall sensibility? If he ever did do another series, all those elements would have to be in place, or he simply wouldn't be interested.

This made him one of the few stand-ups not working every angle to get a shot at a network show, no questions asked. One of the most important showcases and proving grounds for would-be sitcom stars was the Just for Laughs comedy festival in Montreal. Like his contemporaries, Seinfeld appeared at the festival, but unlike his peers, he viewed it as simply another step in his comedic evolution rather than a stepping-stone into television.

What put the Montreal festival on the Hollywood map was its New Faces of Comedy program, which is specifically intended to introduce comics to television executives. To be selected, stand-ups have to be deemed to have the right stuff for prime time, especially a unique point of view, such as Tim Allen's routine about machismo that became the basis for his television show *Home Improvement.*

"We scour the world to find who we think are the most appropriate people for the needs of the industry," says festival director Andy Nulman.

Like the Oscar and Emmy winners before the envelopes are opened, the identity of the comics is a tightly guarded secret; the festival directors want to make sure the comics remain free agents until after their performances so that each network has an equal chance to sign them. "We want to ensure a fair playing field for both the comics and the industry," explained Bruce Hill, the festival's director of programming.

The Hollywood contingent watches the performances from their own secured balcony, which is equipped with note pads, pencils— and TV monitors so they can see how comics play on the small screen. Among the comics who have signed deals as a direct result of the New Faces program are Tim Allen, Drew Carey, Royale Watkins, Greg Girado, and Tom Rhodes.

However, Jerry Seinfeld was not among them. He opted against participating in the New Faces program. His foot in the door would come in a more indirect fashion, and the journey to a network show would take a typically circuitous route.

MUCH to his occasional chagrin, Jerry found himself spending more and more time on the West Coast. Like a lot of New Yorkers, he had resisted buying a condo or house in L.A. out of fear that the roots might become permanent. He was determined to keep his strong bonds with New York; as long as he did, he believed, he would always be centered and grounded.

"New York is the only place that has ever felt like home," Jerry says. "In Los Angeles, people just look at you and sneer. You get the feeling they're thinking, 'You might be a little ahead now, but they're going to overtake you any second now.'

"I miss the dirt, the crime, the congestion, the crumbling infrastructure—I miss everything about it. I also hate the weather in L.A. It has no personality. I want to get drenched and sweaty and frozen. I like that and I miss that. In a sense, the weather reflects the attitude out here—everybody wishes they had no problems. But if problems weren't interesting, why would people want to watch them in movies and stories?"

New York was his hometown and the people his soulmates. Seinfeld felt the city was also the primal wellspring of his comedic soul.

"After living in L.A. for too long, you're not going to be funny anymore," he says. "It just slowly ebbs away because the environment is very unfunny. In New York, they breed it—even the garbage men have it. But out here they exterminate it. Just standing on a street corner or walking down Fifth Avenue I get a rush and five thousand ideas."

Despite his litany of reasons why New York was a superior place to live and work, Jerry had finally given up his apartment and bought a two-bedroom condo in West Hollywood. At the time, the West Hollywood area was part of Los Angeles proper. Subsequently, it seceded to become its own municipality, giving itself the nickname "the Creative City."

West Hollywood is reminiscent of New York City's Greenwich Village, insofar as it is a distinct neighborhood. It is the one community in Los Angeles where people are just as apt to walk or hop on a bike to the numerous coffee shops, restaurants, boutiques, and bars as they are to drive.

It's also the center of L.A.'s gay community, as the Village is of New York's. Seinfeld's association with the area is most likely the genesis of the long-heard rumors that Jerry is gay—that and the fact he's so fastidiously neat. "Yeah, I've heard those rumors for years," he says easily. "I've been told that *everybody* at NBC in New York thought I was gay."

Seinfeld's lack of discomfort over questions about his sexual preferences is just another example of the self-assurance that nearly every interviewer has observed over the years. This extreme self-awareness and confidence gives Jerry the ability to judge himself professionally without any false modesty.

By 1988, Seinfeld would be referring to himself as "America's most imitated comedian" and "the king of observational comedy." To the uninitiated, such self-appraisal could be mistaken for megalomania, but Seinfeld wasn't implying that he was somehow better than any of the rich line of observational comics who came before him. Seinfeld's personal evaluation was based on his belief that at that point in time he was at the top of his game in relation to his peers, even his close friend Jay Leno.

Seinfeld was well aware of his comedic roots, including Leno, Robert Klein, and the man many consider the true king, George Carlin. In fact, it's easy to imagine the following Seinfeld commentary coming straight from Carlin's mouth:

I think the reason people come out to see my show is just really
because they want to go out. I think all of life is going out and
going back. You get to your job, you want to get home; you get
to your home, you want to go out. When you're out you say, 'I
gotta get back.' Wherever you are in life you gotta get the hell
out of there.

Even though George Wallace once commented that so many up-
and-coming comics were now imitating his friend that there should
be a Seinfeld Comedy Cable Channel, in truth, Jerry's style isn't
revolutionary. Although some currently call it recognition humor, to
more veteran comics it's still basic observational humor given a
modern makeover.

"It's nothing new," says Richard Belzer, who was a well-known
stand-up for years before NBC's *Homicide* made him a television
star. "In ten years, they'll be calling it cognizant humor, but it'll be
the same thing. Take a simple everyday event and spin a web with
it."

That is something Seinfeld has proven to be very, very good at.

The Sunday paper is the worst. Here's a thousand pages of
information you had no idea about. How can they tell you
everything they know about every single day of the week and
then have this much left over on Sunday when nothing's going
on?

BY THE time 1988 came to a close, Jerry, now thirty-four, had made
more than twenty-five appearances on Carson and Letterman combined and had signed to host his second HBO special. Like Leno, he
basically lived on the road, making more than three hundred appearances a year. He had been named Funniest Male Stand-up Comic at
the American Comedy Awards and had also been voted America's
Best Male Comedy Club Performer in a poll of nightclub regulars.
By that time, Seinfeld was working primarily in concert halls and
larger venues, such as the Vegas-Tahoe circuit, where he was earning
in the mid–five figures per week.

One of his few regrets was the demise of the comedy album.
Earlier comics such as George Carlin, Bill Cosby, and Bob Newhart
had regularly cut albums of their stand-up material, but the market
had dried up by the time Seinfeld was in his prime. "When I first
started doing stand-up, it was still the ultimate goal," he reflected.

"But within a few years, they'd become obsolete. Now they go right to the back of the record store with Moms Mabley."

Other than that, life was good, and his career was even better. He was one of the very few comics who looked forward to the rigors of constant travel. Most stand-ups find life on the road a grueling but necessary evil, a kind of comic residency program, where your skills are honed in the line of fire. It's also where the less dedicated are quickly weeded out. Michael "Kramer" Richards, for one, tried his hand at stand-up and quickly discovered the road wasn't for him: "Believe me, doing stand-up comedy on the road is a business most comedians don't survive. They turn to women or drinking or get bitter."

George Wallace agrees. "Most comedians don't like themselves, let alone the road because you're with yourself on the road. During the day you get lonesome and you call your friends. *'What's going on?' 'Nothing.'* I ran up thousand-dollar phone bills with calls like that."

Even lifers like Rodney Dangerfield, who helped Jerry out early in his career, have frequently bemoaned how hard it is finding people to talk to while touring, and the resulting loneliness.

Jerry, however, thrived on the constant movement. "Four days is about my maximum to go without working," he said in an interview during that time. "I took a vacation this year, and I just hated it. Going somewhere and just flaking out is not for me."

Being on the road kept Seinfeld's timing razor sharp and offered new challenges every night. He loved the audiences and didn't succumb to the loneliness so many comics suffer. He wasn't bothered by the endless plane trips; the only annoyance was getting stuck next to a chatty fellow passenger who wanted to hear all about what Johnny Carson was really like.

Nor was the constant packing and unpacking a problem. "I throw a couple of sweaters and a jacket into a bag, make sure the answering machine is on, and I go," Jerry said. "If I forget something like underwear, I'll buy it when I get to where I'm going."

Like a superhero going off to do battle in the great unknown, Seinfeld entered another dimension on the road, a parallel universe where he was the lone comic gunman. "I have a very romantic, sentimental attitude about being a stand-up," he admits. "I love being on my own in a strange town, being in the spotlight, with the smoke. I don't even think of it as being in show business; it's more like the guy who's on a surfboard miles out in the ocean."

On the other hand, if you're out to sea you're not around to mind the store. Jerry discovered this drawback when he suddenly found himself the victim of an unscrupulous money manager.

"I was having some trouble getting money from my accountant for a car I wanted to buy," he recalls. "When I went to ask for it, he'd say, 'If you pull it out now, you'll lose all the interest,' which seemed to make sense. Then one day I got a call telling me the money was gone."

The accountant had taken off with about $50,000 of Jerry's money. Rather than bring charges, Jerry decided to make sure he could trust the next person he put in charge of his finances. So he hired his sister to be his business manager. Although she wasn't a certified money manager, Jerry trusted her.

A lot of people claim "it's not about the money," but in Seinfeld's case that maxim has repeatedly proven true. He took the news of the theft with typical equanimity. He knew he would make up the lost money. It simply meant that for now he was short one Porsche, not an insignificant situation.

While stand-up may have been his first love, cars were a close second. Many other East Coast transplants complain incessantly about L.A.'s car culture, but Jerry readily adapted to that particular religion and became one of the high priests of Southern California's Autopia. In particular, he worshiped Porsches, with Volkswagen Bugs a lesser deity. As any car buff knows, the two models are actually related. Ferdinand Porsche created the Volkswagen in the 1930s at the behest of Adolf Hitler, and the popular Porsche 914 of years past was equipped with a basic Bug engine.

"I learned to drive in a Bug," he explains. "It was just the biggest toy. It wasn't part of the adult world, it was the top of the kid world. Everybody has an experience imprinted on their mind about something that happened to them in a Bug."

In the beginning, there was Jerry and one car, which he would tune up himself and upon which he would lavish his total vehicular affection. "I've always liked the idea of a man having his one car. You don't see a really good warrior with, like, three or four swords on his belt. But then I got one car for each coast, and after that the collection sort of grew"—And grew. Numbering sixty cars at last count, it has become so large and valuable that he now stores it in two rented airplane hangars at Santa Monica Airport.

At first glance, Seinfeld's car collection seems out of character with his normally Spartan lifestyle. Jay Leno has publicly teased Jerry over his sparsely furnished homes that take the concept of "uncluttered" to a new, pristine realm. But if one looks beyond the material aspect of car ownership, Jerry's obsession is actually in perfect keeping with his overall Zen sensibilities.

"I like precision-built things," he affirms. "As a kid, I was small for my age, and when you're small, you like small things. In fact, that's what a joke is, a crystallized observation; a small, precision-crafted nugget of truth."

Naturally, for Seinfeld a car is not just a car; it's a personal reflection, an almost spiritual synthesis of form and psyche. "The car is a fascinating combination of social needs, fashion needs, and mechanical design—it's a rolling fashion sculpture. Everyone is in the exact perfect car for them. Even if it's borrowed. And, if you notice, people captain an automobile exactly the way they captain their life. The way they yell or don't yell at people, or when they decide to give, or not give, ground."

In his act he notes:

> *The real problem with boxing is that you have two guys fighting who have no prior argument. They should have the boxers come into the ring in little cars, drive around a little bit, eventually there's an accident.*
> *"Didn't you see my signal?"*
> *"Look at that fender!"*
> *Then you'd see a real fight.*

FOR ALL his aloofness and outward emotional reserve, Seinfeld is not impervious to his detractors. Although his comedy may begin with the premise of pleasing himself, it is ultimately performed for an audience of strangers. Amidst the din of applause, he will search out the one person who doesn't respond. While the praise of fans is fulfilling and as addictive as any feel-good drug, the real challenge is to confront and win over the critics or prove them wrong.

After more than a decade of perfecting his stand-up, by 1988 Seinfeld was by all accounts a polished, smooth performer with laser-accurate timing. He was comfortable with his body onstage and always seemed in complete control, able to command any crowd. For at least one prominent critic, that was exactly the problem. In a review titled *Laughing on Empty,* *Los Angeles Times* critic Lawrence Christon cast a thoughtful and unsparing eye on Jerry:

"Seinfeld is a pleasant, effortless performer who works clean. The kind of likable smoothie who's popular in school because he's a good dancer and gets his date home on time and even chats with her dad. There's no vindictiveness in his act. He doesn't traffic in the mindless hate, or self-hate, that characterizes so many other stand-ups. He uses his body well. His language has imagery and rhythm. He's expressive. He's clear. And he's completely empty."

The critic went on to put Jerry's routine into the context of comedy as art, that is, as representative of human truths. "With the great comedians, the joke serves a coherent body of observations, or at least a theme. [Seinfeld] has a frame of reference. Yeats had a line about 'paying homage to unevent.' Seinfeld pays homage to insignificance, and he does it impeccably."

Christon's observations are not without merit. Seinfeld's stand-up does skim the surface, his observations skipping from crest to comic crest, looking for comic inspiration in small details others would overlook. (Why do we wear cologne? Does anybody really think I smell like that?) He's a master at describing human behavior and pointing out our idiosyncrasies, but he adds nothing to our understanding of them. That is in part because Jerry is so guarded about revealing too much of himself. While his humor may reflect his personality, it does not serve as a window into his soul. Also, he's clearly not interested in the big picture of life. He does comedy to make people laugh, not to make any kind of social or personal commentary. He's funny without being particularly thoughtful or revealing.

"I don't reveal details about myself in my act because I'm not that into myself," he explains. "I'm more into what's going on around me. There's a subtle distinction between being self-obsessed, which I am, and self-oriented, which I'm not. People complain that my comedy doesn't show a lot of personal anguish, but I look at Laurel and Hardy, and they are my icons of comedy perfection—wonderful and simple to enjoy. When the audience applauds, it's not for *me.* It's for the work I've done."

That said, Christon's charge that he lacked *substance*—which implied that he therefore lacked the comedic importance of a Tomlin, Klein, or Carlin—struck a nerve in Seinfeld.

"That review was a turning point for Jerry," says a fellow comic, who recalls Seinfeld's agitation over what he considered a scathing critique. "The gist of the piece said that there was nothing more to Jerry than jokes, that there was nothing underneath his observations to give them substance. But Jerry is the kind of guy who is always looking to make a negative a positive. Rather than get defensive, he decided to take the 'nothing' notion and run with it. Basically, he decided that he would show them just how much he could make out of nothing."

5

The Ratings Were Less Than Glorious

"THERE ARE LEVELS OF COMEDY," SEINFELD NOTES. "THE FIRST LEVEL IS TO make your friends laugh. The second is to make strangers laugh. The third is to make strangers laugh for money, and the highest level is to make people talk like you."

Indeed it is.

Five months after his experience on *Past Imperfect,* Jerry was once again approached about a primetime opportunity. This time it was NBC who called Jerry's manager, George Shapiro, testing the waters on whether Jerry would be interested in trying to transfer his talent from club stages onto the small screen. But NBC's interest didn't come from the primetime development division. Instead, the peacock people wanted to know if Jerry was interested in doing a network special. Seinfeld and Shapiro met with senior vice president Rick Ludwin in early November 1988.

"That was our first meeting," Ludwin remembers. "Our mandate was to find the next Jay Leno. Jerry Seinfeld had started to play bigger venues, just like Jay had, and I set up a meeting. We asked him, 'What do you want to do in TV?'"

During his initial meeting with NBC, Jerry told them, "This meeting is about as far as I ever thought in my whole career: 'Someday I will meet with some really important people in show business.'"

Whether calculated or not, Seinfeld's flippancy wasn't completely genuine. "One result of the Christon review was that Jerry had decided he was going to make the leap and take on television," says an associate. "And he was going to use the very 'nothing' element he had been branded with to do it. But he needed to figure out just the right format to make it work."

Sitcoms, however, weren't at the top of his list. "I wasn't even reading for sitcoms," he recalls. "I couldn't be a summer school teacher with a family and a funny life. Somebody putting words in my mouth, other than me, has never been appealing. I knew I couldn't do it. I was unable to work within the existing form. I had to remake the sitcom to make this work for me."

Seinfeld approached longtime acquaintance Larry David backstage at a comedy club for some advice regarding his NBC experience. David, a local stand-up and former writer for *Saturday Night Live,* was considered by many in the New York comedy club circuit to be the voice of their conscience. He was revered by fellow comics for his intelligence and humor—and complete inability to make any money.

"He was an underground legend in New York comedy circles," explains Seinfeld. "His material was brilliant. It was the best. But he never really made it because he didn't have the stagecraft or the structure. But it was still very hip to like David's material, although I think it's safe to say that he was much more popular among the other comedians than he was with the actual customers."

An edgy performer onstage, David was known for chiding an unresponsive audience if they didn't get his jokes.

"He just wasn't any good at pandering to a group of drunken strangers," Seinfeld recalls. "He'd get so angry and resentful if he'd see someone not listening or someone making a noise that he'd completely fly off the handle. One of the most important traits of being a stand-up is having the right temperament—and his is exactly the type of temperament you *shouldn't* have."

"I can't take adversity," David admits. "I was like John McEnroe. For me, doing comedy in a club was like going to war. But then if they laughed, it was too much pleasure for one man."

But Seinfeld didn't necessarily see David's lack of stage decorum as a total negative. "The thing is, all comedians are cranky," Seinfeld notes. "I never met a funny person who wasn't. To be funny, you've got to be cranky. Now, I'm a contented person, but a thousand and one things *irritate* me. That's what I love about New

York. It's a gymnasium of irritation. I thrive on all the craziness. And that's why New York produces good comedians. It's that constant chafing. If you've got a comedic bent, New York's going to provide you with plenty of ammo."

By that standard, Larry David was a munitions dump ready to blow. Born in Brooklyn, he didn't start out to be a comic. He graduated from the University of Maryland with a degree in history; like many college grads with a liberal arts education, he struggled to make a living. After working variously as a cabbie, a chauffeur, and a salesman, he hit on comedy quite by accident. He went to the Improv one night as a regular paying customer and, while watching the stand-ups, had an epiphany: "I said, 'I could do that.' I had finally found a job I liked. It was a great outlet for saying the things you want to say but might get beat up for otherwise. Plus, I was sleeping as late as I wanted and going to the movies. My boss was my audience."

In 1989, David was already forty-one and still struggling to find the right avenue to vent his comic vision. He had written a pile of screenplays, none of which was optioned, much less produced. He had been a cast member of ABC's late-night sketch comedy show *Fridays* between 1980 and 1982, then had gone on to join the writing staff of *Saturday Night Live* during the 1984–85 season. He had also appeared in a couple of Woody Allen films, *Radio Days* and *Another Woman*. Overall, though, he was still just scraping by.

But by the time Jerry sought him out, David was back on the comedy circuit with his eclectic and obscure brand of observational humor, which included a routine about how people who have such excessive body heat that butter melts on their heads are often mistaken for pancakes.

One night after both Seinfeld and David had performed at Catch a Rising Star, they went to a deli to grab a bite to eat. Jerry remembers, "We were walking around in this deli making fun of the food, and Larry said, 'See, this is what the show should be about.' Because comedians have a lot of very funny conversations in their off-hours."

Ironically, David and Seinfeld had never been close friends. But with a comedic instinct that has proven itself over the years, Seinfeld sensed that David would be able to act as the growth medium through which Jerry's humor could be presented in a funny and pure way on the small screen.

"I chose Larry to work with because when we talked, it sounded like great dialogue," Seinfeld explains. "If you think sexual compatibility is difficult, humor compatibility is far more rare. That's why the original idea of the show was just conversations between me and Larry. There are very few things in life as enjoyable as good conversation."

At the Westway Diner, located in Manhattan at 614 Ninth Avenue, near Times Square, Jerry and Larry came up with the broad outline for a television show they would call *The Seinfeld Chronicles*. Within a span of ten minutes, the idea for the sitcom was born. It would be a show about how comedians come up with ideas for their jokes.

"We were just chatting and came up with the notion that the funniest stuff happens with a comedian during the day, in his life, not at night, when he's working, and that that would be a good show," Jerry says. "I would be the stand-up going around the city collecting material for my act. Then we'd show me doing the material in a club setting."

From those first moments, there was never any question that Jerry would be playing Jerry. "I wanted to be myself," he says. "I didn't want to play a character. I always hated it when comedians come up with these little jobs for themselves on their television series. You know what you really are. You're a comedian. I wanted to be as comfortable as I could, so I stuck with that."

"Basically, Jerry can't act, and he's been pretty up-front about that," says an associate. "He's not a Robin Williams or even a Paul Reiser who's comfortable putting on someone else's hat. He's most comfortable being Jerry, and being Jerry is what Jerry does best."

David and Seinfeld went to NBC and presented their idea to NBC's president of entertainment, Warren Littlefield. Although legend has it that David indeed pitched the show to NBC as a comedy basically about nothing, Jerry sets the record straight: "We said it would be a show about conversation, which is *almost* the same as nothing. It wouldn't be heavy on story."

Littlefield wasn't impressed with the semantics. Putting it kindly, he wasn't particularly enthused about their story idea. Never one to take rejection well, David reacted the way he did to a roomful of hecklers and got into a snit, telling Littlefield in so many words that he didn't know the first thing about comedy.

"I really did kind of lose it," David admits. "I conducted myself in my usual unprofessional manner. The idea we came up with was similar to what eventually went on the air, but we conceived it as a one-camera show. We were laughed out of the building with it."

Not completely. Much to their surprise, Rick Ludwin, an NBC senior vice president in charge of late night, variety, and specials was interested. He was even willing to ante up money from his development budget to shoot a pilot.

When NBC told Seinfeld and David they should find a producer, Jerry turned to his manager, George Shapiro, and said, "How about those guys I did the pilot with last year?" Shapiro put in the call to Castle Rock Entertainment.

Glenn Padnick, president of Castle Rock TV, remembers his reaction: "I was hooked from the first draft of the first script. It was so fabulous. Just everyday stuff, so recognizable and off-the-plot to the max."

From the beginning, Jerry made it clear that he was not going to be merely a hired gun and would be involved in every creative decision. He was looking for a production company that would be a partner, not a boss, and sensed Castle Rock believed enough in the show to give him a free hand.

"Castle Rock really made the show," Seinfeld says now. "They've been behind us a hundred percent from the first episode. They put up the money, they ran interference, they helped develop the whole idea. Castle Rock is responsible for the look of the show and its quality. For example, I wanted it on film instead of video tape, and no one else would have given me that because it's very expensive."

All of a sudden, what had been idle conversation in a diner and afternoons spent writing at David's apartment was turning into a concrete reality. Now Seinfeld and David actually had to come up with the goods on film—as partners. This was untested ground for both of them; going into the pilot, there were a lot of unknown variables, any one of which could have caused the entire project to implode.

The first was how well David and Jerry would work together after spending so many years as the captains of their own comedy ships. For his part, and somewhat out of character, David says he wasn't worried about any possible negative repercussions from working with this particular peer and friend: "Jerry tends to confront and deal with issues as they arise; he'll come right out and tell you directly what's bothering him so you never have to worry that he's harboring any unspoken grudges against you. That's how he is with everyone, because he doesn't like things preying on his mind."

The next was how well they would individually deal with the pressure of the high-stakes game of television. David says, seriously, "To be honest, I think the only thing that really worked in my favor is that right from the beginning I really didn't give a shit whether or not the show was a success. That's not to say I didn't want to do good work, but I wasn't about to let myself be judged by network standards. When you're not concerned with succeeding, you can work with complete freedom."

This is not to say that David, who for years had tried to find steady work in television, was not aware of the opportunity he was being handed. He notes, "The network was already interested in doing something with Jerry, so I skipped a couple of hundred steps right there. I was very fortunate to hook up with Jerry because, believe me, if I had gone to NBC on my own with an idea about, say, a blind deli man, I don't think it would have gone well."

As they worked on the pilot script, Seinfeld and David instinctively divvied up the comic duties to capitalize on their individual strengths, with Jerry focusing on the material and Larry humanizing the situation.

"Some people are better at finding humor in large issues that confront society, but Jerry can go in, take a microscope and examine the tiniest moments, and see the humor in it," David says. "He looks at the small things you can feel, see, and touch."

David, who is as emotional as Jerry is often removed and aloof, had a talent for tapping into the human-behavior side of any given situation and presenting it in such a way as to reveal the universal truth at its core. In other words, he was able to do precisely what Lawrence Christon said Seinfeld's act couldn't: show deeper human truth, albeit a truth borne of angst, through comedy. The synthesis of their wildly different personalities and temperaments blended into a surprisingly coherent comedic form.

In later years, David would look back and say it was a case of blissful ignorance. "I had experience in sketch writing, but I never wrote half hours. The show was fresh because neither one of us knew how a half-hour show was done. We didn't know how you were *supposed* to do it, so we did it our way."

But not without having to draw an occasional line in the sand. "At one of our first meetings with the network," recalls Seinfeld, "they were making all sorts of suggestions, like, 'Why don't we have the characters go to a dude ranch. Then we can get better ratings in Texas.' And Larry said, 'This is the show, and we're not going to change it.' Everyone burst out laughing. What was this guy? Who was I? We were nobodies. But it was that attitude that made the show."

Since the cornerstone idea of the pilot was daytime Jerry's search for material to be used by nighttime Jerry in his stand-up act, Seinfeld and David wrote opening and closing mini-monologues to bracket the interior story line. It was reminiscent of the device used by Jack Benny in his old show.

One of the characters who populated Jerry's TV world was his best friend, George Costanza, a thinly disguised television version of Larry David himself. "I'd like to be George," David would later say about the character. "I wish I was as healthy as George. He's doing the things I want to do."

There was also a strange, off-kilter neighbor who was based on Kenny Kramer, Larry David's real-life neighbor across the hall at the Manhattan Plaza housing complex for performing artists at 43rd Street and Tenth Avenue. As un–New York as it might sound, Larry and Kenny truly did leave their doors open so each could walk into the other's apartment whenever he wanted.

"Kenny was always coming up with these ideas that sounded as if they had been made up for a television show," David recalls. "He would talk you into doing something with him—which would invariably turn out bad for you. Or he'd do something like disappear and leave you waiting in the car by yourself for an hour."

There was a time when Kenny Kramer had visions of playing himself and broached the subject with Seinfeld and David. "Actually, I lobbied to be cast for the part—which is just another word for begging and pleading," says Kramer, a former comedian since turned entrepreneur and general man-about-New-York. "After Larry came up with the idea for the show, they were across the hall creating this television series and they decided they needed a neighbor. So they came across the hall and said, 'Hey Krame, can we base a character on you and call him Kramer?'

"I said okay, *if* I got to play Kramer. They told me I couldn't be Kramer. I said, 'I am Kramer.' Does this sound familiar? Anyway, they explained that NBC would never go for it so I said, *'Okay, do it.'* "

Although Kenny had agreed in principle, he was brought up short when he read the release sent to him by Castle Rock. "They were asking me to give them the exclusive rights to my life story in perpetuity!" he says, indignant. "I said no way. Larry said they'd just have to call the character Bender, and I told him that was fine with me.

"Then I got a phone call from Larry a few days later. He told me that Jerry was in love with the name Kramer and wanted to know if there was any way to work things out. I told him to have the lawyers from Castle Rock call me. They did, and I worked out an agreement with them where the rights that I licensed to them are nonexclusive and I retained all the rights to my life story to exploit in 'any and all media throughout the universe.' In other words," he adds, "I'm the only person in America who can be Kramer and not owe money to Castle Rock or NBC."

The deal also included financial compensation, although what seemed to be good money at the time would later look like so much spare change. "I was given enough money to last me the rest of my life—unless I wanted to buy food, in which case I would have fallen terribly short," Kenny Kramer says. "But you have to understand, at the time nobody had any idea of what a huge show this would be. Larry and Jerry were my friends, and I didn't want to impede them from getting a television show on the air."

Despite all the legal maneuverings, the agreement between Kramer and Castle Rock was not finished in time for his name to be used in the pilot. In the script, the neighbor character is listed as Hoffman, although in the episode, Jerry refers to him at one point as Kessler.

Once he ironed out the deal with Castle Rock, Kenny Kramer became a footnote in television history as the only known person ever to have two TV situation comedy characters named after him. The first time, his full name had been used in the mostly forgotten, and fully forgettable, 1984 NBC pilot *Temporary Insanity. Seinfeld*, however, would provide Kramer with a more enduring legacy, upon which he would eventually build a cottage industry.

Looking at the original pilot script for *The Seinfeld Chronicles*—which would later be retitled "Good News, Bad News" and air as episode 1 of the series—is like taking a trip in a time machine back to a parallel-universe *Seinfeld* (or, to borrow a concept from the series, *Bizarro Seinfeld)*. While the general format and tone of the show are familiar, the characters are noticeably unformed and raw.

Under the direction of Art Wolff, we are introduced to the three main characters as played by Seinfeld, journeyman actor Michael Richards, and noted Broadway star Jason Alexander: Jerry is a comic living in a studio, complete with skylight; Kramer, with normal, flat hair, is the inarticulate and doltish neighbor who lives across the hall; George is a whiny, poor man's Woody Allen clone. Their hangout is Pete's Luncheonette, where they commiserate over their daily travails.

The story line revolves around a pending overnight visit from a woman Jerry met while performing on the road in Michigan. The quandary is whether the visit is platonic or the precursor to a night of romance, so George tries to explain to Jerry the signals to look for. In the end, it turns out the woman is engaged and genuinely just needed a place to crash.

The pilot was shot in April on a soundstage in Los Angeles. After the postproduction was finished, NBC decided to screen the pilot for a select test audience. (All television networks and movie studios spend millions of dollars on marketing research, which includes using test audiences to gauge reaction to new shows.) In May 1989, NBC aired the pilot into selected homes via cable, then conducted a viewer survey.

"The report was really bad," Jerry remembers. In fact, the results were more than just ugly; they were insulting and occasionally hostile.

"You can't get too excited about going two guys going to the Laundromat."

"Jerry's loser friend George is not a forceful character."

"Weak."

"He's just a loser. Who'd want to watch this guy?"

"Jerry needs a stronger supporting cast."

"Jerry is dense and indecisive."

"Why are they interrupting the stand-up for these stupid stories?"

The best critique from the test audience was that the show was "contemporary, unusual, and fairly humorous."

While the Kramer character scored poorly because he apparently reminded some of the test audience of their own weird neighbors, George Costanza fared the worst by far: "George was negatively viewed as a wimp who was only mildly interesting. Viewers said he whined and did not like his relationship with Jerry." As for the overall reaction to Jerry, he was seen as *"powerless, dense, and naive."*

The conclusion of the network researcher should have put the final nails in Larry and Jerry's television coffin: "None of the supports were particularly liked, and viewers felt Jerry needed a better back-up ensemble. No segment of the audience was eager to watch the show again."

When NBC decided to shelve the pilot until the middle of summer, nearly everyone associated with the show had good reason to assume the worst. Networks notoriously burn off unwanted pilots by airing them in the viewer-depleted month of July.

The Seinfeld Chronicles aired July 5, 1989. Not surprisingly, the ratings were less than glorious. Equally not surprising was NBC's initial decision to pass on going any further with the show. But it would take more than a network pulling the plug to kill Jerry and Larry's series.

Even though entertainment president Warren Littlefield agreed with the research conclusion that *The Seinfeld Chronicles* was a series whose time had not come, Rick Ludwin staunchly disagreed. "To this day, I have vivid memories of what was said about the show," Ludwin recalls. " 'It's too New York.' 'It's too Jewish.' An executive who screened it in New York City actually asked me, 'Does he have to be a comedian?' I'm not from New York and I'm not Jewish, but I thought it was funny. I thought it could work. I told people it will be a show that people will turn over rocks to find."

Displaying unwavering faith in the show and its concept, Ludwin did a little creative accounting and used money budgeted for two specials to finance four additional *Seinfeld* half hours. The network brass agreed, with one nonnegotiable condition for the pickup. They needed to add a woman to the cast because, as weak as the overall test results were, the pilot had tested extremely low among women.

When they got the news that they had been resurrected and given an additional order of four episodes, Seinfeld says, he turned to

David and asked, "How the hell are we going to do four more of these things?"

He wasn't kidding. Because of their inexperience in television, neither David nor Seinfeld really had any concept of the amount of work that goes into the creation of a twenty-two-minute episode. As a stand-up, Seinfeld had the leisure of honing his act over many years, but now he and David had to produce four episodes in relatively short order. Unlike most sitcom stars, who get to go home after the day's rehearsal because their only job is to perform, Seinfeld was also not only one of the show's producers but one of its writers, which meant he seldom went home. That was the way he wanted it.

"Why have someone do something for you when they can't do it as well as you can?" he says. Then he adds, "But the hardest thing is switching jobs, because my personality type is to focus in on one thing at a time, like a laser beam."

That is why Jerry decided from the outset that, for one thing, the cast had to be a true ensemble, with the screen time and dialogue evenly shared among Seinfeld and his costars. Although many shows claim to be ensemble ventures, in reality few are; inevitably, egos get in the way. Stories of stars actually counting lines of dialogue or having scripts rewritten so costars won't get the big laughs are legion. But in Jerry's case, he meant it.

"I have no ego about the show, believe it or not," he said. "I don't even care if I am in it, to tell you the truth. If it is a good show, that's all that matters to me."

He also wanted his character to be simply a heightened-reality version of himself, so that his time in front of the camera would be as easy as possible. "We try to keep the television Jerry and the real Jerry as close as we can. We don't want him to do too much acting," David deadpanned. Years later, in the episode "The Pilot," he gave Jerry some dialogue summing up their attitude when the series first started. "I'm the one who's dying, because I can't act," says TV Jerry. "I stink. I don't know what I'm doing."

Actually, real-life Jerry's assessment of the situation was much better balanced: he didn't need to be brilliant, like Carroll O'Connor in *All in the Family,* merely serviceable. He was confident that he could do a more than respectable job.

"Stand-up is a very specific craft, not unlike playing the saxophone," he says. "If you don't know how, forget it. But acting is like riding a bicycle. You may not compete in the Olympics, but you can at least keep the pedals going."

Especially if you are smart enough to surround yourself with co-stars who are talented enough to take up the slack.

6

Kramer: Enter Mr. Hysterical

"I WANTED THE SHOW TO HAVE BALANCE," SAYS JERRY. "IT WAS CALLED *Seinfeld,* but I always wanted it to be an ensemble show."

As Jerry knew, casting for any ensemble show, but particularly a comedy, is a tricky process, and regardless of all the time and thought and second-guessing that goes into it, in the end there is always an element of sheer serendipity. Just because an actor is individually talented and charismatic doesn't mean his or her personality will necessarily mesh with the others to create on-screen magic.

Off-screen harmony is just as important. Jerry was clever enough to understand that terrific costars would only make the show better. And if the show was a success, he would automatically benefit. After all, it was called *Seinfeld.*

Others have not always been so wise. Television history is littered with tales of actors who click on-camera but have such antipathy toward one another that they refuse to speak to each other when not performing. *Evening Shade,* for example, was a Top 25 show, but because of cast incompatibility, the producers gave up rather than go through another season of backstage misery. In a more recent example, *Cybill,* which initially looked like a long-term performer, basically self-destructed because of infighting among the cast that included sniping about who was getting the funnier lines.

In contrast, *The Mary Tyler Moore Show* is perhaps the best example of a show that made maximum use of its supporting players. Even though Moore was the linchpin of her series, it was her interaction with Valerie Harper, Ed Asner, Ted Knight, and Betty White that provided the biggest laughs and embodied the show's central emotional theme: that our friends are nothing less than extended family.

However, there would be a significant and fundamental difference in philosophy between *Seinfeld* and *The Mary Tyler Moore Show*. It is summed up by Larry David's succinct decree of what he never wanted to see on the show: "No hugging. No learning."

Forget motivation; never mind the characters' backstories. All Jerry and Larry wanted was funny. That meant they needed performers who were secure enough to present themselves to the television audience as perhaps less than always likable, because in the *Seinfeld* world "nice" was not funny.

Even though actors portray fictional creations, inevitably they endow the roles they play with certain elements of themselves; who the actors are as people and the life experiences they bring with them are just as important in developing the characters as the writing. So when Seinfeld and David began looking for the actors to play Kramer and George, they were looking for specific sensibilities.

To play the part of Kramer, David called upon a journeyman character actor named Michael Richards, with whom he had worked on *Fridays*. Although there was little physical resemblance between the two, Michael's man-child quality as a performer and his kinetic onstage energy seemed well suited to portraying Kenny's over-the-top life force, which had been incorporated into the TV character.

What's ironic, though, is that away from the cameras Richards is not the bundle of movement he portrays as Kramer. While he's an admitted eccentric like his television counterpart, he is far more low-key, even a bit removed at times. He is also a serious student of comedy who enjoys solitude and reading books on philosophy.

"Michael really is a very serious person who happens to have a side of his personality that is Krameresque," notes Larry Charles, one of *Seinfeld*'s longtime producers. "People who expect him to be a big, goofy guy are in for a shock. I think he wants to put people at ease, yet at times he himself has trouble being at ease."

Richards, who was born July 24, 1949, in Los Angeles, learned to be both serious and solitary as a child. After his father, William, an electrical engineer, died when Michael was only two, his mother, Phyllis, went to work full time to support her only child. With a mother gone all day and no siblings to interact with, Michael learned early how to be alone.

When he was six, he taught himself to ride a bike. "I didn't see it as being lonely," he says. "To me, it was solitude, which I found rather comforting. I used to ride my bike through different neighborhoods just to do it. I always had an adventurous spirit."

When he wasn't biking or taking long walks, Michael would often sit and watch television, particularly fascinated by shows like *I Love Lucy*. To fill the void left by his dad's death, Michael tended to attach himself to surrogate father figures, such as teachers, older male friends, and even Red Skelton. Although as an adult he has forged a warm relationship with his mom, Richards admits they were not particularly close when he was growing up:

"I didn't have much of a relationship with my mother. She worked all the time, so I was left to myself most of the time. I can't ever remember having any deep, meaningful conversations with her. I think she was just so tired from working all day. And that was fine with me. But I get my eccentricity from my mother. She's very reclusive. However, she was also very funny. She used to throw Halloween parties and dress up in outrageous costumes. She had a strong comic sensibility, but it wasn't intentional."

A native Southern Californian, Richards spent his childhood in Culver City, best known in those days as the home of the old MGM Studios. "Because I was brought up in Culver City, I felt a kinship when I watched Laurel and Hardy and recognized a lot of the places they were shooting. I loved them. But as a boy, I was mostly a Red Skelton fan. I used to think of ways to sneak onto the motion picture lots. I liked to play around on the sets."

He didn't equate his intense fascination with the studio with any innate desire to be a performer, although he learned early in life that making people laugh was a great form of self-defense. One day during a kindergarten field trip to the La Brea Tar Pits, Michael somehow managed to wander into a restricted area, stepped into a puddle of tar, and sank up to his knees. When his classmates started laughing at him, he made a joke out of the situation by playing up his predicament with exaggerated movements. It is one of his earliest memories of realizing people will like you if you make them laugh.

Richards claims he didn't feel emotionally deprived at home, which was a small, modest house. Still, he earned a reputation as the local character, willing to do just about anything for a laugh and the attention it brought. He would run the bases backward in neighborhood baseball games and plop himself down in the hallway between classes pretending to be dead.

"Ever since I was a little boy, I always had that clown inside of me," he recalls. "I remember as a kid I would mimic a friend who rode into a tree with his bike. Every time I saw him, I would ride my bike into a tree as a greeting. It cracked everybody up."

However, it was a very unfunny schoolyard incident that occurred when he was ten years old and in the fourth grade at parochial school that left a most lasting impression on Richards: "We were playing tetherball, and a nun came out and told us to stop. But I didn't hear her, and it was my turn to serve, so I let the ball go, and it hit her in the head. I felt so bad because she accused me of doing it on purpose. I agreed to pay for her glasses, so every day I stood in front of the class and put a dime in a glass and she chewed me out. I was humiliated. The glasses only cost a few dollars, but after a couple of weeks I stopped going to school. Every morning my mother would drop me off on her way to work, and I'd walk home and watch TV, take walks, or go swimming."

Eventually the school contacted Michael's mother about his truancy. When her son broke down in tears over his treatment at the hands of the nun, Phyllis took him out of the school and enrolled him in a public school located in the San Fernando Valley. The new, less authoritarian environment proved a boon for Michael, and as a result he discovered his life's passion.

"I first realized I was funny when I was very little and I was able to make my friends laugh," he recalls. "I was always funny, even as a kid. But I never thought I'd be an actor when I grew up until I took an eighth-grade acting class and excelled. After that, I never left it; it was all I lived for. Everything else in school was superfluous. And I've been seeking attention as a clown ever since."

Michael attended Birmingham High School in the San Fernando Valley briefly before transferring to Thousand Oaks, where he was a member of the pep squad. In a curious foreshadowing of life to come, he is remembered for entering classrooms by sliding across the linoleum.

"He couldn't come into class unless he fell over two or three desks," says Lynn Hanks, who was in the same drama class.

"Everything was off the wall with him," agrees classmate Carol

Cooper, now a teacher in Texas. "He was incredible, but I'm sure some of the teachers were ready to belt him."

"I drove my teachers nuts," Richards acknowledges. For instance, after being cast as the Scarecrow in a school production of *The Wizard of Oz,* he would sing "If I Only Had a Brain" as loudly as he could while sauntering down the hall.

During that production, Michael put a water balloon in the Tin Man's costume, which broke while the actor was onstage. "A flood of water came pouring out of the suit," says the classmate. "It looked like he'd wet his pants. The audience howled."

However, school administrators might not have been so amused by Richards's ongoing antics—such as the time he announced over the school's public address system that a catering truck parked outside was giving away free lunches to students. A schoolmate recalls that everyone went running outside only to find a county dump truck filled with fertilizer.

Richards says, "I loved classrooms or any situations where I could upstage my teachers. I was punished a lot, and my grades reflected my behavior. But I was continuously voted the most humorous through high school."

Michael graduated from Thousand Oaks High School in 1967. Despite his desire to be a performer, his mother had a more traditional career in mind. She wanted him to be a doctor. Richards says, "She worked as a medical-records librarian at a local hospital and knew doctors made good money."

In an effort to compromise, Michael, then eighteen, worked as an orderly at the hospital and on an ambulance during the summer after his graduation. When the school year started, Richards enrolled for a brief time at Ventura College, then moved on to Valley College, where he appeared in numerous plays, including Tennessee Williams's *Summer and Smoke* and Samuel Beckett's *Waiting for Godot.* On a lark, he was a contestant on *The Dating Game* in 1968. He wasn't chosen.

It was also during his time at Valley College that he became friends with another aspiring performer, Ed Begley Jr. "Michael is living proof there is intelligent life on other worlds, because he's clearly not of this one," jokes Begley. "He was brilliant. It got to the point where everyone was doing Michael."

While Richards may have excelled at being Mr. Popularity, he struggled in the classroom. Lacking a grade point average high enough to keep him exempt, he was drafted in 1970, as the war raged in Vietnam. Discipline had never been his strength, and the army was a struggle of wills, but he made it through basic training and luckily managed to avoid combat duty. He was trained as a medic and then transferred to Germany, where he wound up being assigned to intelligence.

While overseas, he became interested in the army's race relations and drug abuse program, which used theatrical productions to get its messages across. His commanding officer asked him to put on plays for his fellow servicemen, which Richards did. He began as a writer, then directed and finally performed in the productions. Once discharged, he was able to go back to college on the GI bill. He enrolled at the California Institute of the Arts, a highly respected school just north of Los Angeles.

In 1974, when he was twenty-four, Richards married Cathleen "Cass" Lyons. What made the union so surprising to his friends was that up until then Michael's social life had been practically nonexistent. Nobody realized he had been seriously enough involved with Cass to get married.

"I had no money. I was barely able to keep gas in my car," Richards recalls. "I was doing theater all the time, didn't have a life, and I had never really dated. But Cathleen had just graduated from CalArts with her master's degree, and I had just finished my studies, so we spent that summer traveling. We ended up in Santa Cruz living in a house with a bunch of friends and lived there for a year. The other couples were all married, and they encouraged us to get married too. So we did." Not long after, the couple had their first and only child, Sophia, who is now in her twenties.

In keeping with his inability to stay in one place too long, he eventually transferred to Evergreen State University in Olympia, Washington, where he earned a B.A. in theater arts and studied Oriental philosophy. Initially he intended to become a "serious" actor. Immediately after graduation, he spent six months with the San Diego Repertory Company, performing in a variety of plays. After he returned to L.A., however, Richards was stymied.

At the time, Los Angeles didn't have much local theater, and he had a hard time finding agency representation, which is absolutely mandatory for getting work in television or film. "I tried to get an agent, but he said he already had someone like me. I said I'd like to meet this twin. When I insisted, he ordered me out of his office. I cleared his desk and said, 'You got anybody else like that?' and then left."

As a kid, he had reveled in being a bit of an outsider, finding romance in long walks and solitude. Now, when he was trying to find his niche in Hollywood, being an outsider meant being invisible. "I was sad about it," he admits. "At times I even cried. I wanted to fit in, but I simply couldn't. People were always telling me I was going to be a bum."

In 1979, now thirty years old, tired of sitting around doing nothing, and anxious to perform somewhere, Michael turned to the one venue where anybody can get a chance: the comedy clubs, doing stand-up.

"I only worked stand-up comedy for nine months. I just did it as an adventure. I never regarded myself as a stand-up comedian. But I consider Mitzi Shore and Bud Friedman my second mother and father," says Michael, referring to the owners of the Comedy Store and Improv, respectively. "They gave me the opportunity to start and develop a career. I think of myself as an actor, but I never got out of comedy once I started doing stand-up. I came up with people like David Letterman, Jay Leno, Garry Shandling, and Paul Reiser."

Since casting agents regularly prowl the comedy clubs looking for fresh talent, working stand-up is like doing weekly auditions. Although Richards was never completely comfortable as a stand-up, he was good enough so that doing it helped launch his television career.

After seeing Richards perform his act around town, Billy Crystal gave him his first big break in Hollywood. Richards "He hired me to be on *The Billy Crystal Special.* I got to work with Robin Williams and Martin Mull, who were also on it, it got me my Screen Actors Guild card, *and* I got paid. I was so pleased."

Crystal had been impressed with the way Richards had no particular agenda, other than to get the audience laughing. Ironically, that was one reason why Michael earned the reputation of being the one performer other comics never liked following onstage. He would do anything to get the audience involved, which meant any comic following him was sure to experience an energy letdown by the audience.

Richards's act, he says, "was nothing more than just standing in front of an audience to see what you could get there. I never told jokes. I was a cross between Robin Williams and Andy Kaufman. I loved Andy. He could fool people. He was a great trickster. I knew exactly what he was up to, and I did a lot of that myself before I even met Andy and saw his work.

"My opener was six minutes about a guy who couldn't remember his act. I stood there for minutes not knowing what to say. Just stood there as naturally as possible. But I had to get my hand into my coat pocket without them seeing it and get my piece of paper to find out what my first joke was. They were howling. Ninety percent of humor comes from people laughing at mistakes. As a kid I would crash my bike into a tree and fall down dead. I would walk into a classroom backward. I prefer the comedy of action as opposed to the verbal.

"So I'd move an audience into a whole other area, then these other guys would try to come up there and work on their six minutes for *The Tonight Show*. They were good at it, and it's an art too, but it used to be 'Oh, shit, I'm following Mike. Last night, he set fire to himself.' "

Literally. "I have stood up onstage and lit my tie on fire. I just stood there until the flames got real close to my face. Then suddenly I reacted. I've always been very good with fire. I used to burn toy army men on *Fridays*."

Fridays was Richard's first series experience in television. He recalls that in 1980 "a well-dressed young man from ABC" approached him with an offer to be part of a new ensemble comedy show they were pulling together called *Fridays*. The other cast members included Maryedith Burrell, Melanie Chartoff, and Larry David.

The late-night show debuted in April 1980 and was immediately blasted for being a ripoff of *Saturday Night Live,* which to a certain degree it was: a comedy show that featured a news roundup, live musical guest performers, and lots of off-the-wall sketches and characterizations. ABC nearly canceled *Fridays* after only three weeks. But the ratings improved, and the show stayed on the air for two and a half years.

"One of the best shows was when Andy Kaufman was on," Richards recalls. "We broke out of the sketch we were doing on live television. All of a sudden Andy stopped and threw a glass of water at me. So I stood up and got all the cue cards and threw them around, then we went to black and went to a commercial. We got letters by the thousands after that incident."

Despite all the letters from viewers excited about Kaufman and Richards's improvisation, *Fridays* was canceled in October 1982 when *Nightline* expanded from four nights a week to five. While he harbors some fond memories of the people with whom he worked, Richards's overall experience was much less positive.

"I went into *Fridays* too early, and I was crippled by it," he reflected. "The writers were too young, but producers see money and talent and they exploit it. Comics now only do stand-up for a couple of months and then they're on television. It's hard for someone's uniqueness and maturity to develop and emerge like that."

After *Fridays,* Richards appeared in such forgettable movies as *Transylvania 6-5000, Problem Child,* and *Young Doctors in Love.* He also showed up as a guest star on several series, including *Hill Street Blues* and *Miami Vice,* on which he played villains, *Cheers,* and *Night Court,* an experience that left Richards strangely depressed because "it was so corny." In 1987, Richards was cast as a series regular in the syndicated sitcom *Marblehead Manor,* playing Rick the Gardener.

Although he had become a gainfully employed actor, Richards still felt he was hovering on the fringes. "I've always found work somewhere as an actor. I made five pilots and guest-starred on just about every show that was on between 1982 and 1985, but none of it brought me any notoriety."

Nor did it bring him much in the way of financial security. Just before he received a call from Larry David asking him to read for a pilot he was producing, Michael Richards had a total of sixty dollars to his name. When it was time to cast the *Seinfeld* pilot, Jerry already had Michael Richards in mind for the part of Kramer. Although Seinfeld had known of Michael from his days as a stand-up, it was a spot Richards did on *The Tonight Show* that convinced him Michael was just the man he needed.

"We had other people read for Kramer, but it was pretty much a charade," Jerry says. "I had been a fan of Michael's for a long time, and when I heard he was available, my mind was made up. I had my heart set on Michael. He is one of those natural phenomena—on the level of a Buster Keaton. Michael is a little nutty."

Jerry and Larry were sold, but they still had to convince the network. "They put me through hell," says Richards, who endured three callbacks.

For his final callback, he walked into a room filled with NBC executives as well as thirty affiliate heads. Confronting his audience, Richards decided to go for it.

"At first, I played it straight," he recalls. "Then as we were doing the scene, I started to do a headstand. I fell over backwards on the table and onto the floor but continued to talk to Jerry as if nothing happened."

How could they refuse someone willing to risk bodily harm? After his electrifying audition, everyone assumed he had the character nailed down. But a funny thing happened on the way to the filming. Richards floundered, unable to get a grip on just how the character should be played. He was so unconnected, he came close to being fired the first week.

"My work in the pilot was very bad," Richards admitted. "When I first started this role, I felt the real Kenny Kramer's spirit. I knew I was going to have to get past that. I work slower than most of the others. I push a character, an entrance, a look—a *presence*. It's the presence you bring to the part. That's what makes Kramer so interesting. I've always worked with presences and been fascinated by characters who can charm, characters who can bring an audience into a scene without even speaking. I used to watch Laurel and Hardy do that all the time. And in a show that's very natural, I had to make sure I didn't fall into caricature. I had to find a place where there's a human being, so it took me a while to get Kramer."

Even after years of playing the same character, doing a weekly series was still difficult for Richards because of the speed with which episodes must be rehearsed and filmed. "In films," he explained, "you have time to work on scenes until you get them right. But on series, especially one like *Seinfeld,* there is always a sense of being rushed. And it's hard for me to walk away from something and say, 'That's okay, I got the laugh, that's all that matters,' because sometimes getting the laugh *isn't* enough. Sometimes getting just the right gesture or mannerism is just as important, but there's not enough time to get it down right. Everyone else will think the take is fine, but I'll walk over and ask to do another because I didn't quite get it. On our show, they're used to me by now. They know I *have* to do that. It's a certain kind of torment that I have to go through."

The least social of the group, Michael Richards often kept himself separate from the others, dissecting his performance in private while they sat and talked with each other during breaks.

"Some people are private, and I'm not the type to pry," Seinfeld said. "People know what you show them. He shows me that he's a perfectionist. He is completely committed to go to any length to make a comedic moment work."

Noted Julia Louis-Dreyfus: "There's a look that crosses Michael's face, when things don't go his way, of complete self-loathing. We love him for that. It's a part of his charm and it's why he's so good."

In a case of the pot calling the kettle angst-filled, Larry David said, "He's tortured at times. He makes a lot of demands on himself and always feels he could do it better. Then if he doesn't, he gets so annoyed with himself."

Jason Alexander, who plays George Costanza, recalls, "When the show started, people wrote that Michael was doing a Christopher Lloyd imitation. That had to hurt, because Michael would never copy anyone."

In fact, Richards so fine-tuned Kramer's persona that he was able to sublimate himself almost totally once in character. He had his own eccentric way of preparing, doing a series of exercises including headstands and handstands before each taping to get his body Kramer-loose.

Also, ever since the episode in which Kramer works as a Calvin Klein underwear model, he patted himself down with some of the Eternity cologne the company sent him as a surprise gift. "It gets me in that Kramer state of mind," he said. "The audience doesn't really get that part of it, but the cast sure knows."

Once the cameras started rolling, Richards said, he would just go along for the ride: "I don't play Kramer, he plays me. I just try to get out of his way. It's like I'm channeling him. I put on those shoes and the outfit and push my hair up a little and he's there. The rest of the cast thinks I'm closer to my character than anyone else, but that's not correct. They play themselves. They actually dress that way and talk that way. I push a look.

"It was difficult for me when I started doing the show because they were so natural being themselves. It took me a while to find the character. I had to find a natural eccentricity because I get bored being *natural*. But that's always been my forte, finding a certain quirkiness that truly makes a character.

"In the first ten shows," he continued, "the Kramer I played was a million miles away from what I do now. I played him slower and dumber. Now I play him as a real believer in himself. He really believes in life and certainly says what's on his mind. He's helpful and committed to just about anyone. It's like he always has something going on in his mind when he enters, and that gives a certain intensity to him.

"I think it works because the physical humor comes out of circumstance. Kramer adds a physicality you don't often see, but what people like about Kramer is that he's also a human being."

A human being who rivals Loretta Young in knowing how to make an entrance. "Someday I think there is going to be a videotape rental called *Kramer Enters,* and it will just be his entrances," Seinfeld laughed. "It's like he's shot out of a cannon when he comes through the door."

Richards admits he discovered the shtick of Kramer's entrances completely by accident. "During one scene I was late on a cue and I came in *fast*—and everyone laughed. It's funny when someone comes into a room late. A great deal of comedy comes out of error. It lets us laugh at things that normally just piss us off. So I developed his entrances from there. Kramer comes through the door like he gets involved in life. All of us want to step into life, and Kramer does it with all his heart. He's a catalyst for chaos. He's a guy who's been bomb-rattled by the city."

But it's his eccentricities that have endeared him to the fans of the show. Even the original Kramer admits Richards took the character to places nobody ever imagined.

"If I'd played Kramer," says Kenny, "it never would have flown the way it has with Michael. He's the one who came up with the weird clothes and the physical antics that have nothing to do with me. He has to figure out a new way to walk in the door every week. It takes amazing preparation, minute detail, and a lot of work."

The effort obviously paid off. Despite the pathetic original test screening results, Richards managed to forge a character that was ultimately accepted and embraced.

"I can't tell you why the audience loves this character," Richards admitted. "Maybe it is the eccentricity. I think they enjoy his unpredictable nature and a certain madness that's there. People like him because they like the idea of someone who can get tickets for a sold-out play when nobody else could. I think of Kramer as a kind of scavenger who knows the city and knows life. That's the intensity people feel about Kramer. He's simply connected to his circumstances. He's a wonderful guy, isn't he?

"I never get bored when he's around. I play Kramer as if he's entering life. I come through the door and I believe that character is ready to get involved in just about anything. I can't think of anything that would be wrong for Kramer unless he got into something that was really and totally against the law. I remember one episode was written where he was actually gun trafficking. He got involved with some guys selling guns, and I said, 'No, no, no.' So they cut that whole story line."

To Richards, Kramer is at his best when he's doing a lot and saying very little: "I particularly enjoyed the episode called 'The Revenge,' where I talk Jerry into getting revenge against an owner of a dry-cleaning company by pouring cement into his washing machines, because the guy found some money in Jerry's pants and kept it. In it there's about two and a half minutes of me just grappling with this cement, trying to pour it into the machine with no dialogue. I get the cement to the top of the machine, then dust gets in my eyes, and there's all these reactions.

"I like doing funny rather than saying funny. I've said that a lot, but it is primarily what I'm after. I like the purity of activity itself without speaking to generate the laugh. That was the key to Lucille Ball's show: she got animated and physical. That's why I've always followed the greats like Laurel and Hardy and Charlie Chaplin. Those are the comedies I watched as a child, and now I have the collected works of all of them."

Although Michael Richards started out with a desire to be known as much for his dramatic talents as his comedic abilities, during his stint on *Seinfeld* he came to philosophic terms with his destined role as clown:

"The fool is always the one who takes the fall for everyone else. In many ways, I'm a *lightener*. I'm here to lighten the load. That's my task. And it lightens my own load too, because I'm able to laugh at myself."

7

George: Loving the Unlovable

ALTHOUGH THE SHOW WAS NAMED *SEINFELD,* IT COULD JUST AS EASILY HAVE been called *Jerry and George.* Because of their unique collaboration, Larry David's voice and vision were just as vital to the creation of the show as was Jerry's comic dexterity on-camera, so it was planned from the beginning that one of the characters would be Larry's television alter ego. What they didn't anticipate, however, was that, even more than Jerry's character, George Costanza would become the heart and soul of the series. While Kramer offered the zany comic relief and Zen dimension, and Julia Louis-Dreyfus's Elaine would add feminine spark and an integral opposing-gender viewpoint, George's angst-filled journey through his less than wonderful life would provide the show with its center, tone, and vision.

For the first time, David had found the perfect avenue for venting his anger over all the small daily difficulties that conspire against us. By channeling and filtering his anguish through another character, he was able to win over the audience through empathy and recognition, instead of alienating them with raw emotion the way he had as a stand-up.

If there was ever an example of a role and actor being destined for each other, it's Jason Alexander's portrayal of George. Beyond the superficial physical similarities he shares with Larry David, such as being "follically challenged"—or, in less politically correct terms, bald—Alexander was able to tap into David's anger and frustration without becoming a caricature by underscoring George's inherent, albeit not always justified, optimism.

Of all the main characters, George was the most tricky to play, and it was obvious to Seinfeld and David that they needed an actor who could be funny for the role, rather than a comedian who could also act. Although Alexander's television series track record was spotty, his acting credentials were unquestioned.

Jason Alexander was born Jay Scott Greenspan on September 23, 1959, in Newark, New Jersey; later the family moved to nearby Livingston. His mother, Ruth Simon, a nursing school director, had married widower Alex Greenspan a year before Jason's birth. Greenspan's children from his previous marriage, Karen and Michael, were much older than Jay, twelve and nineteen years, respectively. Despite the age difference, Jay and Karen developed a close relationship.

It was Karen who first introduced her little brother to the world of Broadway musicals. Jason recalls, "I was five years old and listening to Broadway musicals like *Man of La Mancha* and *The Fantasticks* with my sister."

Even though he grew up crazy for musical theater, his first "performances" were merely exercises in emotional survival. Some kids perform for attention and to give themselves an identity; Jay entertained his classmates and peers as a diversionary tactic. If he could make himself likable enough, then the others wouldn't be so quick to tease him about his personal albatross.

"I was a very heavy kid," he says. "I was constantly being harassed, so I was always nervous that I was going to be abused by the other kids. I quickly learned that being called names like 'fatty' and 'fat slob' was no fun. I figured out the golden rule of comedy: if you make the other kids laugh, they won't make fun of you. They may even like you.

"So I'd launch a preemptive strike against other kids by memorizing material on the albums. I became as funny as I could by memorizing every movie script and TV show. And if a comedy album was out, I knew it. I was desperate to have people laugh so they wouldn't be cruel. They'd be so impressed, they wouldn't beat me up. I guess that was a talent, but I never thought it was acting. It was just self-defense. Performing was my defense, and then it gave me power for the first time in my life."

Personal survival aside, Jason had found his passion in Broadway musical theater. It represented all the world's possibilities and potential. The first musical he ever saw onstage was *Fiddler on the Roof* with Zero Mostel, and the experience transformed him. But if *Fiddler* ignited his soul, *Pippin* lit the flame of his ambition. *Pippin* was based on the story of the French ruler Charlemagne and directed by Bob Fosse, who filled the stage with vibrant colors and constant movement. The musical starred Ben Vereen, John Rubinstein, Irene Ryan, and Jill Clayburgh.

"*Pippin* changed my life," Jason says seriously. "I went to this show, and from the minute it started to the minute it ended, it was choreographed to within an inch of its life. You didn't know where to look next. I remember thinking, 'My God, this is what I want to do forever and ever.' I wanted to *be* Ben Vereen, which is why I started taking tap lessons right after that show.

"The theater was everything. It was all I ever wanted to do. I loved doing school plays and local productions. I never thought about film or television because it didn't seem like a possibility. But if I could work on Broadway, that was the be-all and end-all. And I still don't think there's anything more exciting."

However, there was one television icon that Alexander admits was also an inspiration. "I became an actor because of William Shatner. Everywhere I went as a kid, I did the best imitation of Shatner you've ever seen."

Years later, after he was a television star in his own right, Jason had an occasion to meet Shatner, best known as Captain Kirk on *Star Trek,* and was immediately transformed back into a tongue-tied adolescent: "We ended up together in an elevator at a convention in Miami, and I broke into a huge sweat. I didn't know if he knew who I was, so I didn't say a word. I figured he's got enough psychos following him around that he doesn't need one more."

But Shatner impersonations were only a small part of his performance repertoire. His drama teacher at Livingston High School, Robert Lampf, remembers Jay as already being multitalented when he was just a teenager, singing onstage in school theater productions. "I first met Jay in 1974, and within ten minutes I was telling anyone who'd listen, 'This kid was born to be onstage. This kid is going to make it.' He had an aura, a presence, an ability to move people emotionally. Jay had the lead in every high school play, and he was the star of every show. Yet he was totally unspoiled and pretentious."

His undeniable talent had given Jay—who at fifteen adopted the stage name Jason Alexander—an anchoring confidence that belied the insecurity he had felt as a child over his physical self. The drama coach recalls an incident at their high school's annual talent night that pointed up how self-assured Jason was whenever he was on a stage:

"We had a principal at the time, named Leo Hurley, who almost never left his office to mix with the kids. When Leo walked out onstage to introduce Jay as the emcee for our annual talent night, Jay took the microphone, then turned to the principal and asked, 'Excuse me, but who are you?'

"Mr. Hurley said, 'I'm the principal.'

" 'Oh, so that's what you look like.'

"Even Mr. Hurley laughed."

When Jason was sixteen, he joined a local theater company, a children's group called the Pushcart Players. A year later, the group was chosen to appear in a children's program pilot for PBS, *The Pushcart Players: Feelings and Friends.* When one of the lead actors got sick, Jason was chosen as his replacement. It was in his first professional job.

After graduating from high school, Jason went on to study drama at Boston University, eventually graduating with a master of arts degree and the school's Harold C. Case Award for scholarship and service, named after a former president of the university. While still a nineteen-year-old college student, he was cast in his first feature film role in the horror movie called *The Burning,* which was basically a *Friday the 13th* clone that costarred an equally young and unknown Holly Hunter.

After the movie wrapped, he returned to New York and went to work as a casting agent. During August of 1979, an actress named Deana Title walked into the casting office on an open call. Jason scheduled her to come in again, but when she got there she found out she had been called back not for a job but so he could ask her out. She accepted.

Jason and Deana dated for a year until one evening, while walking through Times Square, he pointed to one of the huge electronic billboards overlooking the theater district: DEANA, I LOVE YOU. PLEASE

MARRY ME. FOREVER, JASON. Once again she accepted, and they were married a short time later.

By that time, he was already making a name for himself in the New York theater community. In 1980, when he was twenty, he was cast from an open call for the Broadway musical *Merrily We Roll Along.* Unfortunately, the show's high expectations failed to materialize. Alexander says wryly, "It became a legend as being the first Stephen Sondheim musical to fail."

Although he was fulfilled and happy to be living out his dream of making a career as a performer and working on Broadway, not all of his childhood fantasies were destined to come true. He may have had the soul of a leading man, but he had the body of a character actor.

"What I was able to offer physically was very different from who I was emotionally," Alexander points out. "My heart is Hamlet, but I'm going to be cast as Falstaff. It took me a while, but I finally came to accept that I could be Falstaff with the heart of Hamlet."

Alexander recalls an incident from his theater days that could be lifted straight from a *Seinfeld* episode. "I remember this one time I was doing a show in the Village, and I lived on 90th and York. We had an early matinee that went on at 1:30 instead of the usual 3:00. I was in the cab about 1:15 when it suddenly hit me that I was in big trouble. And I'm being driven by a guy who, when I said, 'Why don't you take the Drive?' said, 'Yes, we'll drive.'

"He was going about three and a half miles an hour. Nothing could get him to move his car one iota faster. Finally I exploded, and then he said, 'Maybe you want to drive the car.' And I said, 'That's exactly what I want to do.' So I got in the front seat of this cab, got behind the wheel, and drove myself to work."

Although Alexander considered himself first and foremost a stage actor, he wasn't going to turn down other work when it came along. "I never really thought about television," he admits. "But it just sort of found me."

His first series experience was in 1984, when he was cast in the CBS sitcom *E/R.* The show starred Elliott Gould as an ear, nose, and throat specialist who is forced to moonlight at an emergency room in order to maintain his huge monthly alimony payments. Jason appeared as Harold Stickly, the hospital administrator. The show lasted one season.

Then, in 1987, Alexander costarred with John Bolger in another

CBS sitcom, *Everything's Relative*. This series, about two opposite-end-of-the-spectrum brothers and their meddlesome mother, played by Anne Jackson, lasted all of six episodes.

Neither failure made Alexander all that unhappy. He left each show with a healthier bank account and was able to return to the theater, performing both on and off Broadway. He appeared in Neil Simon's *Broadway Bound* and in *The Rink* with Liza Minnelli.

All those childhood and adolescent singing and dancing lessons came to fruition when Alexander was twenty-nine and won the 1989 Tony Award for Best Actor in a Musical for *Jerome Robbins' Broadway,* a compilation of vignettes from various Robbins musicals. In addition to his performing duties, Jason wrote narration for the show, which also went on to win the Tony for Best Musical.

Ironically, the high point of his professional life also created an unexpected internal void. "After I won the Tony, I had to reevaluate my life and reassess my ambitions, because I had always thought if I was very lucky and worked really hard, by the time I was forty I'd get to perform on a Broadway stage. Then after that, maybe I'd have a chance to get into a show good enough that I might have a shot at winning a Tony. But everything happened a lot quicker than I anticipated it would. I started working on Broadway when I was nineteen and won a Tony at twenty-nine. So when that happened, I had to adjust my goals."

Out of this career reassessment came Alexander's determination to diversify as much as he could, which included long-term plans to both direct and produce. He broadened his field to include television and, if possible, film. As a result, when he got the call about the Castle Rock project *The Seinfeld Chronicles,* he was more comfortable than ever with the possibility of long-term series work.

At the time, Alexander was still appearing in *Jerome Robbins' Broadway.* "Rob Reiner saw me and knew the *[Seinfeld]* project was happening and suggested me. They called me, and I sent them a tape."

Alexander was already familiar with Seinfeld's work. As a young actor, Alexander had been cast as an extra in a Maxwell House coffee commercial. "It was an ad where stand-ups did bits, ending with something about coffee," he says. "I was in the fake audience. We saw five different guys go through their material. Jerry was by far the best."

Jerry says that when he and Larry David looked at Alexander's audition tape, they knew they had found the right person to play George. "He was so exactly what we had in mind that we never considered another actor."

Still, there were the formalities to go through, so Jason flew to Los Angeles to meet Seinfeld, David, and the other executives in person and to audition formally. He had very little material to work with, which made the audition tricky.

"I only had three pages of a single scene to develop any ideas for the role, so I really had no idea what they wanted," he recalls. "So you take your best guess. It had read to me like a real good Woody Allen script, so I did a blatant Woody Allen impression, which is how I thought of the glasses. The next day, I had the job."

Like Seinfeld, Alexander had been a New Yorker his entire adult life, but after Larry and Jerry were given the go-ahead to film four more episodes, Alexander decided it was more expedient to move to California than to commute cross-country. So in 1989, Deana and Jason relocated to Los Angeles. One advantage was that it put him in the center of the television and film business, which would make it easier to pursue his ambition to direct and produce, as well as to get film acting jobs. The downside, and it was a significant one, was that it meant leaving his beloved Broadway behind.

The biggest challenge for Alexander in creating the role of George Costanza was to put a mental face on the character, which is why he originally saw George as a Woody Allen type. It gave him a place to start. "Yes, if you go back to the early shows, it's quite obvious I was doing a blatant Woody Allen impersonation."

Also, on an intellectual level, Jason initially had a problem accepting some of George's more unusual personality quirks and believing some of the situations in which the character found himself. "In the beginning," he says, "I kept being given things to do that I didn't understand. When there was something I questioned about what the character was doing, I would say, 'Nobody would do this,' or, 'Gee, that would never happen to anybody.' And then Larry would say that it was exactly what happened to him and exactly how he had responded."

For example, Larry David actually joined in a contest with some friends to see who could refrain from masturbating the longest, which became the basis for the episode "The Contest." He also really had left a nasty message on someone's answering machine that he later tried to intercept before it was heard, which was the inspiration for "The Phone Message."

"So," Jason explains, "instead of doing Woody Allen impressions, I tried to do my best Larry David impressions. And once you begin basing your performance on a person who is real, the character gets a lot richer and much more dimensional. George is the nightmare of what Larry thinks his life *could* be."

It's no coincidence that George is by far the most complex among the main characters. A lightning rod for the whimsy of the fates, he can be both pathetic and occasionally, at least to Alexander, heroic.

"George has a lot of good traits," Alexander explained. "He speaks his mind, he has a tremendous amount of conviction at times, he's a risk taker, and he has his heart in the right place. But he has no faith in himself and tries to be everything for everyone, and you just can't do that. That's his Achilles' heel, and that's where everything falls apart. Even though most of George's plans turn to crap, he doesn't think he's a loser—he thinks he's very unlucky. George is very heroic. He's not giving up, and to me only losers give up.

"I think," he continued, "that a lot of George's image as a loser comes from his relationships with women. I never went through any of that. I met my wife when I was twenty years old, and we got married two years later. I always felt loved, I always had a job, and I didn't have parents who were as whacked out as his."

That said, though, Alexander was bemused by how, even though George can't keep a job or maintain a healthy relationship, his character has become a magnet for women. "I have always assumed that everybody would hate George, but I have been told that he has become a very strange sort of sex symbol. And let's face it, the guy keeps getting these unbelievable women. I can't tell you how many people come up to me and tell me that they like me and how much they like George—and how they know someone just like him or that *they* are just like him. And I wonder, 'Why would you be happy about that?' "

Like every actor who has ever played a popular character, Jason had to learn to deal with people who think he and the character are one and the same. "Emotionally I understand him, but I don't know that I *am* him, although I might have been like George had my life not gone so well. Still, if someone calls me George I don't turn around, because I don't assume they're calling *me*. And anybody running up to me to meet George is in trouble, because whenever someone calls me George to my face, I politely but firmly tell them that I am not George; it is a character I play," Jason said, setting up a story.

"So one day I was skiing in Sundance, and these two guys got on my chairlift and said, '*Hi, George.*' I told them I am not George. But then, getting off the chairlift, my wife accidentally skied across my skis and I went tumbling, riding my wife like a bobsled into another skier. I looked up and saw the look in those guys' eyes. I was George.

"The truth is, a lot of performers—and very good actors—are basically who they are in their performances. But I actively make a decision to make each character as different as I can. I always got off on being chameleon-like. However, if the audience wants to believe [that I'm George] now I take the attitude that it's fine."

This isn't necessarily a bad thing, because it brings Jason a lot of affection. The biggest surprise of playing George was how the way audiences have embraced a guy who in reality would be difficult to take in large doses.

That was exactly the feeling of the test audience. But once Jason exchanged his nebbishy Woody Allen mind-set for Larry David's slightly more acerbic, fatalistic outlook, he was able to make George's complex angst empathetic instead of just whiny. In the process, the character went from being the least liked to the one most people identified with.

Just exactly why people are drawn to George is another question, and one that Alexander didn't have any ready answers for. "I don't know why people gravitate to him so much," Alexander admitted. "But he seems to be the character everyone sees as a touchstone. He seems the most realistic. Kramer has become the cult character because he is so outlandish. People will laugh at him, but they don't *recognize* him. George is in the realm of guys that we know. But why we have senior citizens responding to him, why we have little kids responding to him, why we have women in their forties responding to him—nobody is more surprised than we are."

What's most notable about Alexander's detailed characterization of George is that, by all accounts, the actor is absolutely nothing like the character he so convincingly portrayed.

Noted Larry David, who should know, "He's confident. He has a lot of patience, and he always maintains a calm demeanor. He's the exact opposite of the character."

"Jason is not angst-ridden like George," added Julia Louis-Drey-fus. "And he's a great dancer. I don't think George even knows how to dance. And Jason is in the Top Five funny people in the universe."

That last assessment surprised Alexander. "As a group, we all think we're hysterically funny, but I'm not uniquely funny," he countered. "I never thought of myself as being funny, and of the four of us, I am the least naturally funny. If you put us at a party and told us to be funny and entertaining, you'd gravitate toward the others before me. It's easier for me to play Hamlet than a clown. But when I get my head into a character, I can make *that* funny. The way I *look* does it."

For someone with the talent Alexander undeniably has, such modesty might appear disingenuous at first glance. But his castmates confirmed that Jason is truly as unpretentious as he was when he was Mr. Lampf's drama student.

"I don't think he realizes how much I secretly look up to him," mused Seinfeld. "In some ways, he's like a younger big brother to me. And he's a master of many arcane and ancient arts. He's always pulling bizarre skills out of his back pocket, like martial arts moves and magic tricks."

Although he has one of the most recognizable faces in the enter-tainment industry, Alexander has yet to develop the ego to go with it. In fact, he frequently gets tongue-tied when confronted with peo-ple who in his mind are really famous or noteworthy. Once he and Deana were invited to the White House after Alexander performed at a Sondheim tribute at Kennedy Center.

"When I finally get up to the president and Hillary, I've lost all powers of speech," Alexander recalls. "We shake hands with them, we get our picture taken, and it's time to move on, and I realize I've not said a word. So I turn to Hillary and say, 'You have a very lovely home here.' What a schmuck! I mean, it's the goddamn White House.

"But when we come to the vice president, suddenly I'm Mr. Ca-reer Diplomat, introducing my wife and chatting. I'm thinking to myself, 'Why couldn't I have been this way two minutes ago?' It was just so George."

Jason was also a little overwhelmed when he was invited to attend Neil Simon's sixty-fourth birthday party. "I figured there must be thirty thousand people coming to this thing, but when my wife and I arrive, there's only about fifty people there, and I'm the only person

I've never heard of. Goldie Hawn was there, and Steve Martin and Johnny Carson.

"I kept walking by the couch where Carson was sitting, but I was too shy and too intimidated to talk to him, because he wouldn't know who I am. The third time I walked by him he gets up and says, 'You know, I'm sorry I never got to meet you on the show. I'm a big fan of yours.' On the way home, I said to Deana, 'Did we just step into the Twilight Zone?' "

THE *Seinfeld* brain trust—which, in essence, meant Larry and Jerry—could have very well asked the same question when they reassembled to film the next four episodes. While the majority of shows have a battalion of writers, for *Seinfeld* the buck would stop with the two of them.

"We were adamant about not doing a show where ten writers would sit around a table and a script would be written by committee," Seinfeld says.

This meant that Larry and Jerry were flying by the seat of their pants. All everybody else could do was simply hold on and enjoy the comedic work-in-progress.

8

Elaine: Just One of the Guys

"NBC SAID, 'WE'LL ORDER FOUR MORE EPISODES, BUT YOU GOTTA BRING IN a broad.' That was me," says Julia Louis-Dreyfus, summing up her eleventh-hour involvement in the show. "I think they needed a little estrogen."

In light of how much substance and texture the Elaine character has brought to the show, it's ironic to note that Jerry and Larry strongly opposed the idea of having a woman in the cast. In a way, their resistance was understandable considering the original concept for the show: a day in the life of a stand-up comic. During the time when Seinfeld and David had traveled the comedy circuit, it was mostly a boys' club—not that there weren't any female comics, just that the guys tended to hang together in cliques. So it was realistic that Jerry the TV character wouldn't necessarily have a female friend in the mix.

The top NBC executives didn't care. The issue was nonnegotiable. No woman, no show. So Larry and David began considering their options and working out how to introduce the female character while staying true to Larry's "no hugging" admonition. The one thing they absolutely didn't want was for the female character to become a love interest. Seinfeld and David would walk away before they let their show be turned into a romantic comedy. In addition, they didn't want the specter of sexual tension getting in the way of their only real goal—to be funny.

"We didn't want to get into a 'will they or won't they' sex thing, so we got around that by making her an ex-girlfriend," Seinfeld explains. "The ex-girlfriend you can't seem to get past."

Once they figured out the character, they had to find an actress they felt would fit into the rest of the mix. David knew Julia Louis-Dreyfus from the days they worked together at *Saturday Night Live*. He believed she could be comfortable being one of the guys. He sent her two scripts, including one for an episode titled "Male Unbonding," which was unique enough to make her come in to read.

"In the script," she recalls, "there's this scene where Jerry and Elaine are in her apartment and he says, 'Do you want to go out and eat?' She says, 'Yeah.' So then he says, 'Where do you want to go?' And she says, 'I don't care. I'm not hungry.'

"Even though the role was not particularly large, I was most eager to be part of the project. Those lines alone sold me. I thought, 'I've just stumbled onto buried treasure.' There was a relaxed attitude to the writing. It was funny, but not in a predictable way. It sounded like real dialogue rather than the traditional kind of sitcom writing. That interested me as an actress because I could try to be as realistic in my performance as possible and still be funny. I couldn't have imagined it would turn out to be what it did, but I was secretly very excited."

Fortunately for Jerry and Larry, a deal Julia had with Warner Brothers to do her own series had fallen apart just days before she was offered *Seinfeld,* so she was suddenly available to come in and read for the part.

"It was like instant comedy, add dialogue and stir," recalls Jerry. "She's bright, funny, and pretty. That's rare. She's really that amazing combination of daring, spine, and femininity. She was the perfect ingredient that the show was missing. I knew that when we signed Julia, we had a hit show."

Although her performer's gut told Louis-Dreyfus this was a project that could turn into something special, she didn't let her creative impulses get in the way of the business end of being an actress. "I wanted to do the show, so mostly I thought about how I was going to make this deal work," she says bluntly. "It was about making the money right."

Such business savvy and acumen is probably genetic. Julia, born January 13, 1961, comes from a long line of business titans on the paternal side. Her father, William Louis-Dreyfus, was one of the executives of a fourth-generation, family-owned billion-dollar arbitrage firm, the France-based Louis Dreyfus et Cie. (French born, he was actually christened Gerard, but he changed his name to the more American-sounding William as a young man.)

Julia's great-great grandfather Leopold Dreyfus founded the company around 1850 and added the "Louis" and hyphen to the family surname.

"It's *Loo*-ee *Dry*-fus. This is the deal. It's French and it's hyphenated and it's weird," Julia laughs. "It's a drag when you're making reservations. I've actually considered going with my married name, Julia Hall, but all the paperwork I'd have to go through is too much, so I just deal with it."

Despite being heir to vast financial privilege, Julia was no spoiled child sucking on a silver spoon. She experienced her share of emotional turbulence as a child due to her parents' divorce, which happened when she was just one year old. "I have no memory of them as a couple," she says.

When she was four, her mother, award-winning short-story writer Judith Bowles, married thoracic surgeon Dr. Tom Bowles, the dean of George Washington University Medical School. A year later, her father was also remarried, to a schoolteacher named Phyllis.

"I was not present at my father's wedding, but I was at my mother's," she says. "I was a very reluctant flower girl. I wouldn't go down the aisle."

When she was six, Julia, her mom, and Dr. Bowles moved to Sri Lanka, where he had agreed to spend a year working for Project Hope, an international relief organization. The culture shock was immediate and intense for the young girl.

"Being in a foreign country was scary," she remembers. "There were elephants walking around and people in saris. I was the only white girl in this convent school there. One day I saw a chicken run with its head cut off, like *Apocalypse Now*. The cook had cut the head off the chicken, and it took off, which it should have done a couple of minutes earlier. Everyone, including the dog, was chasing after it. It was an awakening in all sorts of ways."

But being far away from her familiar home brought the family closer together. "We spent a lot of time reading aloud to each other at night. We read *Little Women*, and I would look forward to it like it was television."

Over the following years, each of her parents had two more daughters with their new spouses, giving Julia four half-sisters. Suddenly, Julia Louis-Dreyfus found herself a part of two separate and distinct extended families who did not mix at all with each other, making her frequently feel like someone without a country to call her own. By the time she was nine, Julia was commuting, alone, from Washington, D.C., where she lived with her mother and Dr. Bowles, to New York to visit her father and his new family.

"That was kind of hard," she says. "Growing up in two homes was kind of schizophrenic. It was strange, like leading two lives. It was a lot of transition and separation issues and all of that. No matter how much you're embraced by those whom you're with, you're always a member elsewhere."

Family members recall Julia coming home and crying for hours after some of her trips. As her mother wished, she kept the families compartmentalized and didn't talk about one side of the family to the other. Judith had decided that there should be a distinct separation between the two families, with Julia as the only bridge, which made her transitions between the two households that much harder.

"Divorce is not a lot of fun," she says flatly, then adds, "but as divorces go, theirs was amicable. My parents got along with one another, so I wasn't playing referee between them. And I got along wonderfully with everyone—my mother, my stepfather, my father, and Phyllis. In fact, the word *'step'* was never used in any of the homes. I just had two fathers."

In fact, when Julia got married years later to college sweetheart Brad Hall, both Dr. Bowles and William Louis-Dreyfus walked down the aisle with her and jointly gave her away.

"But it was still hard," she recalls. "And it made me desire a very stable family life. That's why stability and knowing what is crucial in my own life and in creating a life for my children is my first priority in life."

Julia's half-sister Amy Bowles-Reyer believes that the experience helped shaped Julia's comic bent in later years. "There is a tragic-comic element to her humor," Amy says. "If there is a morose situation, Julia is going to get the giggles. Her sense of humor is a deflector. She uses it to lighten up a situation, and she uses it to amuse herself. Laughter has been incredibly sustaining for her."

Louis-Dreyfus thinks her family juggling act helped in other ways. "Off the top of my head, I would say the experience enabled me to adapt, to slip into character in a sense."

Although she spent less time with her father than she did with her mother, she was still very close to her dad, who despite being an internationally known businessman is very much in tune with his creative side. He not only writes poetry but teaches poetry classes twice a week at a high school in Harlem.

"The last thing dad would talk about at dinner was business," Julia recalls. "Plus, I never had a head for it. I always wanted to perform. I don't know what steered me in this direction. I guess I'm screwed up.

"But everyone in my family is funny. Even my great-grandmother, who used to do impressions of her first-grade teacher. I grew up watching *Mary Tyler Moore* and *I Love Lucy*. I love them because they didn't have to give up any femininity to be funny. But I'm a fan of anybody who's funny who is a girl."

Even as a child, Julia had a unique bend to her humor. "When I was about four," she says, "I was eating raisins once and I thought it would be funny to put them in my nose. I showed my mom, who laughed and then said, 'Are you going to take them out?' Instead, I snorted them up into my nose, and we ended up having to go to the emergency room."

Whatever discomfort she felt inside about her family situation, Julia never wore her angst on her sleeve. Instead, she is widely remembered as being self-assured, friendly, and funny. It was no surprise to anyone who knew her that she won her tennis camp's Miss Congeniality award.

Since she lived primarily in Washington, D.C., Julia attended the very exclusive Holton-Arms girls' school for ten years. Her classmates there included children from other high-powered or politically connected families, such as Gerald Ford's daughter Susan. Going to school with the president's daughter left some surreal, indelible memories on Julia: "I remember Susan once dressing up as Goldilocks for Halloween and her Secret Service men dressing up as the Three Bears."

Even though she had grown up with an interest in performing, it wasn't until she appeared in a school play that Julia was officially bitten by the bug. "I was doing a class skit in fifth grade, playing a character who suffered from fainting spells. I didn't actually mean it to be funny, but everyone laughed, and I remember thinking, 'Why are they laughing?'

"I like funny. Funny is everything. Funny is smart. Funny is happy. You can definitely fake drama—a few glycerin drops, and you're on your way to an award—but you can't fake funny. You're either funny or you're not."

That said, her brand of funny is more subtle. "People think I'm going to be funny right away, but I'm not one of these people who are *on*. I just have a sort of humorous bent on things."

Never one to sit on the sidelines and watch others, Julia got involved with all aspects of acting, becoming president of the Thespian Society and starring in school plays. She credits many of her achievements to the all-female environment and isn't sure she would have been so involved had she been enrolled in a coed school.

"I don't think an all-boys school is a very needed institution," she says. "But an all-girls school is not a bad idea, because young girls are influenced by social pressure not to excel to the max in a classroom situation. I was president of my class and of the honor council, and I don't know that would have been the case in a coed environment.

"I wish I hadn't gone there for ten years, but I must say I got a real deal out of it. It gives women an advantage in a lot of ways. Because there's no social pressure, you have an opportunity to excel you wouldn't have in a coed situation. It gives you a stronger sense of self. If I had a daughter, I would definitely send her to an all-girls school."

Others think that Julia would have been just as much of an achiever regardless of her surroundings. "Julia just had it," says high school boyfriend Shep Burr. "She was always a leader. Always popular and always funny. I knew she would be a big star."

Louis-Dreyfus says she was just good at making it seem like she was at ease. "When I was nervous, which was most of the time, I could never stop cracking jokes, and when a boy was around, it got worse."

Ironically, one of the things she was most insecure about—her thick, long, naturally wavy hair—later became one of her most noteworthy assets, physically and financially. "I never knew what to do with my hair," she laughs. "In the seventies, it was definitely not cool. I tried straightening it and ironing it and just was never happy with it. Who would have known?"

Louis-Dreyfus's stellar accomplishments in high school meant she virtually had her pick of colleges. She chose Northwestern University in Evanston, Illinois, just north of Chicago, which has one of the finer theater programs in the country. Northwestern students take advantage of the area's rich theater and live performance history, often founding their own companies to play in any of the many venues in town.

When she was a freshman, Louis-Dreyfus joined an improvisational troupe called the Practical Theatre Company, founded by fellow students Brad Hall and his friend Paul Barrosse. "It was really a big thing on campus, and it gave me confidence," she says. "I learned that there's only so much you can learn about certain comedic beats. You either hear it or you don't. And if you don't, you're in the wrong business."

Her participation in the troupe also led to love and romance. "Brad and I had actually first met through mutual friends but it wasn't one of those love-at-first-sight moments. I met him when I was a teenager but didn't start dating him until I was twenty, when I joined the Practical Theatre Company. Then it was love at second sight, and when I fell, I fell hard. On one of our first dates, he went to a 1940s vintage clothing store and bought me pointy, blue spike heels. I was—and still am—mad for him."

Her work with the Practical Theatre Company led her to the famed Second City, the Mecca for aspiring young comics. When Julia got there, it was already renowned as the place that had launched the careers of John Belushi, Gilda Radner, and Bill Murray. So it's ironic that her big break would come while appearing in the Practical Theatre's *50th Anniversary Jubilee* during her junior year, in 1982. In the audience at that performance were talent scouts from *Saturday Night Live* who recruited Louis-Dreyfus and Hall on the spot and made them an offer they couldn't possibly turn down: to relocate to New York City and become the newest members of the Not Ready for Prime Time Players.

"I dropped out of college, and I didn't even consult my parents," Julia says. "They were very supportive because they had no choice. And by the way, I do not advocate dropping out. I think all kids should stay in school, dammit."

The original cast members, including Chevy Chase, Dan Aykroyd, Radner, and Belushi, had already moved on, so Louis-Dreyfus and Hall found themselves working with the second generation, which included Martin Short, Billy Crystal, Joe Piscopo, and Eddie Murphy. Having come from a theater and improvisational background, Louis-Dreyfus was unprepared for the self-serving world that was *Saturday Night Live.*

"I was naive," she admits. "I had no professional experience outside of Chicago theater, so coming into the huge machine of that show was tough. The schedule alone of doing a live television show every week is very difficult. On Monday there is no script, and on Saturday you're going to be on live. The pressure is on. Plus, a few of the writers were doing drugs, and it wasn't a funny kind of wasted.

"And for a woman at that time, it was particularly difficult. I hope it's different now. But then the show was very male-oriented and very competitive. It was definitely not an ensemble. Everyone was vying for material every week. I was extremely young and naive and wasn't equipped to turn things to my advantage. It was a real induction, a very hard experience. It wasn't fun."

Even so, she still managed to get herself noticed with parodies of Linda Ronstadt, an incest-minded Marie Osmond, and Liza Minnelli, as well as for her *Julia Show* bit, in which she played a talk show host who forces her celebrity guests to listen to her only talk about herself. One thing she always wanted to do was to sing *"I Am Sixteen Going on Seventeen,"* from *The Sound of Music,* while doing a striptease; she never got the chance.

Despite the locker-room mentality that permeated the show—and, perhaps, despite her inability to promote herself as successfully as some of the men in the cast—she stood out. When she did make it on the air, she was the only woman, so her appearances were in sharp contrast to the other skits and bits and characterizations.

"It's true," she says, "while there was a big disadvantage being the only woman, it was also a big advantage. Every now and then I would think it would be nice to have another girl on the show, and then they would hire one and I would not be the only girl anymore, and I would rethink that fantasy and chuck it."

Looking back now at the work she did on *Saturday Night Live* leaves Louis-Dreyfus somewhat ambivalent but appreciative that she survived it. "I'm not one hundred percent embarrassed by things I did," she says, "but some of the stuff wasn't funny. You were always having to gamble, which made it a lot like graduate school. But I'm totally grateful to have had the experience. It taught me about everything."

It also served to bring her and Hall closer together. "I don't feel as if we grew up together, but I feel as if we shared an enormous amount of experience together. I don't know, to tell you the truth, how our relationship endured back then. It was a difficult time. I guess we just liked each other enough so that we weathered it."

Julia Louis-Dreyfus stayed with *Saturday Night Live* for three years before she and Hall, who had left the show after two, decided it was time to move on together, both professionally and personally. They relocated to Los Angeles, where they were married in 1987. Hall eased away from performing and concentrated on producing and writing. He would eventually get a writing job on *Brooklyn Bridge,* the critically acclaimed autobiographical series from Gary David Goldberg about a Jewish family living in 1950s Brooklyn, and would later produce *The Single Guy,* a critically panned series that was artificially kept afloat by being fortuitously slotted between *Friends* and *Seinfeld.*

While Hall looked for writing work, Louis-Dreyfus got acquainted with the Hollywood casting agents. Within a year she landed her first series: the NBC yuppie sitcom *Day by Day,* which starred Linda (*Lou Grant*) Kelsey and Doug Sheehan, who was just coming off a four-year stint on *Knott's Landing.* The premise had Kelsey and Sheehan playing downwardly mobile yuppies who leave high-powered jobs to open a day care center.

Louis-Dreyfus was cast as Sheehan's former business associate Eileen Swift, who finds the whole idea of trading money and glamour for sandboxes abhorrent. "I played an ass," Julia says easily. "She's a conglomerate of a lot of people I've known who are like her who think values are something you get in Saks after New Year's Day."

The network premiered *Day by Day* as a midseason replacement in 1988, then put it back on the schedule the following October, buried on Sunday opposite *Married . . . With Children* and *Murder, She Wrote.* Not surprisingly, it was canceled at the end of the season; it went off the air in June 1989, just one month before NBC aired a pilot called *The Seinfeld Chronicles.*

One of the biggest hurdles for actors to overcome in auditions is the mist of desperation that can seep through and taint the reading. However, because Louis-Dreyfus had just come off a series and wasn't worrying at that moment about paying the rent or having to take a job as a waitress, she could approach the material freely without trying to second-guess what anyone else wanted. If she didn't get the job, it wasn't the end of her world.

"It was one of the more relaxed auditioning experiences I ever had," she says. "We were going to read the scene together, to meet and see if we got along. Jerry was eating a bowl of cereal. I said, 'To hell with it,' and just sat on the floor, and we talked for a while. I had a good feeling about him as soon as I met him. He was exactly where he should be as a levelheaded person. I think the appeal of Jerry Seinfeld is that people watch him and feel as if he's just like a friend of theirs.

"When I read for the part," she adds, "I went with the attitude that Elaine didn't really give a shit. I played her as cynical and sort of noninvolved. And it turned out that was exactly what they were looking for."

What Jerry was looking for was a small-screen version of his vision of the ideal woman. "That's what Elaine is to me," Seinfeld explained. "She's sexy and someone whose every opinion you want to know."

Unlike Jason Alexander and Michael Richards had been for their roles, Julia was not necessarily the first choice. Approximately a hundred actresses eventually read for the part. But she was the one who brought the right combination to the role of Elaine Benes as envisioned by Seinfeld and David.

"It was like we were connected somehow," said Jerry. "It's like having a dance partner. Julia is one of my favorite people. We eat cereal together, which is a bonding thing on our set."

He also appreciated her attitude toward the show. ("I have no agenda except to be funny," she said. "I don't profess to offer any worldly wisdom. I'm an actress, not a politician.") and her work ethic.

"Julia is very no-nonsense," Jerry added. "I can't imagine anyone more able. I've seen her work pregnant, ill, exhausted—and she never complains. She'll wear a beautiful Armani suit to rehearsal, and if she had an idea for a scene, like to fall down, she'll just do it, which is something I cannot get used to. If I was wearing a T-shirt and jeans I would be asking, 'Is the floor clean?' But for Julia, it's all about the work."

With Louis-Dreyfus in place, Larry and Jerry could begin to construct the next four shows around the characters who were now set. Contrary to her experience on *Saturday Night Live,* the *Seinfeld* guys didn't feel the need to pound on their chests, and her gender wasn't a point of contention, which meant the end product was of a much higher quality.

"It's consistently good and groundbreaking, which *Saturday Night Live* wasn't when I was there," she said. "It's also a calm working environment. It's very fun, and we have a good time. I think that we all think the show is funnier than it actually is, because we're having such a good time doing it and because we really do enjoy each other's company and the work experience is that much better as we go because of it. And the fact that I happen to be a woman doesn't keep me from getting good material every week.

"The bottom line is, here I'm just another actor in the cast. Everyone treats me pretty much like one of the boys, which I take as a great compliment. And in return, I treat each of them as one of the girls," she laughed. "Elaine is one of the guys but hasn't forgotten she's a gal. Although most of the humor on the show is not gender-specific, she definitely gives a feminine sensibility, which is crucial."

Like Alexander and Richards, Louis-Dreyfus has had to deal with people blurring the lines between her television persona and her real-life self. To her, there was really no comparison. "I'm one hundred percent *not* like Elaine. I'm married. I don't hang out with a bunch of losers. And I don't put up with a lot of crap. I don't really even look like her, because I don't have her hair and makeup person at home."

To point up the differences, Julia imagined what a series called *Louis-Dreyfus* would be like. "There would be no supporting characters. Just me on a stool dressed in black, under a spotlight for a half hour. I'd open with a song, do poetry in the middle, and close with a song. There would be no jokes. It would be very serious. And I would discourage any network from buying the show, because it's not going to be funny or particularly entertaining."

While playing Elaine, Louis-Dreyfus felt so estranged from her on a personal level that she wasn't sure she'd want to socialize much with her. "I suppose she could be a friend of mine, but in a very distant kind of way. She looks like a stable character because she's up there with psychopaths like George and Kramer, but in fact she's cuckoo. She has a tendency to move in all these directions and spin out of control. So I would be friends with her only from a distance. I didn't really intend to make her so despicable. The writing led me that way. I think they just like the way I play nuts.

"The reality is," she added, "these four characters are a pathetic group and they should disassemble promptly. If you stand back and look at what happens every week, they do terrible things to one another and yet they continue to hang out. This is a sick group of people. She's obviously had bad role models, but if Elaine had had functional relationships growing up, she wouldn't be on this show. She is not a grounded person. But actually, no one on the series is grounded. That's why their relationships tend to crumble."

Yet Elaine and her friends are adored by millions. Does that say more about the quality of the show or the mental health of the audience? For Louis-Dreyfus, the answer lay in the gray middle ground: "There are a lot of female characters who are well written. But Elaine has opinions and is kind of nuts, and I think she is very much like a lot of single women out there."

According to Carol Leifer, a longtime *Seinfeld* writer, Jerry took special care to make sure Elaine never veers off into bitchy. "Jerry really watched out for the Elaine character," she says. "Elaine would never just be mean. If she lashes out, she wants to make up for it. She might get mad at them, but then she'll get them tickets to *Sunset Boulevard.*"

In other words, he didn't mind her being confrontational as long as it didn't violate the premise that these four friends are a unit, whether they like it or not. Of course, that's just how many of us respond and react in our friendships.

"I also think she's possible to identify with because she's not defined by a relationship with a guy," added Louis-Dreyfus. "She's her own person, for good or bad."

"I'll tell you why her character has taken on some celebrity," Seinfeld offered. "You have on this show three very strong, well-drawn male characters, and she is cast against them. She matches their strength with femininity. That's what makes it special. She's not a loudmouthed bruiser. It's a feminine strength. She really is a magical comedic performer."

As the show became more and more successful, her male costars certainly got their share of fan mail, but Louis-Dreyfus probably got more "crush" letters. "Yes, I've gotten a couple of proposals. In fact, I'm thinking of leaving my husband for these people," she joked. "Once a kid invited me to go to his prom with him. It was very sweet, and I considered it, but there was the corsage and I'd have to get a dress. . . . Plus, I never had any fun at my proms. That's why I decided not to go, based on past prom experiences."

Through both instinct and serendipity, Seinfeld and David put together a cast Larry felt comfortable writing for and Jerry felt comfortable performing with.

"When you cast people, they read and you like them, but you don't realize who you got until you start working together," Seinfeld points out. "Obviously it turned out wonderfully well for us. Also, I think I have proven pretty convincingly that you can do very well, even if you're a bad actor, when you surround yourself with spectacular talent."

In the end, Julia Louis-Dreyfus, Jason Alexander, and Michael Richards would not only share the spotlight with Seinfeld, but they would become so individually elemental to the synergy of the ensemble that without any one of them, the dynamics and unique chemistry of the show would collapse.

9

How Episodes Were Put Together

SINCE THE PREMISE FOR THE SERIES WAS A LOOK INTO HOW A COMIC DEVEL-
ops material from everyday life, Seinfeld and David borrowed liber-
ally from their own lives not only to come up with episode ideas and
characters but to create the *Seinfeld*ian universe the characters
would inhabit. For example, after Jerry moved out of the suburbs
and into Manhattan during his days as a struggling young comic, he
lived on the Upper West Side at 129 West 81st, which is where TV
Jerry lives.

To flesh out Elaine, Jerry and Larry made her a composite of two
people. The first was comic Carol Leifer, Jerry's ex-girlfriend, who
would become one of *Seinfeld*'s staff writers during the series' fifth
season. The other model for Elaine was Monica Yates, whom Larry
used to date.

As for the ideas for the early episodes, Seinfeld readily admits they
came directly from Larry's fertile mind and strange occurrences in
his life. Once Larry wore a suede jacket that got wet while he was
meeting Monica Yates' father. The experience became the inspiration for the eighth episode, "The Jacket," in which Jerry is forced to
spend time with Elaine's brusque father, who doesn't want to be
seen on the street with him after Jerry turns the coat inside-out to
protect it from the rain.

David tended to view using moments from of his life as necessary.

"We just want to do jokes, but we have to come up with a story for them," he deadpanned.

"Most of the stories are from Larry's life, almost all of them," Seinfeld said. "He just has a tremendous wellspring of ideas. I mean, he just fills notebooks with ideas. I try to help him, but Larry really is the designer of the show. There are just some people who literally have funny lives, and things happen to them that sound like stories. He has that kind of life."

David begged to differ. "It appears I have that kind of life, but I really don't think I do have that kind of life. My life has been pretty depressing, actually. I feel I am completely devoid of experiences. Other people, they travel, they do things. I go for acupuncture or see something strange on the subway. Big deal."

But it's precisely that eye for detail that made Seinfeld approach David in the first place about becoming his partner.

"We have always tried to get small with this show and do little stories that become big stories," Jerry explained. "This show is about minutiae. Most of life is consumed with minor events, and we use them as a place to start and then we make them funny. It's about the little things that everybody experiences, the small, quirky, and unusual things that happen to people in their lives.

"I wanted our show to be about the thousands of little dilemmas that television and the movies never touch on because they are too small. They don't think there's enough in it to make a whole show, but to us that's the richest stuff in the world. We take minute problems and have discussions about them, and that is what real people do. And people really enjoy seeing these characters deal with these things; a lot of people are concerned with those things."

The biggest irony about Seinfeld doing a sitcom is that he never liked the form. In fact, his dislike of the genre is what made *Seinfeld* the anti-sitcom. And his desire to break all the network sitcom rules is one reason he made a decision early on to play his hand out at NBC rather than find a home for the series in the alternate television universe that is cable.

"Jerry had an opportunity to take the show to a cable network, who had flipped for the show," reveals Michael Richards. "But even though NBC had only ordered four shows and wasn't as promising as the cable offer, which wanted twenty-four episodes, Jerry chose the four because he had a lot of faith it was going to happen."

Richards adds, "I was always the most pessimistic—I never expected it to go any further."

"I actually would have preferred to go to cable or the Fox network," Larry David admits. "I like small. I don't like a lot of attention. With my stand-up act, I liked to go on at one in the morning when three-fourths of the audience had already gone. Then there's no pressure. I like situations with no pressure."

However, Jerry wanted a primetime network platform from which to work. His desire to reconfigure the face of sitcom by returning to a purer form is why Jerry was not influenced by *The Mary Tyler Moore Show, Cheers, M*A*S*H,* or any other contemporary show that combined comedy with varying degrees of sentimentality. The tenor of the show, and even the set itself, would hark back to the idols of his youth, Abbott and Costello.

"The Abbott and Costello Show that ran in the fifties was definitely the most important ancestor of my show, because of its emphasis on comedy more than anything else," Seinfeld said. "Everybody on the show knows I'm a fan of them. So we're always joking about how we do stuff from their show. George and I will often get into a riff that has the rhythm from the old Abbott and Costello shows. And sometimes I'll hit George in the chest the way Abbott would hit Costello. Even George's middle name, Louis, is an homage to Lou Costello.

"I love playing straight on the show, like Abbott did, because it's largely a lost art. How many times have you heard me start a bit with the line 'Now let me get this straight'? I mean, the structure of it and the character interaction is our invention, but I like the show best when I feel it's something Abbott and Costello might have done. Even the street we have, we made it look like the funny little street in *Abbott and Costello,* where everything and everyone is just around the block."

The four ideas chosen to comprise what in network parlance would become known as *Seinfeld*'s first season (a "real" season typically consists of twenty-four or twenty-six episodes) would set the foundation for the ultimate direction the show would take. It was filmed before a live audience, but because nobody knew anything about the show, tourists at Universal Studios were brought in to fill the seats.

During the course of each show, Jerry would perform several stand-up routines that related to the events of the episode. Judging from the in-studio reaction, the audience enjoyed what they were seeing. But the real test would occur when the episode was aired into people's homes.

Episode 2 (the first episode of the short order), "The Stakeout," introduced Elaine and established her clearly platonic relationship with Jerry. She will go with him to a sure-to-be-awful family reunion if he will go with her to a birthday party so she won't be alone. At the party, Jerry finds himself in a quandary. He's smitten by a friend of Elaine's but feels it's inappropriate to ask Elaine for the woman's phone number. Instead, he and George stake out the lobby of the building where the woman works.

This episode also introduced Jerry's TV father (originally played by Phil Bruns, who soon would be replaced by Barney Martin) and George's fictional alter ego, Art Vandelay, who is usually described as an importer-exporter. Besides Julia Louis-Dreyfus, there was another pivotal addition to the personnel of the show at this point: Tom Cherones, the series' sole director until he abruptly left after the 1993–94 season.

Many people mistakenly remember "The Stakeout" as the first *Seinfeld* episode. *The Seinfeld Chronicles* tends to get lost in the collective consciousness, largely because of a promo NBC aired prior to rerunning "The Stakeout." It features Jerry and Julia sitting next to each other on a couch. Jerry tells the viewers how many episodes have been done and comments that this particular episode was "the first one we did." As the promo fades to black, Jerry and Julia get into a clinch, as if they are about to kiss. His "we," intended to mean Julia and Jerry, apparently struck people as meaning the series itself instead.

In episode 3, "The Robbery," Jerry's apartment is robbed after Kramer inadvertently leaves the door open. When Jerry contemplates moving, George, then working as a real estate agent, finds him a great apartment but then decides he wants the apartment himself, which results in neither of them getting it. This was the episode in which Michael Richards barreled through the door to Jerry's apartment because he was late on his cue and discovered the "Kramer entrance."

In "Male Unbonding" (episode 4, and the script that won over Julia Louis-Dreyfus), Jerry tries to "break up" with a needy and obnoxious childhood friend. When the guy bursts into tears, Jerry capitulates, discovering it's no easier than breaking off a romance.

This episode introduces a recurring theme in *Seinfeld:* it isn't easy to get out of relationships, and we often stay in them, even if they're dysfunctional, because it's less trouble.

In his act, Jerry has noted:

There is no easy way to break off any relationship. It's like mozzarella cheese on a good slice of pizza. No matter how far you pull the slice away from your mouth, it just gets thinner and longer but never snaps.

Episode 5 (the final episode of the truncated first season) was "The Stock Tip," in which Jerry loses money as a nervous stock market investor, delighting Kramer. It also features a bad weekend date and Elaine being dumped by her boyfriend because she's allergic to his cats. Jerry's favorite superhero, Superman, is referred to twice.

"THE EPISODES I really like are when you twist the stories in ways the audience doesn't expect and yet still manage to combine them into a point at the end," Seinfeld says.

In each first-season episode, Cherones wove the seemingly disparate threads of action around and through each other in a style that is now a unique hallmark of the series but at the time seemed meandering compared to other sitcoms. Because it wasn't the recognizable sitcom format—a central "A story" issue to be resolved, with a related "B story" to give the supporting characters something to do—it wasn't the kind of show people could watch with comfortable familiarity.

"If you ask what the stories are about on this show, you're going to get answers that don't make sense," Jason Alexander noted. "And when you read the scripts, sometimes they don't even have jokes. Jerry in his stand-up has jokes, but his comedy isn't jokey. It's a cumulative thing."

When the four episodes aired, from May 31 to June 21, 1990, the ratings were, politely put, uninspired. Once again, the research people strongly recommended against picking up the show, explaining in excruciating detail why people simply weren't getting it and why it wasn't capable of garnering an audience. The question of finding an audience also concerned Jerry.

"At one point, I thought it would be four shows and out," he admits. "I envisioned people coming up to me in clubs years later and saying, 'You were robbed. They never gave you a chance.' And that I would never work on network television again."

However, as he had done after the pilot, NBC executive Rick Ludwin stubbornly refused to accept the results of the network's very highly paid marketing research department and went on a one-man campaign. "I had a feeling it was too good to walk away from," says Ludwin, unable to articulate exactly why he was so sure *Seinfeld* was worth the struggle he knew he would face in trying to give it another chance.

Had the series been developed under the auspices of the prime-time entertainment division, unquestionably *Seinfeld* would have been permanently pulled at this juncture. However, apparently through sheer force of will, Ludwin prevailed on entertainment president Warren Littlefield to order thirteen more episodes for the 1990–91 season. It was a personal victory for Seinfeld because, by anybody's standard, the amount of control he had over his series from the first episode was unheard of at the time. But then, that had been a nonnegotiable condition of his involvement.

"One big reason, I think, is that I didn't want it [a series] for a long time," Jerry muses. "So by the time I got to do it, I had clout. I had a following and I already had perspective when I got the show. I was already a successful comedian, so it wasn't like, 'I'll do anything. Whatever the network says, I'll go along with it.' When I got the series, I felt like I could take it or leave it, and that's a good attitude to have. If you are too desperate to please, I think it hurts the product."

Creators and producers of many other series tell horror stories of head-butting with and interference by the network. With *Seinfeld,* Ludwin admits, he and the others kept a hands-off approach.

"The good shows run themselves," he says, "and it became clear early on that these guys had a fix on who these characters were and what was funny. It makes our jobs a pleasure to go into a table reading, laugh along with everyone else, shake hands, thank them, and then go back to our offices. That's the best situation you can have. I think one of the few notes I gave was to tell them they got the lyrics to the Bugs Bunny theme song wrong."

Once they received the half-season order for 1990–91, Jerry and Larry knew they would have to hire a group of writers to help develop scripts. Even so, every script went through their hands and, more often than not, a Larry David rewrite.

"It was somewhat of a collaborative effort between me, the writers, and Jerry but we rarely met as a group," explains David. "We didn't want to do a show where fifteen writers sit around together. Basically the writers wrote the scripts and then Jerry and I went over them. Usually there were a few ideas, a few premises, for each show, and then we went from there."

In January 1991, NBC scheduled *Seinfeld* to air at 9:30 P.M. on Wednesdays following *Night Court* and opposite CBS's very popular *Jake and the Fat Man* with William Conrad and ABC's Jamie Lee Curtis–Richard Lewis vehicle, *Anything but Love.*

Larry David, for one, foresaw doom and said at the time, "I'm sure it's not good. We're not really compatible with *Night Court,* and Richard Lewis is one of my best friends, so I try not to think about it. But if it's a good show, people will find it."

As if the show weren't facing a difficult enough situation, *Seinfeld*'s heavily promoted return was preempted by the start of the Gulf War, delaying its airing until later in January.

"It was pretty much a disaster," David says about their sputtering start. "But I was very comfortable having the show be unpopular. There's something about popularity that throws you a bit. I'd never had that kind of pressure before."

The first episode of the official second season (episode 6 of the series) "The Ex-Girlfriend," finally aired on January 23, 1991. It is a classic David-Seinfeld script about sexual politics. Jerry finds himself unwillingly sexually attracted to one of George's ex-girlfriends; Elaine confronts a guy to find out why he has stopped saying hello to her. Meanwhile, Kramer obsesses over fresh fruit.

Episode 7 is included on many critics' Top Ten list of *Seinfeld* episodes. "The Pony Remark" has Jerry offending an elderly relative with a remark about how immigrants shouldn't have ponies. When she dies, he's torn between attending her funeral or playing in the softball championship. He also muses on funerals in his stand-up segment:

We don't understand death. The proof of this is that we give dead people a pillow. If you can't stretch out and get some rest at this point, I don't see how bedding accessories really make a difference.

In episode 8, "The Jacket," Elaine's Hemingway-esque father is introduced. Julia Louis-Dreyfus says Alton Benes's demeanor goes a long way toward explaining her character's dysfunction. Jerry explains, "Her father was a tough bruiser who was intimidating and mean—and we've never seen her mother. Elaine doesn't get along with him and he doesn't get along with anybody, and that would account for her hanging out with these other bad role models."

Episode 9, "The Phone Message," was a case of art imitating life. After leaving scathing messages on his girlfriend's answering machine, George has to figure out a way to erase the messages before she has a chance to hear them. Larry David had created the same predicament for himself once.

Once again, the show's progress resembled that of salmon swimming upstream. While some people did respond to the show as Larry had hoped, *Seinfeld* was still running third in households behind *Anything but Love* and *Jake and the Fat Man*. Rather than sacrifice episodes in an obvious losing cause, NBC took the show off the air after February 13, 1991, and put it on ice temporarily.

While his series waited in suspended animation, Jerry kept busy. In the spring of 1991, he appeared on NBC's *Spy TV: How to Be Famous* and Showtime's *Aspen Comedy Festival*. Larry waited, fretted, and worried. As it turned out, *Seinfeld* sat collecting dust until April, almost a full year after the first short order had aired. By the time the last of the thirteen second-season episodes aired, almost two years would have passed since the original pilot had been broadcast.

"At this rate," Castle Rock executive Glenn Padnick cracked, "we'll be in syndication around 2010."

But the wait turned out to be propitious. When NBC finally put *Seinfeld* back on the schedule, it was positioned to follow *Cheers,* which would finish the 1990–91 season as television's top-rated show. Finally *Seinfeld* performed well, but its success was not unqualified. "There were still people not sure about the show and who doubted it could survive on its own without the help it got from *Cheers,*" Jerry recalls.

And the fact was, *Seinfeld* would not be getting any help from *Cheers* in future seasons. Although networks claim they do not negotiate specific time slots, according to NBC sources the Thursday 9:30 P.M. slot "belonged" contractually to Paramount, which produced *Cheers* and another show on the NBC schedule, *Wings*. Because *Cheers* was so important to the network, Paramount had been able to exert enough control to negotiate that *Wings* would occupy the Thursday 9:30 P.M. time slot for the 1991–92 season.

On the basis of households reached and ratings compiled after eighteen episodes spread out over two years, the show's future looked dim—so dim that Rick Ludwin was ready to grovel once more at the feet of Warren Littlefield. He was surprised to discover he didn't have to, because *Seinfeld* was turning out to be a demographics gold mine. "Warren told me that even though the show wasn't doing so great in the ratings, it was attracting the kind of audience the network wanted to attract," Ludwin recalls.

"That kind of audience" was viewers 18–49, with emphasis on the subcategory of viewers 18–34. How well a show does with the 18–49 group determines the amount of money advertisers pay the network to air their commercials during its time slot. And a show with a particularly high number of 18–34 viewers will generate far more income for the network than a show that skews older, because advertisers believe that people in that age range have the most disposable income and spend their money more freely. Consequently, for example, the struggling *SeaQuest DSV* actually made more money for NBC than *Murder, She Wrote*, a Top Twenty series, was making for CBS.

Seinfeld was attracting an affluent crowd interested in seeing themselves on-screen. Not coincidentally, the same group comprised the bulk of Jerry's comedy club audience at that point in his career. The show was becoming the comedic flip side of *thirtysomething*, which could make burned pesto sauce seem relevant and riveting and had also appealed to the sought-after 18–49 group.

Seinfeld concedes, "What gave us the chance to keep going and develop was that despite being very low-rated in the beginning, we had a very desirable demographic. Even though we were technically bombing by normal standards, the people who were watching were very appealing to advertisers."

So, based on its strength in the advertising-friendly demographic, *Seinfeld* was renewed for the 1991–92 season—but, again, only for a half-season of thirteen episodes. And it would be sent back to Wednesday nights when the fall schedule debuted the following September.

At the time, Jerry could only joke about what seemed to be monthly changes in scheduling. "This show started like a garage band. We aired four times one year, thirteen times the following year, and then were on opposite the Gulf War. So we've really been through it all. We're still against *Jake and the Fat Man*. And I don't know, but every time I look, he gets a little fatter."

Despite all the maneuverings and network politics, many fans of the show believe that Larry and Jerry's early work on the series, especially during the 1991 short season, contains some of the best *Seinfeld* episodes ever produced. Of the thirteen episodes, Larry and Jerry had written six together with Larry adding two more on his own. The other five scripts were closely supervised and in most cases rewritten by David, although he took no official credit for doing so. By not handing the writing of the series over to a roomful of staff writers, Seinfeld and David were able to maintain tight control over the tone and timbre of the interwoven stories they were presenting.

Again, Larry borrowed heavily from his life, turning his own experiences into reality-heightened, absurdist commentaries on the things that tend to consume our lives so completely that we hardly take the time to step back and look at the humor in them.

Although by this time critics had already begun to sing the praises of the show's Byzantine story lines and well-defined eccentricities, *Seinfeld* was getting clobbered in the ratings. NBC pulled it off the air until they were able to position it after *Cheers*.

SEINFELD returned to the air on April 4, 1991, the first Thursday-night, post-*Cheers* appearance for the series. Episode 10 was a milestone for another reason as well: it was the first episode written by someone other than Larry or Jerry. "The Apartment" had been submitted on a freelance basis by Peter Mehlman, a former journalist. Jerry had hired him onto the staff after reading his dryly amusing article in the *New York Times* about star-spotting.

"I had never written dialogue in my life, other than making up quotes," Mehlman says. But Jerry was more interested in outlook and perception than in technical skills, and "The Apartment" showed that Mehlman was on the same comedic page as his two bosses. The plot revolves around Kramer moussing his hair, Jerry worrying over what it would mean for Elaine to move into an apartment above him, and George wearing a wedding ring in hopes of attracting on-the-make single women.

Episode 11, "The Statue," was written by Larry Charles, a staff writer who was known for his unusually dark humor. Although "The Statue" was rather tame by Charles's standards, with the main story line centering around an old statue Jerry finds in a box of stuff his grandfather left him, an episode that aired a few weeks later, "The Baby Shower," includes a fantasy sequence in which Jerry is shot to death.

"So many places ask you to shave off your edge," Charles commented, "but at *Seinfeld* they ask you to sharpen it."

The episodes aired up to this point had been created without much interference from NBC. The network's only concern revolved around the relationship between Jerry and Elaine. Seinfeld had thought that by making her an ex-girlfriend, any need to address the issue of sex between them could be bypassed altogether. He thought wrong. "They wanted us to *clarify* the relationship," David says dryly.

NBC executives strongly suggested that they would like the *Seinfeld* brain trust to move Elaine and Jerry into a *Moonlighting* or *Cheers* kind of romance—even though the added romantic element proved detrimental to both those series. *Cheers* probably survived only because Shelley Long left; the case of *Moonlighting,* the sexual tension between Cybill Shephard and Bruce Willis was the heat that fueled the show, so when their relationship was consummated, it effectively signaled the end of the series.

But network executives tend to be creatures of habit, and to them, sitcoms need to have a romantic angle. Although Jerry wasn't about to let that happen, he conceded the need to address the issue in order to satisfy the powers that be—and perhaps some viewers, as well.

"We wanted to do it without making a big deal about it, just break down that wall of teasing," he explained at the time. "I hate that 'will they, won't they' crap on television. We just hope someone out there is enjoying the effort we're going through to make this nonstupid."

Julia Louis-Dreyfus, for one, was also against the idea of making Elaine and Jerry a twosome again. "They were toying with the idea of making us a couple, but fortunately they decided not to, because Elaine's relationship with Jerry is unusual, and nothing like that had ever really been done," she says, then explains her take on the characters' past relationship. "They weren't together for a long time. Elaine was attracted to Jerry by his humor, but it was the rest of his personality that led to their breakup."

First aired May 2, 1991, "The Deal" begins with Jerry and Elaine sitting in his apartment watching television late at night. A movie they come across makes them start talking about whether they could start having sex again without ruining their friendship. Their agreement to have "this and that" seems to be working until Jerry decides to give Elaine cash for her birthday. In the end, George, who says all along it simply can't be done, is proven right.

However, two years later, in the first episode of the fifth season, "The Mango," Jerry and Elaine were once again brought together sexually. "We came back together for one episode after I admit to Jerry I faked every orgasm, so he could have another chance to sexually fulfill me," Julia Louis-Dreyfus explained. "There was pressure from above to get those two back in the sack. I think, though, it's better for them to be apart because it provides more conflict."

"It's safe to say the network wouldn't mind seeing Jerry and Elaine together every week," noted Larry David, making it clear NBC executives have had a hard time seeing that.

"You know," Seinfeld said, "the network's kind of like your aunts and uncles. I mean, they are our superiors, but we don't *really* have to listen to them. It's like going with your uncle to Disneyland."

With "this and that" taken care of, the show was able to go back to concentrating on what it did best: bringing into clear focus the trials and tribulations of our daily lives. This ability to transform the mundane into the universal is what makes "The Chinese Restaurant" a classic *Seinfeld* episode and one that many viewers and critics have included among the show's all-time best.

On their way to see a revival of *Plan 9 From Outer Space*, Jerry, Elaine, and George go to a Chinese restaurant to grab a quick meal. The entire episode has them waiting to be seated. Meanwhile, Jerry sees a woman whose name he can't recall; George needs to use the phone, which others refuse to relinquish; Elaine becomes crazed with hunger. In the end, they never get to eat.

After seeing the episode, some NBC executives developed stomach pangs of their own and began voicing their concerns about the show. "They felt the shows were not big enough," explains David. "Not enough action, not enough plot. So I said, 'Well, I quit.' Jerry said not to worry, so I said, 'I'm going to do the same show. Nothing's going to change.' And they said okay. I thought, 'Wow. Saying no—what an amazing, powerful thing that is.'"

The final new episode aired in *Seinfeld*'s second season was "The Busboy," in which George feels obliged to take responsibility for a busboy after inadvertently getting him fired. However, this was only the twelfth new episode to air. An additional show, "The Stranded," which was originally supposed to air on July 17, 1991, was held back. When it finally did air in November 1991, Jerry appeared prior to the show and explained that the episode had been shot earlier, before George lost his job, and he wanted "to let you know that we know you know."

With eighteen episodes shot, Larry and Jerry felt confident that they had a firm handle on the show and where they wanted to take it. They were pleased with their small writing staff but were vigilant about always keeping hands firmly on.

As the 1991–92 season premiere approached, *Seinfeld* had been honed, refined, defined, and cultivated like few shows before or since. Instead of jumping into a new season while still working out the nuances of a developing show, the cast and writers of *Seinfeld* were a cohesive unit, tested and strengthened by more than two years of blending together.

But everyone was also aware of one other truth: if they didn't succeed this time, there would be no more chances.

10

TV Jerry Versus Real Jerry

WHILE *SEINFELD* WOULD STILL BE UP AGAINST THE SECOND HALF HOUR OF *Jake and the Fat Man* when the 1991–92 season premiered in September, the show was given an unexpected and fortuitous break. Surprisingly, it was provided by rival ABC, when that network moved *Anything but Love* to 10:00 and tried out the new show *Sibs* in the 9:30 time slot.

On paper, *Sibs* looked strong. Marsha Mason starred as the eldest of three sisters whose two younger siblings, played by Margaret Colin and Jami Gertz, unexpectedly move in with her and her husband just as their only child has gone off to college. But the audience reaction was tepid, and *Seinfeld* was able to outperform *Sibs* surprisingly easily.

For some reason, NBC wasn't content to leave *Seinfeld* where it was finally performing well. As if trying to see just how much it could make Larry David suffer, in early 1992 the network moved *Seinfeld* from 9:30 to 9:00, opposite ABC's *Doogie Howser, M.D.* Although the Neal Patrick Harris series still beat *Seinfeld,* the family comedy suffered its lowest ratings of the season.

Despite losing the time period, *Seinfeld* was beefing up, albeit a pound at a time. Satisfied with its performance, the network ordered nine more episodes to give the series its first truly full season—although it would be considered the show's third. As a bonus, NBC also renewed the show for the 1992–93 season, giving Larry and Jerry their first full-order renewal.

When the 1991–92 season ended, the Top Five shows for the year based on ratings were, in descending order, *60 Minutes, Roseanne, Murphy Brown, Cheers,* and *Home Improvement,* Tim Allen's powerhouse for ABC. *Seinfeld* finished out hovering in the middle of the ratings pack, ranked in the 40s, but had continued to increase its 18–34 demographic fan base. It had also started to attract the attention of critics, who praised it for its unconventionality and often characterized it in terms of Jerry's stand-up—not completely surprising, since many comics developed shows around their best-known material.

"There are a lot of great comedians who never got to do the Great Thing. What *Seinfeld* has meant to me is that I got to do it," Jerry said. "I started out as a nightclub comic and made it as that. Then I went on and fulfilled that potential every comedian has. Every comedian, if he's good enough to make it as a stand-up, has the essence of comedic greatness. But to take it to the next step and build something around that essence is very hard. So the show means that I took the ball all the way into the end zone, which very few of us have done."

However, Seinfeld knew that his show had evolved into something quite different, taking on its own life force. "In the end," he reflected, "I don't think it had anything to do with stand-up. I think that when you sit down and try to do something to please yourself, which is what we did, it gives you a chance to come up with something new. That's all this was—two guys who didn't have any experience in the television business who wanted to do their own thing. That is what helped us do something so original."

Another thing also helped the show develop was Seinfeld's lack of ego when it came to sharing the spotlight with his costars.

"He's one of the most generous people I know," claimed Michael Richards. "When he sees the success of the show, he shares it with us. It's not just the Jerry Seinfeld show. We're definitely there for each other. I know everybody says that, but when you're at this stage of the game, a lot of people start letting their egos fly. Deep down, he's eternally grateful for what he has. That point of view came out of twenty years of honing his craft. It takes a long time. Along the way you develop soulfully."

"Jerry is a very generous boss," said Jason Alexander. "He shares lines and is always on an even keel."

* * *

THIS is not to say he didn't get antsy, especially when he stayed away from performing at comedy clubs for too long. Unlike some other actors in television series, Jerry neither turned vegetative during hiatuses nor looked to do a quick TV movie or to use his small-screen popularity as a springboard to movie stardom. In fact, he expressed himself forcefully on the subject: "Everybody else is trying to do this bullshit—to be a star or be a hunk, to be a celebrity or to be a host. What about *be* a comedian? That's what I want to do. Look at all those people from *Saturday Night Live,* going into those dumb movies. You want to say to them, 'What happened to what you were trying to do?' "

When Jerry had any time, he headed immediately back on the road, even though he was already tired from the strain of doing the show. Fortunately, his years on the road had taught him a valuable skill for stand-ups: being able to sleep anywhere, anytime. But Jerry was willing to suffer a certain amount of exhaustion in order to maintain the ties to his lifeblood.

"I miss doing stand-up when I'm away from it," he said. "I'm obsessed with the mechanism of comedy; it's unconquerable, dark, and mystical. A sitcom could never give me what stand-up does. Stand-up is more legitimate, more honest than doing a television series. Stand-up is a kind of grimy, sweaty, smoky, far less controlled business. I don't get that bead of sweat rolling down the middle of my back doing the show like I do in stand-up.

"Stand-up is a black and mysterious art, and you can't pretend it. Real stand-up has a certain ring to it, a certain energy. You can't write a monologue and hand it to someone and expect it to sound like the real thing. Being in front of a live audience, you're being reviewed every seventeen seconds. It's like going on a job interview every minute.

"I'll never give it up. I am a comedian. That's what I do. The show has come along, and that's been great, but doing stand-up is really my first love. There are certain things that you do in life that when you are doing them, you get this feeling, 'This is what I'm supposed to be doing.' Something just feels right."

Jerry would frequently drop into local clubs like the Improv to try out new material he was planning to use on the show and to keep in fighting shape. As he put it, "Stand-up is like a knife—if you don't use it, it gets dull."

The L.A. locals were always happy to see him, but his appearances didn't create much of a stir beyond the room. However, life on the road had become quite a different experience since his show had started gaining a wider audience.

When Seinfeld had gone back to stand-up after the truncated four-episode season, the television series had made no discernible impact on how comedy club audiences responded to him. After the second installment of episodes, he found himself being nudged into cult status; his concert dates now included more fans drawn by their enjoyment of the show.

The 1991–92 season was a breakout year. Suddenly Jerry went from being a comic with a television show to a television star who did stand-up comedy. Instead of thirtysomethings and college kids, Jerry was now playing to families, senior citizens, and TV fans of all persuasions.

"It's a mania," he acknowledged at the time, referring to the fan adoration that would lead audiences to scream with laughter at the slightest amusing one-liner. "It's madness. This isn't about comedy. This is about suddenly being hot. I've gone from being a comedian who made it to being a guy from a TV show. But the people who like the show are going to like my act and vice versa."

However, along with that change of perception came a sudden increase in value. During his hiatus as early as 1992, Jerry could earn $200,000 and possibly more for a single night's work. A contract rider put together by his personal management company, Shapiro/West and Associates, Inc., not only indicates what Jerry was making and that he got paid the same day he performed but also gives insight into the perks that accompany personal performances for someone of Jerry's stature.

The promoter was to supply "all local ground transportation via limousine" with a "professional driver with or from a professional car service only." Jerry would be provided with a "comfortable, private dressing room," where "freshly baked sliced turkey, plain tuna fish (mayonnaise on side), whole wheat bread, mustard, mayo, cole slaw, lettuce and tomato, and a fresh vegetable tray with dip, along with bottled carbonated and non-carbonated mineral water (Evian)" would be available. For the performance itself, the "promoter agrees to supply (1) follow spot . . . to supply on stage a wooden stool, Evian water, and one mic[rophone] stand with a round base and long-corded mic. . . . There must be *no* 'dance floor' or any other type of open area aside from seating areas in front or to the sides of the performance area."

Considering the lifestyle of most young stand-ups traveling the circuit, specifications like these seem to highlight the celebrity aspect of Seinfeld rather than his comedy—a point that concerned Jerry: "This isn't something I've cobbled together after the show became a hit just in order to make some extra money. I want people to know that comedy is my life's work, that a lot of years and time have gone into this."

THAT said, Jerry *was* pleased, and somewhat astounded, that the show had started to seep so deeply into the public's consciousness. During a 1991 New Year's Eve performance, members of the audience held up banners that read THESE PRETZELS ARE MAKING ME THIRSTY. They alluded to episode 28, "The Alternate Side," in which Kramer gets to say that one line in a Woody Allen movie.

"The reaction to the show has been amazing," Jerry said. "Part of me still doesn't believe it. We did a show that featured a Pez dispenser [episode 31, "The Pez Dispenser"], and afterward we got a call from the Pez people saying their sales had gone up nationally— and they were giving us the credit for that. You hear something like that and you think, 'Oh, come on.' "

Not everybody was a fan. One critic complained of the show's "smugness. What emanates unmistakably from the whole Seinfeld group is how enormously pleased they are with themselves." A Los Angeles producer questioned Jerry's public "take it or leave it" attitude toward the series. "He tries to be cool and aloof, but you can see he's calculating his every move. He acts like he's not needy, but to me he seems to be the neediest person on earth."

But these sentiments were in the minority among those familiar with the show. Trying to figure out why the show had such appeal, Julia Louis-Dreyfus suggested that the situations it explored were so universal that they struck a chord with all kinds of different people who otherwise might not watch a lot of television.

"It's a word-of-mouth kind of show," she said. "It has broad appeal because everybody has a lot of nothing going on in their lives, whether they live in New York, Des Moines, or Seattle. Plus, we have no big messages, no moral, no pretense. We're not curing cancer. We want jokes. Now, you look at shows and it's 'The meaning. The artistry. Who am I reaching?' "

She also objected to some critics who considered *Seinfeld* a primer getting along with the opposite sex. "Let's not kid ourselves. A television show isn't going to make a difference when it comes to communication between the sexes. In fact, none of these characters communicates particularly well—these people never really listen to one another. That's one of the things I love about the writing on our show. Each character has their own agenda, and no one feigns concern about anyone else's. They are there for one another, but they usually let one another down. I'm so tired of . . . television in twenty-two minutes trying to teach a life lesson. I'm glad if people enjoy the show and my check clears."

"It is a bit presumptuous to think that you can really teach people a meaningful lesson after twenty-one minutes of bad one-liners," Seinfeld agreed. "You can't get philosophical in the last minute and expect it to hit home. That's the big thing with us. You don't see where we're going.

"On other shows, most of the time, within a few minutes, you know what the story is and you know how it's going to work out. In our show, we don't resolve the problem. Sometimes things just get worse and then it is over. Sometimes it gets better. It's more stimulating. We try to avoid familiar patterns."

In fact, during a 1992 interview with Barbara Walters, who asked exactly what his show was about, Jerry did his bit to ensure that nobody would ever look to his series for inspiration or answers to life's questions. "It's about nothing," he said. "It's like Regis and Kathie Lee."

To his audience, however, Jerry was very much something. If he had any doubts, all he had to do was look at the true bellwethers of pop culture popularity. Not only did his name appear as an answer to a *TV Guide* crossword puzzle clue, but he began finding himself in the tabloids.

However, considering his clean living and his genial personality at work, there wasn't a lot of dirt to dish on Seinfeld. So the articles about him were more benign than barbed. The *Star* ran a headline that screamed: SEINFELD'S BIG PROBLEM: TOO MUCH MONEY AND NOT ENOUGH LOVE. The article had Jerry confiding to various insiders and friend that the only thing missing in his life was his "dream woman." Since there was nothing in Jerry's life that made for scandalous copy, the tabloid instead took the poor, poor, pitiful Seinfeld tack, using the following captions in the article:

Sad—He earns $80G a show but doesn't know what to spend it on.

Sad—Pal Jay Leno twisted his arm to buy a $3M mansion and a $50G Porsche.

Sad—He's lonely and convinced he'll never find Ms. Right.

Both the *Star* and the *Globe* ran features about Jerry's "obsession" with the size of his head, which were actually based on a kernel of truth. Jerry *had* joked about his head in the past, and Julia Louis-Dreyfus admitted that on the set of *Seinfeld* the cast had spent time measuring their heads and faces. "I'm the shortest person, but I had the widest face," she noted.

Seinfeld was beginning to stand out among the dozens of comedies on network television, and the industry and fans alike started to recognize Jerry as something special. In May 1992, he was named the funniest actor on television at the annual American Comedy Awards. The show garnered nine Emmy nominations that year, including Jerry's for Lead Actor in a Comedy Series, which he suggested was pretty good for someone who admittedly isn't an actor.

Typically, he was gracious about the nominations but refused to take them too seriously even if he was excited that *Seinfeld* was obviously being appreciated. "I am going to react if I don't win," he joked prior to the Emmy ceremony. "You know how they always show the losers sitting there with the brave smiles? Well, you won't see that from me. You'll see me shaking my head and the program flying."

As it turned out, Jerry lost to *Coach*'s Craig T. Nelson. However, the *Seinfeld* crew didn't go home empty-handed. Larry Charles and Elaine Pope walked away with an Emmy for Writing in a Comedy Series for "The Fix Up." In that episode Elaine and Jerry play matchmaker with George and a friend, then Kramer gives George a defective condom, making George think he might have gotten the girl pregnant. The episode contained the *Seinfeld*ian phrase "My boys can swim!"

WHILE Jerry was busy revitalizing himself out on the road, Larry David was recuperating from the mental and emotional wear and tear the series continually caused him. The success of the show had done little to diminish the sense of unease and angst that had dogged him for what seemed his entire adult life.

"I'm a person just trying to make it to the end," David said in a 1992 interview. "Our shooting schedule is grueling, brutalizing, and dehumanizing. I've compared it to a prison sentence. I've said, in fact, that I would prefer to be in prison if I could guarantee I wouldn't get raped.

"I work so hard now, so unrelentingly, that I don't have much time to know how miserable I really am. That's one of the good things about working on television. The person I was then is the person I am now, only with more money."

A lot more money. In fact, both David and Seinfeld had begun to reap substantial financial rewards from the show. In March 1993, David asked for, and eventually received, a salary of $125,000 per episode, which translated to over $3 million for the next season's twenty-six planned episodes.

One reason for David's salary demand was that prior to the 1992–93 season, Jerry's salary tripled, from $40,000 to over $100,000 an episode. This in addition to his extremely lucrative stand-up appearances meant Jerry was in line to become a mini–Hollywood mogul.

"We were just negotiating my contract, and I was prepared to accept what they were offering," Seinfeld says. "And my mother told me, 'No, you ought to get more. That's not right what they're offering.' And we're talking insane amounts of money, more money in a week than what my father would have made in five years. But it's not about the money to me. Besides, I'm rich already."

His friend George Wallace says dryly, "Oh, yeah, crazy money. Sometimes he would call me up and tell me how much he was making. I just hung up on him."

Jerry had finally started spending some of that money. After years of living in his Spartan condo in West Hollywood, he broke down and bought a home. Part of the reason he had waited so long was that he didn't want to feel he was putting down roots in L.A.

"I work in Los Angeles, but I live in New York," he clarified. "And I have fun in L.A. because that's the business and I have a lot of friends there. L.A. is good for working because the city is no distraction at all," he added pointedly.

In his act, Seinfeld says one of the things he loves most about New York is that the city is packed with humanity.

It's every different type of person piled one on top of the other. That sign we have in front of the Statue of Liberty, "Give us your tired, your poor huddled masses?" Can't we just say, "We'll take whoever you got. Give us the sad, the slow, people who can't drive, if they can't stay in their lane, if they don't signal, if they have bad credit, if they have no credit . . . in other words, any dysfunctional, defective slob you can somehow cattle-prod onto a wagon, send them over"?

"He has an amazing place in New York and still wants to be known as a New Yorker," says a friend, "but with the success of *Seinfeld,* he knew he had to establish himself in Los Angeles."

The house that finally won Jerry's heart was a $3 million home in the Hollywood Hills on Sierra Mar Place that had originally been built in the 1960s by George Montgomery. A subsequent owner gutted and refurbished it, creating an architectural showcase with views of both the ocean and downtown Los Angeles, a theater, a guest house, and a pool fifty-five feet long. Besides, he liked the area where the house was located. To his way of thinking, "The Hollywood Hills is the only vaguely urban environment in L.A. I miss New York every second. I can't get enough of it. I might have a house in Los Angeles, but I'm heterocoastal."

Although Jerry could now afford all the trappings of fame and indulge his Porsche passion, he made a conscious effort not to succumb to his celebrity. He never pulled tantrums or flashed his rank on the set. He maintained close contact with his family—always an excellent grounding source—regularly flying his mom, sister, and nephew out to L.A. for visits.

He shunned taking lavish vacations and, although he made several best-dressed lists, didn't become a clotheshorse. Although he could afford to fill his home floor to ceiling with toys and trinkets, he maintained his austere sense of personal space.

"I've seen a lot of people fall into the trap of thinking you're as important as you are being treated, and he's smart enough not to fall into that trap," commented Julia Louis-Dreyfus.

Longtime friend Carol Leifer took both his achievement and his equanimity about it in stride. "I'm not surprised at the success Jerry's had. He's disciplined without being rigid; hardworking without being fanatical. When he does his stand-up tour now, it's like being with a Beatle, with people banging on the limo and leaving gifts—but it rolls off his back. For someone who's been in therapy, he's the most together person I've met."

Although Seinfeld didn't let himself be swayed by his ever-increasing notoriety, he was not oblivious to it. "When I get dressed in the morning, I'm going out to do a show. I go to the supermarket and I kind of think about how I look, which I didn't before."

At the same time, he managed to remain detached from his stardom. "I saw it happen with Jay [Leno], and it was interesting to watch. But he handles his celebrity differently than I do. He wants the table in the restaurant facing the door at the front so the maximum number of people will know that he's there. He walks through the airport with no sunglasses. He can't wait to meet people.

"Even though all this attention that I'm getting now is very nice, I don't seek attention. But it's perfume. I smell it. I don't eat it. So I'm enjoying it but I'm not buying it."

However, he has been known to use his celebrity, but in ways unrelated to self-promotion. Although Seinfeld has frequently said his job is that of comedian and not politician, he uncharacteristically became involved in what was a blatantly social and political issue following the 1992 Los Angeles riots caused by the acquittal of the four policemen charged with the brutal beating of Rodney King.

The Los Angeles riots had been the worst widespread public unrest in decades. The nation watched in fascinated horror as pictures of beatings, looting, and arson beamed into people's homes on the nightly news. In Los Angeles, a citywide dusk-to-dawn curfew was put into effect. As the sun went down, carloads of young men wielding baseball bats could be seen driving on side streets through L.A.'s tony West Side.

It was a scary and surreal time; longtime neighbors turned on one another as a mob mentality began to take control of the street. In the aftermath, Los Angeles was a raw wound oozing suspicion and anger; the depth of the damage to the spirit of the community transcended personal politics and became a concern that cut across income level and profession.

Feeling the need to do something, Seinfeld called on his old friend George Wallace to join him for two benefit performances in an effort to use laughter as a means of healing the city, with the proceeds donated to the Rebuild L.A. Fund.

"I was very angry about the Rodney King verdict and the resulting damage. I was extremely shocked with the racist, social ignorance that caused that to happen," Seinfeld explained prior to the performances. "I just have to do something because it bothered me so much. I thought this would be the best thing that I could do as far as making a dent in the problem. Not even a dent, maybe a scratch. That it would be a positive act in the face of a lot of pain.

"The reason this was so upsetting to so many people was because it was so visible, and there's where television comes in. When it's this visible, people should stand up and say, 'Stop. This is no good.'

"All comedy, in a sense, is relieving some irritation, and irritations come in many sizes. My comedy tends to be based on small ones. This just happens to be a big irritation. As a stand-up, you really only react to the culture, reacting the same way everybody else reacts. I'm actually doing this because it's something I can do. I'm not taking advantage of my position. If I couldn't do *this*, I would go out and volunteer to help in some other way. If I was Ross Perot, I could send a check."

In our day, self-serving personalities all too often shamelessly use the misfortune of others as a self-promotional tool; those closest to Seinfeld knew that Jerry's only agenda was to try to help. The human tragedy of the riots was too great to ignore.

"This [benefit] was his idea, and it's just basic and vital to him," explained a friend, comic Larry Miller. "He thought he could show that this divisiveness is a disgrace."

It is possibly the only time in his career that Seinfeld has so openly revealed his personal beliefs. Although some of the inner Jerry seeps out in his stand-up, his stage persona requires keeping a cool distance between him and his audience; he is the detached observer and commentator on our daily foibles. His is not an intimate comedy, and by standing just to the side of those in his audience, he is better able to control the ebb and flow of his act's rhythm. On this occasion, though, he allowed a brief glimpse of his private side personal morality. For the moment, at least, his comedy was very much about something.

11

A Phenomenon Is Born

NORMALLY, A SHOW THAT HAD FINISHED THE PREVIOUS SEASON IN FORTY-second place would be considered marginal at best, but *Seinfeld* was riding a humming wave of increasing awareness and acclaim. Jerry himself was an even more visible presence in the American psyche since becoming the new spokesperson for American Express, at a stipend of $1 million a year. The clever *Seinfeld*-ian spots helped change the company's musty, old-money image to one of yuppie exuberance.

The NBC marketing machine rumbled into overdrive to keep the buzz going—or, as some might say, to manufacture it. If you tell viewers long enough that your show is "appointment TV" and sell it as if you didn't want it to be crassly popular and preferred having an eclectic audience, you encourage a jump-on-the-bandwagon mentality.

Even as the network was touting *Seinfeld* as the future—a trend-setter that would redefine television comedy—Jerry found himself constantly amazed and bemused by the twisting and turning fortunes of his show. "I knew we had a good show, but I don't think any of us could have imagined what it became. This is the series that managed to get on the air by sneaking in through the back door and became successful while never having to compromise its vision."

The strength of that originality and vision was going to be sorely tested when ABC decided to make *Seinfeld*'s Wednesday night slot a primetime battleground. It was touted as the biggest matchup since

The Simpsons took on—and dethroned—*The Cosby Show*. Despite its low ranking, *Seinfeld* was clearly a show that was generating a lot of interest and pulling in the highly desired 18–49 demographic, so NBC had decided to move it up by half an hour to the 9:00 P.M. slot, where it was paired with the new sitcom *Mad About You,* starring Jerry's close friend Paul Reiser. In the chess game that is primetime scheduling, ABC countered by moving its ratings powerhouse *Home Improvement* from its comfortable Tuesday 8:30 P.M. slot to opposite *Seinfeld*.

It was a somewhat risky move. Although *Home Improvement* had been ranked fifth for the 1991–92 season, cradled between two other family comedies—*Full House* and *Roseanne*—on Wednesday night it would have to be the anchor. It would follow a past-its-prime *Doogie Howser* (which in fact would not return the following season) and lead into a new comedy, *Laurie Hill,* starring DeLane Matthews and featuring Ellen DeGeneres in a small supporting role.

Tim Allen was not overly enthused with his show's new time slot but was powerless to do anything about it. As the media played up the "showdown" aspect of the scheduling, Allen made it clear what he thought about it all. "Jerry and I are in the same position," he said. "We have empathy for each other, but we're in the middle of this. They make their own decision at the network. The childish point of view is that I would like to have stayed where the show was most secure. But as a businessman, I understand what ABC is doing, and I applaud their confidence in our show after only one season on air. This is trial by fire."

Jerry also refused to get drawn into a verbal war. "I'm kind of flattered that they have to send in these powerhouse shows to hold us down. It's like they are trying to tie these huge weights to our balloon. It's funny to me that networks even have to even think about us. It's hilarious to me, and delightful, that other networks make programming decisions based on what we're doing."

Instead, both comics let the network brass do all the posturing.

"This is a competitive business, and we're not going to stay out of anybody's way to do them a favor," said Robert Iger, ABC entertainment president. "I happen to be a fan of Seinfeld's—he's a very talented comedian—but I really have no second thoughts about moving Tim's show. Initially, everybody said this was a time-period hit, until everybody realized that in many cases, *Home Improvement* was improving on its lead-in. Which is significant because *Full*

House is a powerhouse unto itself. Creatively, *Home Improvement* is a solid show, so moving it is not a concern."

NBC entertainment president Warren Littlefield also expressed no concern for how *Seinfeld* might fare against a solid hit show. "When *Cosby* was on Thursday, it brought more viewers to the plate—the number of households using televisions went way up," he noted. "And that's what I think will happen here. When everyone has their schedule in place, I think it's certainly possible for more than one show to succeed in a particular time period."

In truth, *Home Improvement* ran roughshod over the competition and would jump two spots by the end of the 1992–93 season, finishing at number three behind perennial winner *60 Minutes* and *Roseanne*.

Although *Seinfeld* was holding its own, it was clearly being outperformed by Allen's family-centered juggernaut. If ABC's intent had been to snuff out the fires of a show it felt was a potential breakout hit for NBC, it seemed to be doing a good job of it. *Seinfeld* continued to suffer from mediocre ratings, languishing in the mid-40s.

Then came *the* break. Ted Danson, who had gone from bit-part movie anonymity to being one of television's highest-paid performers on *Cheers,* earning an estimated $450,000 per episode for the 1992–93 season, abruptly decided to call it quits after eleven years. The producers immediately announced they would not continue the show without him, signaling the end to one of the most honored sitcoms in television history—and creating a huge void in NBC's Thursday night programming.

Cheers creator and director James Burrows explained, "Our thinking was, we rolled the dice twice and came out winners when we replaced Nick Colasanto with Woody Harrelson and Shelley [Long] with Kirstie Alley. We didn't want to take that risk again. It is better to leave too early than too late."

The one upside of the pending *Cheers* cancellation was that Paramount had suddenly lost the leverage to keep *Wings* on Thursday nights.

NBC wasted no time shuffling the schedule, not wanting to wait until the following season to groom *Cheers*'s successor. Although the move raised eyebrows within the television community, Warren Littlefield went on a gut instinct and moved *Seinfeld* back to the post-*Cheers* slot on February 4, 1993.

After almost four years of relative obscurity, the show finally jumped to unexpected heights—from number forty to number ten within a week.

"They tried every other place they could think of, but we needed that Thursday spot," Jerry noted, tongue in cheek.

The subtext of his comment is worth noting: viewer habit should never be underestimated. It's the reason *Family Matters,* for instance, could air on ABC Friday nights at 8:00 P.M. and be a Top Ten show, then lose 40 percent of its audience when it moved to CBS, despite airing *on the same day and at the same time.* Was it that *Seinfeld* was suddenly so much better, or merely that it was given a time slot that regularly attracted a large number of viewers, regardless of what was on, whether it be *Cheers, Diff'rent Strokes,* or *Seinfeld?*

This is not to say *Seinfeld* didn't deserve a bigger audience. The dramatic improvement in ratings just shows the serendipity of scheduling. Had *The Larroquette Show,* another comedy praised by critics, been given the Thursday 9:00 P.M. slot and *Seinfeld* been moved to Tuesday at 9:00 P.M. instead, the fates of both shows could have been dramatically different.

On March 4, 1993, *Seinfeld* outperformed an original episode of *Cheers.* Then it continued to beat the venerable series, the first time that had happened since *Taxi* managed it back in 1982. The buzz had turned into a roar, so much so that NBC eventually awarded *Seinfeld* the highly coveted *Cheers* slot for the 1993–94 season.

"We went from number forty to number two over the course of a week," recalled Seinfeld. "It was exciting and fun. And it was nice that the ratings finally matched people's enthusiasm. It had been hard when people would say, 'This is the funniest show on television,' and you'd wonder why it was so lowly rated."

As usual, Larry David took a darker view of their good fortune. "As I've said before, if people didn't watch us on Wednesday, I don't want them watching us on Thursdays. Every day I pray that this show will be canceled. I'm just a simple caveman. I don't understand why people are watching us now when they didn't watch us before. I don't have good feelings about anything."

As IT happened, and probably not coincidentally, the move came during what is arguably the show's most consistent and groundbreaking season, its fourth.

The early episodes had to work around the fact that Julia Louis-Dreyfus had just given birth to her first child, Henry. "They had hidden my pregnancy the second half of the previous season by having me wear lots of layers and carry around large objects," she said. Elaine's absence was explained away in the two-part season opener by having her traveling in Europe with her psychiatrist boyfriend.

The show also picked up where it had left off in the third season finale by having Kramer still in Los Angeles trying to break into acting. This gave Seinfeld and David the opportunity to move the show away from the familiar confines of New York cross-country to L.A. In the first part, Jerry and George go looking for Kramer, who ends up a suspect in a string of serial killings committed by "the Smog Strangler." Murder is not normally the stuff of knee-slapping humor, but somehow, they got away with it.

In the second part, Kramer is released from jail after another murder is committed while he is incarcerated, but he still refuses to leave with Jerry and George. In a somewhat anticlimactic ending, Kramer reappears in New York a few days later. But the tone for the season was set.

There was a new element to the fourth-season episodes. For the first time there is a season-long story arc, beginning with "The Pitch" and ending with the one-hour season finale, "The Pilot": TV Jerry is asked by NBC to come up with an idea for a television series, and George suggests a show about "nothing." The episodes became more Byzantine than ever as the real-life backstory of the creation of the *Seinfeld* pilot intersected with the characters it had begotten—art and life imitating and feeding off each other simultaneously.

Larry David seems to have taken great pleasure in retooling his early experiences at NBC, especially the encounters with the character of Russell Dalrimple, based on NBC executive Warren Littlefield. (In a bit of typical television typecasting, the actor hired to play Littlefield's alter ego, Bob Balaban, was cast to play Littlefield again a few years later in the HBO movie *The Late Shift,* which recounted the events surrounding Jay Leno being picked over David Letterman to succeed Johnny Carson.)

Julia Louis-Dreyfus returned for the fifth episode of the season. With the cast back at full strength, the season shifted into an even higher gear.

One of the hallmarks of *Seinfeld* had been the writers' ability to distill the essence of a show into a catchphrase. For instance, there was "shrinkage," which afflicted George after a dip in cold water. ("I'm very proud to have brought the concept of shrinkage before the American public," says Seinfeld) and "Bubble Boy." In the episode of the same name, Jerry agrees to go visit a sick fan, who turns out to be so obnoxious that George gets into a fight with him, dispelling the universal notion that all ill people are noble beings.

Since the lines between fiction and reality were already being blurred beyond recognition with the "pilot" story line, Larry David decided to expand his horizons in the "The Cheever Letters," in which the father of George's girlfriend, Susan, turns out to be a secret former lover of author John Cheever.

Then on November 18, 1992, came "The Contest." So to speak. After George's mother ends up in the hospital after falling down in shock when she walks in on George masturbating while leafing through *Glamour* magazine, he swears he'll never sexually satisfy himself again. When Jerry challenges him to a contest of self-denial and George accepts, Elaine and Kramer also want in on the bet.

This was uncharted prime time territory for a network show and even Larry David thought he might have crossed a line with this one.

"I had the whole scenario worked out," he recalled. "I just thought NBC would say, 'there's no way we'll let you do this show.' And then I would quit over it."

"When I first heard about the show's topic, the blood did drain from my face," admits NBC executive Rick Ludwin. "But after reading the script, there was no way I could object. The subject matter was handled so tastefully."

Based on a real-life contest in which Larry David was once involved, "The Contest" was destined to become a quintessential *Seinfeld* in that it showed how much one can get away with if enough creative wordplay is used. Once again, code words ruled the day, with the phrases "Master of His Domain," when referring to the three guys, and "Queen of the Castle" for Elaine, used when referring to abstinence.

"I enjoy the art of euphemism," explained Seinfeld, "especially compared to the shove-it-up-your-nose kind of stuff they usually do on television."

Kramer was the first to pay up his $100 for the winner's kitty. Elaine came in a close second after being overwhelmed with fantasies about John F. Kennedy Jr. "I had hoped to hear from John,"

Louis-Dreyfus admits, "because I would have loved to hear his comments, but I never did."

Although NBC solidly backed the quality and taste of the show, several nervous advertisers pulled out at the last minute, which proved to be their loss. Even though "The Contest" was aired opposite ABC's *The Jacksons: An American Dream*, *Seinfeld* still managed to post its highest rating ever on a Wednesday night.

By the time "The Contest" was repeated on April 29, 1993, the first night of that year's May sweeps, *Seinfeld* was a Top Ten show on Thursday nights, and advertisers were crawling over each other to sign up. Tom Cherones would win a Directors Guild of America Award for his work on the episode.

Although the show generated a lot of notice for its controversial subject matter, Larry David contended: "It's one of my favorite episodes not because I got away with something, but because it was funny." Television Academy voters thought so too, voting him the Emmy for Outstanding Writing in a Comedy Series for his work on "The Contest."

"The Pick," in turn, reveled in embarrassment. Not only does Jerry lose a girlfriend who thinks she caught him picking his nose, but Elaine is mortified to discover that the Christmas card she sent out shows her nipple, or "nip" as it is referred to in the episode.

"Not that there's anything wrong with that" became the next *Seinfeld* phrase to infiltrate the consciousness of television viewers. In "The Outing," a college reporter mistakenly reports that Jerry and George are gay—not that there's anything wrong with that.

"The Junior Mint" was another example of clever writing enabling Jerry to go where no other sitcom had gone before. Jerry has a date with a woman whose name he has forgotten, but he knows it rhymes with a female body part. Could it be Mulva? Actually, it was Dolores. In real-life offices all across the country, people chuckled around the water cooler the next day about the "naughty" implication of her name.

However, not everybody laughed. This episode became the crux of a multimillion-dollar civil suit filed by Jerrold Mackenzie, a former Miller Brewing Company executive employee who was fired from his $95,000-a-year job after discussing the episode with a female coworker. When the woman claimed she didn't get the joke, he copied the page of a dictionary containing the word "clitoris"—so he wouldn't have to say it—and put it on her desk. He claimed in his lawsuit that Miller Brewing had used the incident as an excuse to fire him and that he was the victim of wrongful termination. The jury agreed, awarding Mackenzie $26.6 million, $18 million of which was punitive damages.

It seemed to be the season of controversies. When certain groups got wind of "The Handicap Spot," a mild swell of protest wafted up to the executive offices of NBC. In the story, George parks his father's car in a handicap parking spot. When a disabled woman is injured because George has taken the space, an angry mob trashes the car. Later, Kramer falls in love with the woman, and George's father gets arrested for parking in the spot.

The network was concerned enough to put the episode on ice for a while, and at one point there was some speculation that "The Handicap Spot" might not be aired at all. However, both Seinfeld and David claim they never had to adjust an episode at the direction of NBC, nor were they ever in danger of having a completed show pulled.

Because the series had originally been developed by Ludwin in the specials division, it wasn't always subject to the same scrutiny and interference that others shows endure. Jerry believes that hierarchical difference was a big reason for the show's ultimate success: "We weren't meddled with at all, and we were able to keep the originality of it intact. Even when they didn't like what we were doing or understand it, they put it on the air."

(In a casting note, when "The Handicap Spot" originally aired, Frank Costanza was played by actor John Randolph. The following season, in "The Puffy Shirt," the role was played by Jerry Stiller. After *Seinfeld* went into syndication, "The Handicap Spot" was reshot in the spring of 1995 with Stiller.)

The fourth season ended with a special one-hour finale, "The Pilot." Russell Dalrimple, who has developed an obsession with Elaine, green-lights Jerry and George's pilot and clears it for production. All the guest characters from the past season offer their comments on the pilot when it airs, and they all think it's terrific. However, when Russell disappears, the fate of the pilot is in the hands of the new president, who is convinced that Jerry just can't act.

SEINFELD was now a full-fledged hit, on the verge of phenomenon status, and the attention the show and its stars had received before was nothing compared to the white-hot interest in them after the

1992–93 season. But not all of the critics were happy with the show's new-found popularity.

In October 1992, *TV Guide* gave *Seinfeld* a thumbs-down in its "Cheers & Jeers" column: "In seasons past, before Jerry and his pals became one of NBC's most highly touted shows, *Seinfeld* concerned itself with the little things in life. Entire episodes were dedicated to waiting for a table at a restaurant, riding the subway, or losing a car in a mall parking lot. This season, however, there's a cast of thousands. Characters who used to wander no further than the corner diner now travel the world. And there's a continuing plot that finds Jerry and George pitching a TV series to NBC. We're glad the show is finally getting some recognition, but we can't help but feel that something—or is it nothing?—has been lost in the quest to become more than a cult favorite."

Typically, Jerry took both the accolades and the occasional criticism in stride. "It's very easy to get tricked by television, but I had been around for a while and I had seen enough that I knew the routine," he explained. "Even though it was new to me, I didn't suck it in like I might have had I been in my early twenties and let it really throw me off kilter. In fact, I don't think I could have handled it very well if it had happened when I was younger. But I had been on the sidelines for so long that by the time I was called in to play, I knew the game."

Julia Louis-Dreyfus, however, wasn't so sanguine. "I'm blown away," she admitted.

Castle Rock's Glenn Padnick was equally beside himself. "We're all giddy; the company has been energized. I must have thought *Seinfeld* was in danger of being pulled probably a million times—until just a few weeks ago"

The show's rocketing popularity immediately translated into other career opportunities. Jason Alexander and Julia Louis-Dreyfus were selected by Rob Reiner, one of Castle Rock's founders, to star in his next film, *North,* playing husband and wife. Michael Richards began doing ads for the Gap. As he had done over previous hiatuses, Jerry headed out for an extended eighteen-city stand-up tour, which sold out within days.

He had also agreed to write a book—not an autobiography, a humor book—for a $1.5 million advance from Bantam. "That's quite a lot of money for doing essentially the same act he was doing when he was poor," said one caustic observer.

Seinfeld ignored such sour grapes and approached his new role of author with his trademark manner. "I am a very amusing young man, and people seem to be interested in these useless little ideas I have," he said during a gathering of booksellers. "There seems to be some money in it. What we're doing here is trying to somehow conceptualize this small quirk in my personality into a huge publishing fortune. Because the nightclubs, the television series, the American Express commercial is not enough. I won't be satisfied until you all hate me!"

Irwyn Applebaum, president and publisher of Bantam, said Jerry contributed "an unusual amount of book-specific promotion by a celebrity. Would that all of our authors had twenty-plus million people interested in them every week. If only five percent of the people who watch the show buy the book, then it'll be a bestseller.

"Part of our plan all along was that there would be a tremendous amount of promotion Jerry would do in the fall, then as we headed into spring, when Jerry set out on his concert tour, there would be another chance to visit cities and do book signings and appearances. It was the kind of full-tilt energy he's put into every aspect of the book."

Not everyone was as charmed as the booksellers. He had recently been voted first in *Spy* magazine's annual ranking of the year's worst people, places, and things, for "mating stand-up with a sitcom to form the mutant genre 'sit-up,' for the comment, I just hate everybody and everything. That's why I'm so funny,' and for owning 25 pairs of sneakers including a pair of Air Seinfelds." Former winners included Al Sharpton and Ross Perot.

But such sentiments were becoming more and more in the minority and Bantam was betting the bank that Jerry was a publishing gold mine. His book would include most of the routines he had honed over the previous seventeen years.

> *I have no plants in my house. They won't live for me. Some of them don't even wait to die; they commit suicide. I once came home and found one hanging from a macramé noose, the pot kicked out from underneath. The note said, "I hate you and your albums."*

Jerry planned to write it while on his summer tour, and its release was set to coincide with the 1993–94 season premiere of *Seinfeld*. If there had been any concern over such a big investment in an untried author, the publisher's fears were allayed the day Bantam advertised that the *Village Voice* would be giving away free copies of *SeinLanguage*. People began lining up at seven in the morning for the 9:30 A.M. giveaway, and the books were all gone in seven minutes.

Less than a year after its release, *Seinlanguage* had sold over 1.2 million copies and was into its twentieth printing. It had surpassed General Norman Schwarzkopf's *It Doesn't Take a Hero* to become the second-largest-selling hardback in Bantam's history, trailing only the *Iococca* autobiography.

Once again, Jerry was the man with the Midas touch.

Soon, every company wanted a piece of *Seinfeld*. At one point, an idea of having the cast's pictures appear on a box of Kellogg's Nonfat Granola was floated; the marketing possibilities were obvious. However, Julia Louis-Dreyfus's attorney, Thomas Hansen, warned Castle Rock in a strongly worded letter that putting his client's picture on a box of cereal would be in breach of her contract, which prohibited no product endorsement without her direct consent. The idea went away.

WHENEVER a series suddenly takes off, it's almost a given that there will be speculation about spinoffs. Both NBC and the *Seinfeld* actors put that speculation to rest immediately. "No, there will be no spin-off," Jerry promised. "We're family."

His comment wasn't just hyperbole. The primary cast members had developed a sort of us-against-them mentality, forged during their years of working to satisfy each other first and anyone else second. The depth of that unity was proven in a bizarre incident involving studio neighbor Tom Arnold, who was then still married to Roseanne.

The contretemps began shortly before the end of the fourth season. Louis-Dreyfus came to work at the MTM Studios in Studio City, where the series was shot, and found her regular parking space blocked by sandbags being used for nearby construction work. The security man on duty directed her to park in a spot marked for Tom Arnold, who would later claim that Julia did it of her own volition and was using the security guard as a scapegoat.

When Arnold drove onto the lot in his $250,000 Turbo Bentley and saw another car in his space, he had a tantrum. "I was late for rehearsal and blew a fuse," he said, admitting he then wrote an obscenity-filled note and left it on the car's windshield. He claimed he had no idea who the car belonged to.

After Louis-Dreyfus returned and found the note, she and her three costars confronted Arnold near the *Seinfeld* soundstage. According to an eyewitness, she called him an ass, which started a shouting match between the two of them. The next day, the incident escalated when the *Seinfeld* crew took back production equipment they had previously lent to the staff of Arnold's series, making it clear the repossession was in response to his note.

According to Arnold's representatives, later that day his parking-place nameplate mysteriously disappeared, which precipitated a furious reaction from both Arnold and Roseanne, who was now involved. Roseanne took a Polaroid of one of her crewmen mooning the camera. In addition to leaving the photo on the car with the epithet JULIA LOSER written on it, she also allegedly soaped the windows, writing BITCH and other obscenities.

For Seinfeld, who is usually unfailingly polite, the outrageousness of the pettiness and bad taste involved was unacceptable. "Tom Arnold gives a whole new meaning to the word 'moron,' and I don't care how much clout his wife has," he was reported as saying. "I'd always heard he was a lowlife jerk, and the note on Julia's car and everything else reinforces that. Only someone with the IQ of pond scum would do that."

To which Roseanne replied, "They're idiots. Seinfeld and his crowd are so arrogant they think they're doing Samuel Beckett instead of a sitcom."

To which Jason Alexander commented, "I am willing to bet that she has never read *anything* Beckett ever wrote."

Worried about the incident escalating further, NBC finally stepped in and effectively issued a gag order. The network believed—probably correctly—that nobody would win a war of words with Roseanne, who at the time was one of the most powerful women in Hollywood, with the number two series and a reputation for vindictiveness.

Eventually the furor died down, even if the rancor never fully dissipated. One can assume that nobody on the *Seinfeld* set felt particularly bad when Arnold's series, *The Jackie Thomas Show,* was canceled by ABC despite being ranked fourteenth; it was the highest-ranking show of the season not to be renewed.

Later, asked to comment about the parking-space incident, Julia

Louis-Dreyfus smiled sweetly and demurred, saying only, "All in all I consider myself very lucky. I don't think life could get any better."

The following September, *Seinfeld* reached a pinnacle that would have seemed impossible, even laughable, just two years earlier. At the 1992–93 Emmy Awards, not only did Larry David win for "The Contest," Michael Richards took home the statue for Best Supporting Actor in a Comedy Series.

Neither of those wins was particularly shocking, and David's had actually been anticipated. But when *Seinfeld* won for Outstanding Comedy Series over such traditional fare as *Murphy Brown, Home Improvement,* and *Cheers,* a collective gasp shuddered through Hollywood.

The onetime primetime outsiders were suddenly television royalty.

12

On the Set With Jerry, Larry, and the Cast

AMID THE HOOPLA CRANKED UP BY NBC'S ABLE MARKETING AND PUBLICITY departments, *Cheers* went off the air May 20, 1993, with a ninety-minute finale, which featured the return of prodigal former series star Shelley Long. After being in the Top Ten for eight straight seasons and with twenty-six Emmys on its shelf, *Cheers* bowed out gracefully and passed the torch to *Seinfeld*. A show steeped in sitcom tradition was making a perfectly timed exit, opening the door for a cutting-edge program intent on redefining the genre.

But groundbreaking doesn't come easy, and the very process of getting a *Seinfeld* episode up on its feet was unique among sitcoms. The difference was not so much in the nuts and bolts of rehearsing and filming but in the close scrutiny that was given literally every word of the script and in the amount of hands-on supervision Jerry and Larry demanded over the series' first four seasons and into the 1993–94 season, their fifth.

"*Seinfeld* is not a typical sitcom," staff writer Larry Charles agreed. "We don't do things as a committee. It is not just sitting in a room throwing out punch lines. We don't have a grand scheme. We are not as concerned with punch lines as we are in finding the truth of the situation. That's where the real laughs are for us. From week to week we just try to do the funniest possible show we can.

"Basically, Larry [David] and Jerry make the executive decisions, but it is based on Larry's syntax. He just goes with his feelings about things. He lies down on the couch and says, 'This is what we will do.' The script does evolve over the course of a week, but it evolves based on Larry's take on it."

That didn't always sit well with some on the writing staff. "After you'd write a script, Larry would completely take it over, and that's the last you'd see of your script," one former staffer complained after leaving the show. "The writer is just a cog in the system. Larry is definitely the man behind the curtain."

"Scripts do evolve, but it all depends on the script," countered Seinfeld. "Sometimes we hardly change it. Sometimes . . . nearly every line is rewritten. If the script is not written by Larry and me, the changes can be fairly drastic."

One of their artistic commandments was originality, which is why they seldom, if ever, accepted spec scripts from nonstaff writers.

"Everyone thinks they understand the show," complained Charles. "They think it's easy to write, which is the first mistake."

"I'm doing something that seems so taken from their own lives that they can't help but assume that everything in their lives must be as funny," offered Jerry. "But they're wrong. I take it as a comment on my skill as a comedian that it seems like nothing. It *should* seem like nothing. It should seem like something anyone could do."

Stories could be in development for months before being woven together into cohesive episodes. The other writers had to clear every idea for every subplot with Jerry and Larry. It is testimony to the Seinfeld-David craft that when viewing the episodes, you don't see the effort. Just as an actor's acting should be invisible, a script should be seamless and not come across as forced. But a *Seinfeld* script also needed something much harder to achieve—uniqueness.

"We don't ever want something in our show that could have happened on another show," Jerry explained. "Almost anything we do is offbeat, and we try to step into real life. If it's not quirky and odd, if it seems like something you could see somewhere else, I don't want it."

This meant that the writers—a staff of eleven—needed to find a new wellspring for ideas, not simply reinvent plots that had been passed down through the television ages. Remember the *Mary Tyler Moore* episode in which Mary begins to laugh hysterically at the funeral for Chuckles the Clown? Jerry and Larry insisted on that kind of originality for every episode, week in and week out. The burden of maintaining such a seemingly impossibly high standard of creativity weighed most heavily on the head writer.

"For Larry, the show is blood and agony," noted Jason Alexander.

"There are so many shows to do, and it's such a daunting prospect, that all you can think about is the next show," Larry himself admitted. "The hardest part of this show is coming up with the ideas. I like something tiny that just expands."

Jerry once commented, "You start out with an idea and you have an idea, then the idea has you. Many people ask, 'Where do you get your ideas?' But the real, secret truth is that nobody knows where their ideas come from. They just make things up. Nobody really knows the truth to that question. It is a mystery. If jokes come into your head, you become a comedian. If songs come into your head, you become a songwriter or a musician. But you don't *really* know where the music is coming from."

One specific idea, which became "The Barber," was developed after one of the staff recounted the stress, anxiety, and guilt he had experienced in changing hairstylists.

"Somebody comes up with an idea for a show," explained Seinfeld. "It could just be one line, but hearing that line makes you laugh. 'Jerry picks his car up from the valet, and there's a smell that won't come out.' Or 'Jerry and Kramer go to watch an operation, and a Junior Mint falls into the body.' It's not like 'Jerry's nephew comes to visit for a week.' That *doesn't* make you laugh. Virtually every show that we've done can be boiled down that way."

Even the most promising ideas from the staff eventually had some direct input from Larry and Jerry. (Carol Leifer, who wrote some of *Seinfeld*'s more memorable episodes, including "The Beard," "The Understudy," and "The Rye," before leaving to develop her own series, understood perhaps better than most how to work with them on development. "If you pitch something once they're not crazy about, you can always bring it up again a few months later, because sometimes they'll forget they rejected it the first time," she joked.)

"Larry and I do a lot of the writing—actually, Larry does most of it—even though we don't take credit for it," said Seinfeld. "Our way works, just to be funny, that's really it. We go straight for the comedy. Other shows are supposed to be funny and then start telling you warm stories. I just want a little laugh here. This show is about comedy, not about characters. It's not about people's lives. It's just about what's funny, and that determines the story lines. Sometimes we're just a thin layer above a sketch show. And the great thing in the chemistry between Larry and me is that if it passes through both of us, it almost always works."

WHAT makes the David-Seinfeld synergy so intriguing is that two acquaintances managed to forge their disparate personalities into a powerful comic mind-set.

"My theory on Larry and Jerry is that they are the Lennon and McCartney of comedy," noted Leifer, who had dated Jerry for a while when they were both starting out. "When Larry did stand-up, the comedians would love it because he's on the edge—cerebral, dark, and brooding—while Jerry has a pop sensibility and a talent for conveying it to the masses. He's lighter and fluffier and quick with the one-liners. He has said that if he hadn't gone into show business, he probably would have gone into advertising, which he would be very good at."

"We weren't really close friends," Larry acknowledged. "Obviously, we're much closer now—you *have* to get closer if you've worked the way we've worked. You either get closer or you end up hating each other. We definitely have disagreements, hundreds. It's usually over a line, sometimes it's over a word—literally a word. In the beginning, I would scream, but I no longer do."

That they could be in tune enough to argue over the value of a single word indicates they had a unique meeting of the minds.

"Most people are not equipped to discuss the things I want to discuss. They haven't thought about the things I have, and they have no ideas about it," noted Jerry. "That's why Larry David and I go on forever. He's equipped to discuss anything. Obviously there is a partnership between me and Larry, but we are also very similar in terms of sense of humor and what makes us laugh. That's just the luck of the chemistry between us. If it makes us laugh after so many years of dealing with this substance of humor, then it's really funny. We can pretty much say that if we both think it's funny, it *is* funny and the audience will like it.

"And I always start with me. I don't think, 'Here's something that other people will like.' I start with what I like. And Larry has a brilliant flair for staging and direction. There is no show without him. He has, more than me, created this enterprise. My skill has been to help him interpret his ideas. He filters things through me. I contribute lines and jokes."

EVEN in the best of weeks, the work load on *Seinfeld* was overwhelming and incredibly time-consuming. Usually, if a show makes it to a fifth season, the work week gives the actors as close to a nine-to-five existence as they'll ever get, because the production has settled into a familiar groove. But because *Seinfeld*'s mission was to avoid that very thing, everyone had to be ready to put in the necessary hours.

Usually, sitcoms work a Monday through Friday schedule, with weekends off and a hiatus week for every three weeks of filming. Of course, *Seinfeld* was not your usual sitcom. "On this show . . . the schedule is not worth the paper it's written on," Jason Alexander commented. "It's not unusual for us to start on a weekend, so you can't make weekend plans, and you can't swear to the hiatus week."

In the beginning, Jason Alexander acknowledged, it was annoying to have such an up-in-the-air working life, but the actors all understood that the extra work was the consequence and price of consistent quality. "When they feel they have a script ready is when they feel they have a script ready. What they put on the table is always worthwhile," Alexander said.

Unlike Chris Carter of *The X-Files,* Seinfeld and David never really mapped out an entire season; they basically worked week to week. Even the season-long story arc about the pilot in 1992–93 was only very loosely conceived. "All we knew for sure," Jerry says, "was that the first show would be the meeting at NBC and the last show would be the filming."

"We are in a complete state of panic virtually week to week trying to come up with a great story," staff writer Charles admitted. "In that panic-stricken mode, we throw around ideas and we think about stuff. I compare the show to *The Twilight Zone.* It is about behaviors that we don't like to admit about ourselves—that we are sometimes greedy, sometimes selfish. Jerry is like Rod Serling—a guide to take us to those lower depths.

"*Seinfeld* may be about nothing, but being about nothing really means we're about everything. The show is extremely dense with actual information. The episodes are almost like albums to me, and they get better with repeated viewing. All the in-jokes that are kind of dropped into the show really enhance the experience for the fan."

Jerry tried to explain further: "Our show is actually about details. We joke that it's about nothing because there's no *concept* behind the show; there's nothing intrinsically funny in the situation. There's no thread, no higher concept. It's just about four people. That's the concept—no concept."

Every week began with an informal table reading, the first opportunity for the actors to see the script and for the producers to hear it read aloud. Afterwards network and studio execs had the chance to "give notes"—that is, to offer their opinions, suggestions, concerns. This practice is standard in the industry and can turn tense and confrontational, but in the *Seinfeld* universe, executive scrutiny was almost perfunctory.

"We're pretty unsupervised," Jerry said. "We just do the show. I don't want to offend anybody, and I'm not trying to get away with anything. It's just another funny story."

However, it was frequently a funny story broaching topics that on another sitcom might not make it past the network's standards and practices department. "We always do a subject in the highest moral standards," Jerry said. "We don't try to get away with anything in terms of language or in terms of subject. The thing is to do it the right way."

The *Seinfeld* trademark of using code words proved to be a valuable device for getting a point across "the right way." For instance, in "The Rye" Elaine complains about her musician boyfriend who "doesn't do *everything*" when it comes to lovemaking. Enough said.

"This is Larry David's brilliance," Charles enthused. "He has the innate sense to take any provocative subject and find just the right tone to make it acceptable for the viewers. He is totally fearless. But he also knows how far to go."

Typically, Larry shrugged off such praise, deflating his own balloon. "I just do what fits the story—the story is the thing."

Jerry in turn dismissed Larry's humility: "If I may be so immodest, it takes some pretty skillful writing to do these things and make them comfortable for people to watch on a mass level. Anybody can write a funny show about masturbation. But can you do it in an artful way that offends no one and is funnier than if you had come right out and talked about it? That takes skill. I want to see if I can do what I want to do without pushing people's moral envelope. If we can't, then we won't do it."

Even after notes were dealt with, the script was not set in stone.

More often than not, Larry would make changes over the course of the filming week. Frequently, it was the small details that threatened to stymie the process.

"For example, there were times we got tired of always going to the coffee shop," Jerry said. "That was one of our bigger questions every week—where are we going to go? Because we're doing the life of a comic and there's really no place to go, because all he does is hang out with his friends."

Occasionally the three costars might make a suggestion, but Louis-Dreyfus, Alexander, and Richards probably contributed less than actors on other shows. Also, there was no ad-libbing, except perhaps by Jerry.

"We don't try to write and they don't try to act," Alexander said. "They write stuff that on the page doesn't seem like a joke, but they know we'll make it funny, which is a big compliment to us."

"The writers are more than willing to hear what I have to say about a certain issue or a line or the way a scene is going," noted Louis-Dreyfus. "Sometimes they incorporate my ideas if they're good and sometimes they don't."

While those types of issues were being settled, the camera blocking of the show—meaning where the actors will physically be on the set during the scenes—and other technical details were worked out under Larry's supervision. Jerry, in turn, would work on the show's opening and closing monologues, which he would usually test-run at local comedy clubs before committing them to film. (Unfortunately, in the syndicated version of the series each episode has been shortened by about ninety seconds to provide extra time for commercials, and it is often the stand-up material that has been excised.)

Of all the episodes they worked on together, Seinfeld and David claim, there were only about three that they were unhappy with— although neither will identify the episodes they considered disappointments. Jerry will, however, talk about one particular show that worked out even better than they anticipated.

"We did an episode called 'The Parking Garage' where we couldn't find Kramer's car in a mall parking lot and we spent the entire episode looking for it. And we didn't really have an ending," Jerry says.

The episode was unusual in that it was shot not before a live studio audience but on location in an actual parking lot. It was more time- and labor-intensive than most, with the cast filming the show over the course of two fifteen-hour days, which they spent mostly on their feet.

"That shoot was difficult for many reasons, and we shot into the wee hours of the morning and were so giddy it was amazing that we got anything done," says Julia Louis-Dreyfus, who also considers "The Parking Garage" one of the series' highlights. "We had these microphone packs on our butts, and we were so exhausted. Instead of getting in makeup chairs to get touched up, we lay down on the floor. The original ending was that after we finally find the car, we get in and then drive around unable to find the exit. And the last shot we did was of the end, when we were supposed to climb in the car and go."

"The cameras were rolling, and Michael turned the key and the engine wouldn't start," says Seinfeld, picking up the story. "If you see the show, you'll see four heads inside the car just going back and forth in laughter."

"We were all laughing so damn hard," recalls Louis-Dreyfus. "Jason and I were in the backseat trying to control our hysterical laughter while the camera's running. But it was like God had given us a better ending to the script."

On more routine weeks, once the show was filmed, the audience was sent home, then the cast and crew completed whatever pickup shots (reshoots) were necessary before finally calling it a wrap. In the early seasons, everyone would pack up and head to a nearby deli, appropriately named Jerry's, where they sat at a round table near the front door. After Louis-Dreyfus and Alexander became parents, they often begged off to go home and be with their families, but Jerry would continue the tradition to the final days of the show.

From week to week, the waitresses would take turns serving the group. The reason for that varies depending on who is talking. Some waitresses claimed Jerry would regularly leave a 50 percent tip; others would complain about how stingy he was.

Sitting at the restaurant, the gang would discuss what worked and what might not have worked as well as it could have, nit-picking at the episode while enjoying the relief that came from having another show "in the can." But Jerry and Larry's down time was short-lived. There was always another show to prepare for production.

"It's a tremendous amount of work, and the pressure really never leaves," David pointed out. "Just because the audience loves you doesn't make it any easier. You never feel like you've got it wired. Being famous only makes it more embarrassing when you stumble."

Even though Jerry enjoyed the process of filming and had more fun with it than Larry did, he also admitted the work load was all-encompassing. "I certainly won't want to live like this the rest of my life," he said going into the 1993–94 season. "It's an exhausting show to do. But if people say I'm a workaholic, I just kind of laugh. You never hear people say someone just has a good work ethic. There are so many lazy good-for-nothings out there that you're supposed to feel guilty for accomplishing something.

"Let me tell you," Jerry added, "workaholism is one of the smallest problems I have."

Jerry accepting the 1997 Emmy for Best Comedy Series. (Note Larry David in the background below.)

The cast and producers pose for a group shot after the Emmy win.

Jason Alexander, Jerry Seinfeld, a pregnant Julia Louis-Dreyfus, and Michael Richards at the 1997 Screen Actors Guild Awards, where they won for Best Comedy Ensemble.

Jerry helps Shoshanna blow out her birthday candles on her eighteenth birthday.

Jerry has some fun with his People's Choice Award for Favorite TV Performer.

(*Above*) Jerry and Shoshanna pose at the 1996 People's Choice Awards.

(*Left*) Golden Girl Estelle Getty with Jerry at the 1997 Golden Globe Awards.

Jerry and Shoshanna arriving at the 1996 Emmy Awards.

(*Above*) Jerry and Julia Louis-Dreyfus show off their Golden Globes at the 1997 ceremony.

(*Right*) Jerry chats with legendary Hollywood columnist Army Archerd at the Emmys.

Between takes on the set of an American Express commercial, Jerry acknowledges some diehard fans.

(*Right*) Even the Hollywood paparazzi are targets of Seinfeld's humor as Jerry and Shoshanna ham it up for photographers on Sunset Boulevard.

(*Right*) Jerry and
Shoshanna strolling
down the street in
Beverly Hills.

(*Below*) Jerry's
Porsche gets ticketed
for an expired meter
in Beverly Hills.

After his break-up with Shoshanna, Jerry out on the town alone.

Michael Richards, Jerry Seinfeld, Julia Louis-Dreyfus, and Jason Alexander celebrate the supporting actor/actress Emmys received by Richards and Louis-Dreyfus.

Betty Seinfeld with her son at the Emmys.

Jerry at the *Vanity Fair* Oscar party in 1998 as he faces the future.

13

"I'm Not Windexing My Toaster Three Times a Day"

WITH THE EMERGENCE OF *SEINFELD* INTO MAINSTREAM AWARENESS, AND AS the shows became a staple of conversation among a growing legion of viewers, more and more fans became curious about where TV Jerry left off and real-life Jerry began. When characters are invited into homes week in and week out, the lines between fiction and authenticity can become blurred and indistinct. In this case, the delineation was especially vague, because in many regards Jerry was playing Jerry. Even Seinfeld couldn't separate the two.

"I think the difference between the real-life me and TV Jerry is kind of like Nice 'n Easy hair coloring—it's me, only better," he joked. "You know, a little wittier and a little more resourceful, a little more likely to get involved in annoying situations than I am in real life. In the show, I play myself as I was before I got the show. I understand that people would like to think that they're looking into my actual life, and it would be fun if that were true."

Seinfeld has pointed out that we all have different faces we put on, depending on the situation we find ourselves in, and performing is just another situation: "It's like two different faces that you can switch back and forth. When I'm by myself, I act one way. On a date or in public, it's heightened, and when I'm doing stand-up, it's even one step higher than that.

"When I get up onstage, that's not really me. I don't talk in jokes and routines all day—that's just my act. But then again, it *is* me, because that's what I've been doing just about my entire adult life. I found an acceptable image that was really pretty much me, and that's how I've done everything. That's why I was able to do the show and why I've succeeded as a comedian. I wouldn't have the energy to maintain an image."

It's interesting that those who knew him both in front of and away from *Seinfeld*'s camera have differing opinions on where sitcom Jerry ends and the reality Jerry takes over.

"Real-life Jerry never gets involved in any unusual situations," said Larry David. "The real Jerry usually knows what's going to happen every day, but TV Jerry gets into a lot of pickles. I don't think there are many surprises in Jerry's real life."

According to Carol Leifer, real Jerry "likes to do simple things, like hang out at the mall, just to walk around." As for TV Jerry, "it's interesting because you can't really define his character, so ideas for him [from the writers] have to be real specific. To me, much of his appeal is that he's a boy-man. Jerry's got a quality that makes him boyish and innocent, allowing him to get away with things that might be creepy in other guys."

The two Jerrys share a love of cereal, often mixing three different types together, muffin tops, and cities. "I get very nervous outside a city. I like nature, but only until it gets dark," Seinfeld admits.

"TV Jerry is about eighty percent the same as real Jerry," Jason Alexander estimated. "One of the differences is that TV Jerry doesn't like to be seen in intimate situations, such as kissing on-screen or any other sexual activity."

Seinfeld agreed. Both TV Jerry and real Jerry are not huggers. "There are many things I'm embarrassed to do on the show, usually something with a woman. I go to great lengths to keep myself from feeling at all awkward, because I hate it. Comedians are generally very self-conscious people. There is nothing like having your own show. I can't recommend it more highly to you. To be able to say, 'I don't think I want to do that.' "

Early in the series' run, Alexander decided to organize a prank that would make him squirm. "Once for Jerry's birthday, I thought it would be funny if I hired a stripper who started coming on to Jerry, because he's very shy about that kind of stuff. But then his mother came to the set—for the first time ever—so I had to go tell the stripper to put some clothes on. It was like I was speaking Martian to her, since her whole job is not to wear clothes. Finally, she ended up in this weird bathing suit thing. Afterwards, Jerry's mom says, 'She should have been naked. Jerry could use naked.' "

Julia Louis-Dreyfus saw a much clearer distinction between the man and the character. "He's playing the television character Jerry Seinfeld with such aplomb that everybody believes that's really him and feels as if they know him. But they don't. Real Jerry is a very serious guy with a television show. And he works hard at it."

Bill Maher, a friend since Seinfeld's early days on the comedy club circuit, said, "Those of us who knew Jerry way back when, and knew his apartment and life, know that's what the show is."

A cornerstone of the series was David and Seinfeld's refusal to sugarcoat the baser human behavior often displayed by the four friends, so TV Jerry is not a particularly nice or generous character. Think of when he knocked down an old lady to steal her loaf of marble rye or didn't want to watch the dog of a stricken fellow airline passenger because it was just too much trouble.

"To me, we show respect for the audience's intelligence," Seinfeld said. "People are not always nice. We all have selfish instincts. We did an episode, 'The Junior Mint,' where Kramer was trying to get me to come watch this guy's operation and I didn't want to go. Finally I said, 'All right, just let me finish my coffee, and we'll go watch them slice this fat bastard up.' I just said it to be silly, but everyone laughed—and we ended up getting it on the air. That show was a real turning point because it opened a lot of doors. Once that happened, the horses were out of the barn."

While real Jerry has never been known to physically assault the elderly or insult hospital patients, he *can* come across sounding a bit too flip and superior at times. When he was granted an honorary doctorate at Queens College, he was asked to address 3,300 graduates. Seinfeld's stand-up riffing didn't play well with everyone.

"I spent several wonderful years here at Queens College," he said. "I would say the best parking spot I ever got was my junior year. I want to thank the professor who allowed me to pursue an independent study in stand-up comedy, and I really feel that worked out pretty good.

"My only regret is that if at the time I could have foreseen I would be standing here today, when my parents were pushing me to become a doctor, I would have said to them, 'All right, all right, just let me tell jokes to strangers in nightclubs for eighteen years, and I'm sure they'll make me a doctor.'

"I've always been proud to be an alumnus of Queens College, and it's truly a wonderful feeling to know you are all so proud of me. Good luck."

That was the entire commencement address. After less than two minutes, he was ushered to his limo by a phalanx of campus police.

"It was a little more casual than I had hoped," school spokesman Ron Cannava said later. "We had hoped he would have taken the opportunity to say more."

Speaking backstage at the 1994 Golden Globe Awards, Jerry might have been wiser to say less. Seinfeld sounded oblivious and callous when he commented that he thought the Northridge earth-quake—one of the costliest natural disasters in American history—had been sensationalized by the media. "What I saw in the paper on the news was scarier than what I saw driving around. My dental floss fell, but that can be repaired." Several news outlets later pointed out that an event that left sixty people dead, tens of thousands displaced, and many more financially ruined wasn't fodder for jokes.

Despite an occasional misplaced or inappropriate joke, real Jerry possesses a generosity of spirit that is seldom seen in his TV alter ego. It's a side of himself that he tends not to put on public display. He overcame some of that reserve when discussing his feelings about the Rodney King verdict and the ensuing riots, but Jerry is not the kind of celebrity who attaches himself to high-visibility causes or makes any pretense that he believes it's his job to be a social activist. His job is to be funny for his public.

More often than not, Seinfeld seems to deal with being a public figure by using comedy as a protective shield against revealing too much of his more vulnerable self. He fends off questions he doesn't want to answer, but always politely. When asked if he had any marriage plans, Jerry declined to comment on the question but did apologize sarcastically: "I hate to go counter to the great American tradition of revealing things about your personal life [to the media] before you do [to] the people who are actually *in* your life."

Many celebrities complain incessantly about how fame has made their lives miserable, but to Jerry fame was just another aspect of his job. He acknowledged without rancor that his life had become "everybody's business, . . . and I honestly have no problem with that. Luckily, I have no seriously aberrant proclivities."

Still, Seinfeld believes that as a celebrity "you want to be a little tough to grasp, because people don't like things they can fully understand. And I think people want to see you enjoy what you've done. If I were depressed and complaining, people would say, 'Oh, for crying out loud—what does it take?'

"The most amusing and bizarre thing about celebrity is when total strangers start talking to you. I'm walking down the street; someone comes alongside me and says, 'So how come Elaine and you got together only that one time?' They don't say, 'Excuse me, could I talk to you?' We just start talking as if we've been talking for blocks, and this happens all the time.

"But," he adds, "people want to get to know the people they see on TV. That's why they read interviews. That's why they watch talk shows. Other cultures accept performers as they see them. Americans see performers they like and want to know, 'What's behind that? How did they get to be that way?' "

Although Jerry does seem to truly enjoy his lot in life, he also makes a very specific distinction between what he does and who he is. This is why he doesn't travel with an entourage, prefers to drive himself rather than be chauffered, and feels more at home in smaller, cozier spaces than in a mansion befitting one of the most powerful men in television. Even if others view him differently, Jerry has worked hard to maintain his personal sense of self.

"I had just bought this house, and it's pretty impressive, in the Hills overlooking the city with a beautiful pool and everything," he recalls. "And I said, 'Gee, I don't know if I'm going to feel comfortable there.' And my mother said, 'Oh, it's always easy to get used to better.' And I think in a way, that's sort of what happened to me. But I have no interest in the trappings of success, the *'star'* junk. People act very baffled by how easygoing I am, but I feel very privileged. To me it's all Disneyland."

From the earliest point in his career, Seinfeld has always said his life was never about becoming rich and famous. It was about getting the chance to make people laugh. "It's not about money. I'm not like Jay," he jokes, referring to friend Leno. "He once told me about a place to get a VCR a hundred dollars cheaper. This is lunacy. The man is a millionaire. I just looked at him. A hundred dollars? If it's on the next table I wouldn't bother, just to save a hundred dollars. I always feel as if you get more if you pay more, so I try to pay the maximum."

In light of this attitude, an item *USA Today* reported in January 1994 seems more fiction than fact. The paper said Jerry had been seen at a Miami International Airport newsstand buying magazines and newspapers and allegedly tried to wangle a free pack of Certs from the cashier. When she refused, he supposedly told her to keep the few cents' change from the $20 bill he paid with and snidely remarked that her tip would have been bigger if she had given him some mints.

It was the core of meanness that seemed out of place. Besides, as castmate Jason Alexander noted, "Jerry is one of the most generous people I've ever met."

And one person who seems not to be impressed with wealth. However, even though money isn't his main or even secondary focus, it does allow Jerry to revel in his few indulgences, such as the pristine collection of Porsches stored at Santa Monica Airport. Among the sixty cars is a rare Spyder 550, the same model James Dean was driving the night of his fatal crash.

"There are only forty left in the world," Seinfeld points out. "I considered bringing it into the house, but it's aluminum, and I was afraid it might get dented. Whenever life gets too crazy, I think about the cars."

While TV Jerry motors slowly through the crawl that is Manhattan traffic, real Jerry enjoys the open road and feeling the power of his world-class performance cars. "Some people want to fly planes, but I don't get that. There's no sense of speed. You could be doing 250 mph in the air and you can't tell."

In May 1994, Jerry took a driving course at the Skip Barber Racing School in Sonoma, during which he got to drive Formula Fords at over 100 miles per hour. When the instructors gave out the students' rankings at the end of the course, Seinfeld came in first. However, one thing the experience taught him was that he didn't necessarily want to join Tom Cruise and Paul Newman on the pro-am racing circuit.

"You could kill yourself, because the car and the pavement don't know you're learning," he says. "They rated me one of the potentially best, and it is something I could really do, but I wouldn't, because it's too much like stand-up as far as being a crucial-results environment."

Both TV Jerry and real Jerry indulge in their passion for sports, particularly the Mets. "Comedy writers are almost always sports-obsessed," Seinfeld points out. "Because if you've chosen to make comedy a career, it means you love to waste time—and that's what sports are about.

"My ultimate evening at home is watching a night of baseball or anything else that's a media event. I enjoy the sense of community, even though it is completely bogus. But when you know that everyone's watching something, it's a great community experience."

It's not unusual to find Jerry playing in an impromptu game of softball, even while at work. Several years ago, actress Alexandra Wentworth received a surprise visit from Seinfeld while she was working on the Fox series *Hardball,* which ironically, was about a hapless baseball team. After making some pleasant small talk, Jerry confessed the real reason for his visit. He and some friends had been playing baseball outside on the studio lot when someone smacked the ball through Wentworth's Saab's windshield. When Jerry first she thought it was a joke, but it wasn't. Without her having to ask, Seinfeld had her car fixed and even rented her a Lexus to drive while the repairs were being done.

"He was incredibly nice about the whole thing," said the somewhat surprised actress.

That seems to be a recurring response. Most people assume someone in Jerry's position automatically develops a more-famous-than-thou attitude. Seinfeld posits that he's too immature to take himself that seriously, as proven by his manner of dress, which is more Gap-influenced than Armani-oriented.

"I would call my fashion style New York Immature. The guy who refuses to give up jeans and sneakers from his twenties. Comedians have a thing about their feet. They almost never wear shoes when they're not being paid. But more than that, it's clinging to your youthful mood. I always wanted to be ready to play ball if anyone suggested it—I didn't want to have to go home and change clothes. I like to have something playful on my feet. I've always liked sneakers; that was something I responded to even at six years old. I drove my mother crazy about getting me sneakers."

"I always knew he'd find a way to keep wearing sneakers," comments his mother, Betty.

Seinfeld has become famous for his sneakers, particularly his preference for clean, smudge-free shoes. His overall neatness, in fact, has become a bit of an albatross for Seinfeld and the focus of teasing from his friends and work associates. Even his mother chides him a bit.

"Jerry's a perfectionist, but he's not a show-off or pushy. You never know when he's around, because he walks in and disappears into the shadows," she says. "He does yoga for an hour and a half a day and doesn't eat sugar or red meat. And his closets are so neat you love to just stand and look at them. Everything is arranged perfectly."

Some of his comic friends say they enjoy visiting his house just so they can make a mess and annoy him. Jerry's the first to make light of his Spartan living. "I like to go to other people's homes so I can look in and see the life there. If you come to my house, you don't see any life. I remember an English teacher in college; I was in his office talking. He asked me what I liked, and I said I liked driving, because you're inside and not moving yet you're outside and moving. He told me I was the most vicarious person he'd ever met. And I am very satisfied with vicarious experience."

Seinfeld doesn't smoke and drinks sparingly. To Jerry a night of heavy drinking means having a second glass of wine with dinner. (He turned down a lucrative beer commercial several years ago, prior to becoming the American Express spokesman.) He eats health foods such as tofu hot dogs, studies Zen and yoga, and recalls the Scientology classes that he once took as very beneficial.

"I learned a lot and I had a good experience with it," he says. "I've always had the skill of extracting the essence of any subject I study, be it meditation, yoga, Scientology, Judaism, Zen, whatever it is. I go in to get what I need. To me, these are supermarkets where I go in to get my supplies, then I leave."

Because of Jerry's innate sense of self and confidence, he didn't need Scientology or any other discipline to feel good about himself. He had a clear vision of what he wanted to do with his life and lived an uncluttered existence in order to remove any unnecessary distractions from his pursuit of his goals. Some of his friends and associates thought Jerry lived an almost too-pure life. Once during an interview, the *Seinfeld* writers chimed in with their take on Jerry's notorious neatness, targeting his dental hygiene.

"As soon as he puts down his food, he flosses."

"He flosses so much, there are grooves in his thumbs."

"If he could floss while eating, he would."

"I do not overfloss," Jerry countered. "It is generally considered a very good thing to do for your teeth. I floss twice a day. That's what my dentist told me to do, so I do it."

In the same session, one writer cracked: "He doesn't just have creases in his pants, he has creases in his ankles."

"Let's face it, people do not like happy people," Jerry sighed in response.

Larry David came to his partner's defense. "Let's not turn him into Howard Hughes. He likes to keep a neat apartment, but it doesn't make the guy psychotic."

Writer Elaine Pope agreed. "I know a lot of single, successful guys like Jerry, with the expensive sports car, the high-tech furniture, and the empty refrigerator."

"It's not like I'm Windexing my toaster three times a day," Jerry says dryly. "What I do is highly developed living backed up by solid, rational thinking with a foundation in logic. I'm not compulsive. People keep trying to find this raging psycho inside of me. The truth is, I'm basically sloppy, but I overcompensate that weakness by being excessively neat. There is not one thing I do that is not defensible."

Seinfeld has maintained his childhood fascination with Superman. He integrated his hero into both his series and the American Express campaign, appearing with an animated version of the superhero in a recent commercial. He believes *Superman* is "really the most important show, because it deals with life on a *super* level," he says, trying to explain the cultural significance of the character. "Imagine if you had all of these powers, and look at the problems you would still have. The problems just increase to match the size of your ability. Even though you are super, life has many nuances. I watch and discuss Superman daily."

But even superheroes have their Achilles' heels. Although he was not particularly angst-filled as a youngster, he did have certain insecurities, and they were very *Seinfeld*-ian. For years, Jerry was small for his age, which exacerbated his concern that his head appeared ever so slightly too big for his body. As an adult, he would incorporate his obsession into his act.

Sometimes people tell me that I have a big head, but I just tell them it's because I have a bigger brain. All people have big heads. I think people should look more like salamanders, be-

cause their *heads are more in proportion to their bodies. People
are more like horses—they have huge heads in proportion to
their bodies. Now I know why Mr. Ed talked—because he was
really a human being.*

The *Globe* tabloid would take this bit of self-obsession and turn it
into a full-fledged phobia, writing: "As an adult, he would always be
conscious of trying to make himself look more in proportion by
wearing baseball caps, or padded blazers and oversized button-
down shirts to make his body look bigger than it really is." The
paper went on to point out that there is actually a psychiatric term,
larguscaputophobia, for a person who fears his head is too big. The
full-page spread also included a "scientific" test to check whether a
person's head is in proportion, which "proved" Seinfeld's head was
indeed too large for his body.

Once can only assume Seinfeld appreciated the creativity that
went into the article. In fact, a 1998 *Seinfeld* episode dealt with
George's fury at being told his neck was so big it would stretch a
cashmere sweater completely out of shape.

One function of celebrity that Seinfeld does seem to enjoy is his
ability to help others professionally. He has been known to come to
the aid of other performers and series unsolicited. He once phoned
NewsRadio creator and executive producer Paul Simma with an offer to appear on the show when it seemed in danger of being canceled. Jerry played himself, the first time he had guest-starred on a
series since becoming Jerry Seinfeld. Whether or not it was a turning
point for the show, it was typical of him to take the time to offer
support to someone he didn't know but whose work he respected.

He is also quick to critique work he feels lacks truth, such as *The
Bridges of Madison County.* According to Jerry, author Robert
James Waller "manipulates the female psyche so deftly, so *ruthlessly.*
The main character is a guy who's fifty but in absolutely rock-hard
condition. After he spends three days with this woman, he never has
another relationship for the rest of his life. Waller has invented
something irresistible, unattainable, and nonexistent."

Then there's the strange case of Ted L. Nancy and his book, *Letters From a Nut.* This unusual book is a collection of prank letters,
such as a note to a baseball card company asking if it wants a
collection of Mickey Mantle's toenail clippings. What makes the
book intriguing and sent the antennae of Seinfeld fans all aquiver is

Seinfeld-ian feel of the book's concept and execution—that and the fact that nobody seems to know just who Ted Nancy is, nor could any journalist find evidence that the person really exists. The book's agent, Dan Strone, claims he has never met Nancy and deals solely with Seinfeld, who wrote the introduction and whose name is on the cover.

When asked directly if Ted Nancy was a figment of his too-fertile imagine, Seinfeld denied it. "I am not Ted L. Nancy—when would I have the time to do that? Ted's just a guy I'm helping out. I'm a comedy facilitator."

But not necessarily a fantasy facilitator. Dan Tanenbaum, a freelance copy writer from Toronto, was making a minor name for himself because of his rather remarkable resemblance to Jerry Seinfeld. He had visions of becoming Jerry's protégé the same way Vicki Lawrence had been taken under Carol Burnett's wing after they met and Carol noticed their physical resemblance.

"People are constantly coming up to me saying, 'We love your show!' or asking, 'What are you doing in Toronto?' They also say, 'I never realized how short you are,' " laughs Tanenbaum, who's five feet, eight inches tall. "The more I deny it, the more they don't believe me. So I let them take pictures with me. Who's it hurting?"

When Tanenbaum and Seinfeld finally met at Detroit's Fox Theater, the fantasy of Jerry becoming his mentor died a quick and inglorious death. "It was a little discouraging," Tanenbaum admits. "All he did was glance at me and say, 'Yeah, he looks a little like me.' And that was it. I guess I had let my imagination run away with me."

Jerry is too grounded to buy into strangers' flights of fancy, and it's that same ability to center himself that enables him to be a trusted friend. Usually he uses his humor as a means of communicating with those around him, but on occasion he employs it as a way of comforting others, as he did with his friend Marjorie Gross.

Gross joined the *Seinfeld* writing staff in 1994, later becoming one of the producers. Born in Toronto, she had started as a stand-up, then went on to write for *Newhart* and *Alf*. Popular, ebullient, and outgoing, Gross—along with Carol Leifer—brought an important female view and sensibility to the show in episodes including "Bania," "The Secretary," "The Fusilli Jerry," "The Understudy," and "The Shower Head."

Just as she was coming into her prime, Gross was diagnosed with ovarian cancer. When it was decided she needed surgery and chemo, Jerry kept her on staff at full salary so she wouldn't have to worry about money or insurance.

Despite the best care available, Gross's condition steadily worsened. Several months before her death, she wrote an article titled "Cancer Becomes Me" for *The New Yorker,* describing what it was like to be dying from the disease. Seinfeld could only admire her strength and ability to maintain her humor in the face of her own demise. It was their bond of laughter that brought Jerry and Marjorie closer in her last days.

Marjorie's brother, Jonathan Gross, says his sister's best friend, actress Sharon Stone, brought some Buddhist monks to the hospital in an attempt to cheer Marjorie up, but she kicked them out. However, she spent considerable time with Jerry, despite what Jonathan calls Seinfeld's "problem dealing with death." No doubt, her cancer brought to mind his own father's death from the same disease a decade earlier. Despite that memory, he sat with Marjorie and sang to her some of her favorite Beatles songs, such as *"All You Need Is Love."*

"Jerry was very good to her throughout her ordeal," Jonathan says. "She went through a lot of pain and suffering, and his kindness made it easier for her to bear. He cried with her when the pain was bad, and he laughed with her when they shared moments of humor. He was on the phone with her frequently offering encouraging words. He visited her at home and in the hospital when her spirits were low. I guess he's really a soft-hearted and big-hearted guy."

Marjorie Gross died on June 7, 1996, in Los Angeles. She was only forty years old.

Through the extreme highs and lows, both personal and professional, Jerry has consistently maintained his personal center and an almost surreally even temper. He has an instinctive capability to ferret out what is important and what isn't.

"Jerry's the opposite of anxious," Julia Louis-Dreyfus said while working with him. "He knows about anxiety, he can spot it, but he keeps it away from himself."

"Between his Zen, his former Scientology, his mega-memory, and probably his Vulcan mind techniques, he has no trace of anxiety or stress in his whole system," added Jason Alexander.

This is not to say he doesn't have a temper or won't speak out when he feels the situation warrants it. After fellow comic Bob

Goldthwait—who had long waged a verbal tirade of insult against Seinfeld—appeared on Greg Kinnear's late-night NBC talk show wearing a KILL SEINFELD T-shirt, Jerry lodged a complaint with the network, based on rather practical considerations in this day of celebrity stalkers. "I don't care what he says about me," Jerry said, "but to wear that kind of shirt with all the crazies out there is totally irresponsible."

Even when he is most agitated, Jerry exudes the aura of a confident man eminently at peace with himself, his abilities, and his life. At the same time, he is not one to become too comfortable, knowing it's the challenges in life that are the real point and keep you feeling most alive.

"I don't have much of a fear or panic response to anything," he said after the show had hit its stride. "There were years in the beginning when we were aging by the minute, but now I don't feel pressure. We've slain every dragon. But I don't think this feeling will be long-lived, though, because you eventually need another dragon.

"I am my job. Everything else in life pales by comparison to the interpretive experience. Every time something funny is discovered, it's an absolute miracle. And the most amazing thing is when I only have three minutes to think of something funny."

For instance, in one episode involves a scene with TV Jerry, George, and George's father, Frank, whose car has been completely totaled. It was late, they were shooting outside, and everyone was cold and tired.

"We needed a line," Seinfeld recalled. "What can I say? I love that. We were going to make the joke with the camera shot, but once we were all standing by the car, it needed a line. So I said to Frank, 'You know, a lot of these scratches will buff right out.'

"Here's what it comes down to: you need talent, you need brains, and you need confidence. Those are three things you need to do virtually anything. Confidence is a fascinating commodity, and that's what I've gained from this show. I didn't want money or fame or any of the things any normal person would want. I wanted the confidence I would have if I could do it. And that's what I wanted from day one."

Then he added, "There's no upper limit on the usefulness of confidence, as long as it doesn't bleed into arrogance."

14

Jerry's Idea of a Perfect Date

AFTER THE 1992–93 SEASON, NBC RENEWED *SEINFELD* FOR TWO FULL seasons instead of the typical single year. It was a pointed show of faith by the network and a testament to the single-minded persever- ance of both Jerry and Larry David, who had refused to compromise their creative and comic vision, even when the future of the show seemed bleak, at best.

The success of *Seinfeld,* however, had not come without a per- sonal price for both men. Beyond the day-to-day stresses and pressure inherent in doing a series, because they insisted on being involved with every decision the show effectively became their lives, particularly in the early years when *Seinfeld's* fate hung in the bal- ance.

During the months the series was in production, Jerry, like Larry, practically lived at the set. During hiatus, he would hit the road with his comedy concerts. Between the two, very little time was left for nurturing romantic relationships—not that Jerry had ever seemed eager for one that went very far.

"I used to do this joke," Larry David recalled: "If you're over forty and never married, you're either gay or something's wrong. I think Seinfeld might be approaching the tenor of that joke."

Jerry dismissed the conjecture over his apparent resistance to get- ting married by blaming it on his commitment to his work and career. "I've had a number of legitimate relationships, but not in the past few years," he said in 1993. "I've been too busy, and it's been too difficult." In his stand-up routine he notes that dating is not exactly a mindless activity:

Dating is pressure and tension. What is a date, really, but a job interview that lasts all night? The only difference between a date and a job interview is that in not many job interviews is there a chance you'll end up naked at the end of it.

But the fact is, many highly successful people manage to balance, however precariously, a serious relationship or family with a heavy work load—even Larry David, who arguably worked longer hours than anybody else on the show. He married Laurie Lennard in 1993, and they soon had children. Some speculated Jerry avoided deep relationships because they tend to get messy; casual dating, on the other hand, can be neat and clean, with no pesky emotional baggage.

Jerry admitted to being comfortable with women storming out on him because of his willingness to keep things relatively superficial. "Even Superman can't make a commitment. If he, with all his powers, can't get it together, why should I be able to?" he once commented, only half joking. "My ex-girlfriends would say that I'm immature and not willing to make the sacrifices for a permanent relationship, a serious commitment."

On another occasion, he pointed out: "I'm never lonely, even when I'm alone. That's another reason I'm a good comic; a lot of time alone never bothered me."

Seinfeld's mother, naturally, believes her son is ideal husband and father material, if women would only do things his way. "He'd make a perfect family man," Betty says. "He adores children. One day he's going to meet somebody who is going to knock him off his feet. If she would just go along with everything he wanted . . . I think that's why he's having trouble. It's impossible."

Jerry addresses that very issue in his stand-up.

Men want absolute, total control over every single aspect of everything. Girls want grown men. Women know there's no such thing.

Some of Jerry's acquaintances suggest that perhaps it's more than just resistance to commitment and preoccupation with work that has kept him a bachelor for so long. "At first women are impressed with Jerry's neatness, but he can start to drive them crazy after a while," comments one friend. "He likes things done *his* way and is somewhat uncompromising about it."

Seinfeld himself readily admits to his obsession with order: "If someone walks into my house, even if she's very smart and very aware, there's nothing she can move. Even if she moves it back to where she thought it was, I will notice."

However, he's a little less anal when it comes to his cars, claiming he doesn't mind a date driving one of his prized autos. "If a woman has a certain *command,* then I'm comfortable with that."

Another positive quality Jerry says he has is a lack of possessiveness. "I'm not the jealous type, because I'm too cocky."

On a more serious note, Jerry made a case for staying unattached during the early days of his show. "The women who go out with me have to be extremely patient," he said. "I don't place a high priority on it. I have to get my work done, and then, if there's time, I'll go out with someone who's willing to wait for me to get it done. A good relationship takes time and commitment. So does a good career. I'm at a point in my career where it needs a lot of attention. It's like I've just given birth to triplets and I've got to get them on their feet. That's what I'm nurturing right now.

"I'm just one person trying to get it all done. It's not a problem for me, but it is a problem for my dates, which is why I'm not involved. The kind of woman who would put up with that is not the kind of woman I want. Now, if there were someone willing to do it and make the sacrifices, I might do it."

Then again, he might not, because all the signs pointed to the fact that Seinfeld was in no hurry to leave his bachelor days behind. "I love being not married," he admitted. "It's a very free, unfettered life. I'm way too young for me to get married. I would think your fifties would be a wonderful time to get married. Right now, I'm too busy with other things to really look at any relationship in a serious way."

Even so, Seinfeld already knew what qualities his bride must have: "I don't want my wife to work. I've had enough career for both of us. The wife needs to be fun-loving. Let's have fun. People aren't as fun-loving as you think. They all have other things they have to do."

Although Jerry undoubtedly loved women and dating, romantic relationships never seemed to be of primary importance to him; that place was reserved for comedy and his stand-up career. "Even as a kid I didn't have much interaction with girls," he admits. "I kind of withdrew from social activity. I didn't like the group mentality—I preferred to focus in on one person. I still do. You go to parties and it's all breezy bullshitting. I like that up to a point, but then I'm bored by it."

Small for his age and wearing braces, Jerry didn't possess the big-man-on-campus kind of confidence that some young men are born with—or fake. Since he couldn't impress girls with physical prowess, athletic ability, or movie-star looks, he stayed in the background, content to get a laugh by making jokes.

It wasn't until he was in college that Jerry discovered sexual gratification—of any kind. "I'm willing now to admit that as a teenager I never had sex. And I was the master of my domain," he jokes, referring to the code phrase from "The Contest" that denoted refraining from masturbation.

"I didn't discover masturbation until after I lost my virginity. My college roommate told me. I don't understand how everybody else knew about it and I didn't. Nobody told me about it. I didn't know this technique was available to me. But when I discovered it, I thought, 'I'm never going to get upset about a woman ever again.'

"I don't remember how I learned about sex itself, whether my parents showed me a book or played a record or what. They swear they told me all about it, but I don't remember. I think I learned from that David Reuben book, *Everything You Always Wanted to Know About Sex but Were Afraid to Ask*. I read it when I was in high school, and it was very helpful."

Jerry says he had his first sexual experience when he was twenty years old. "I was never pushy, but I do remember being upset about it having taken so long. I hated the idea of upsetting a woman in any way, so the slightest amount of resistance would deter me. I had no persistence at all. I still don't. If a woman is at all reticent, I'm out of there, because it kills the mood for me. I'm still very shy about such things."

Even in college, romance always seemed to take second place behind his stand-up dreams and the work at hand, so his relationships never invited permanence. Later, once he started working the club circuit, his dating opportunities dwindled further, and Seinfeld was not inclined to indulge in a series of one-night stands. "Who wants a groupie anyway? It sounds like some kind of grotesque fish," he once cracked.

The phenomenon of people wanting to go out with or sleep with someone they don't know simply because they see the person up on a stage or, especially, on television both fascinates and concerns Jerry. "I find it astounding. I don't know them, but they know me. The basic fact of electronics seems to get past a lot of people. They get to see me, but I don't get to see them. Maybe some people are that indiscriminate, but I am extremely careful about who I spend my time with."

Still, he understands the appeal certain careers have for some women. "Women need to like the job of the guy they're dating. If they don't like the job, they don't like the guy. Men know this, which is why we make up phony, bogus names for the jobs we have. 'Well, right now I'm the regional management supervisor. . . .'

"Men, on the other hand, if they are physically attracted to a woman, are not that concerned with her job. 'Slaughterhouse? That sounds interesting. Listen, why don't you shower up and we'll get some burgers and catch a movie.' "

"I am fascinated with women because, for one thing, there's this whole language of appearance in which women are very fluent and men aren't, such as makeup colors. That's what's constantly amusing to me about women and what gives them the alien quality I think men find so fascinating.

"I also love watching women put on their perfume. They're very careful. They have their little areas where they think we're going. They always hit the inside of the wrists. Women are convinced that this is the most action-packed area that could ever happen. Why? Is this in case you slap the guy so he'll still find you intriguing?"

Just as Jerry has very specific likes and dislikes in cars or home furnishings or comedy, he has very defined ideals about women. "I like women who are sweet, smart, and sexy. I tend not to like ugly, dumb, hostile women," he says. "Comedy is about perception, and to me a good relationship is about two people's points of view playing well together, someone you enjoying comparing notes with. And I take a lot of notes. And I warn anyone I date that everything is fair game."

Most people get sweaty palms at the prospect of going on first dates, but Jerry revels in the challenge. "I like first dates because I enjoy the tension. I've been on one blind date, but I couldn't stand it even though she was sweet, smart, and sexy. I was uncomfortable because it hadn't been *my* choice."

He used the experience as fodder for a comedy bit.

I was fixed up one time and couldn't deal with it. The whole time we were out, I could feel the puppet strings of the fixer-uppers on me. I couldn't even operate my body. I go to put my arm around her . . . SLAP! Sorry, I can't control my arms. This whole evening wasn't my idea. I'm just a puppet.

"To me, the ultimate date is dinner and a movie, where the woman lets you know you don't have to dress up," Jerry says. "My fantasies are all of normalcy, because I don't get to do a lot of those things. I'm a great fan of the mundane. I can't imagine a more fabulous evening than to have enough time to do that. And then you have coffee later. That's just orgasmic for me. I don't usually initiate things outside my pattern but I will 'come with.' However, a lot of women don't like to go to the movies in the early stages of a relationship, because they want to spend time getting to know you. I don't really feel that's necessary," he adds, tongue firmly in cheek.

Carol Leifer dated Jerry, as well as Paul Reiser, very early in their careers. "I got into stand-up because of Paul," she says. "We dated in college when we were both at the State University of New York at Binghamton. In 1977, we went to the Comic Strip together, and Jerry was the master of ceremonies, and he passed us both on the audition. We all really go way back."

From a romantic viewpoint, Jerry and Carol were obviously not a match made in heaven, and they broke up in 1977, although they remained close as friends. "When a male and female comic date each other it's incestuous and masturbatory," says Seinfeld bluntly. "It's two self-involved people who want the approval of strangers. It's not good."

Possibly the closest Jerry had ever come to matrimony was in the early 1980s, after he had moved to Los Angeles. According to other comics who knew him at the time, he fell in love with a young woman who worked as a hotel manager. "She was beautiful," recalls one stand-up. "And Jerry really seemed mad for her, and when he told everyone they were engaged, it seemed to be the real thing."

The wedding had been set for February 1984, but after a six-month engagement, Jerry and his fiancée abruptly called it off. The answer to why varies with the source. According to Betty Seinfeld, the relationship soured after a New Year's Eve disagreement. As he always liked to do, Jerry had booked a performance on New Year's Eve in New York City, and the girlfriend, who was already tiring of

Jerry's constant traveling and life on the road, drew a line in the sand.

"She didn't want to spend her New Year in a hotel room while he performed," recalls Betty. "She wanted to go out to a club and have a good time. That's when Jerry realized she just wasn't the girl for him. Jerry needs a woman who will support a family life and his career."

According to a fellow comic, the relationship soured after Jerry flew to Europe to meet the girl's parents. "Supposedly, Jerry and the parents didn't really get along very well. What we heard was that rather than marry into that kind of situation, Jerry decided to call the whole thing off. But even then, it seemed somewhat of an excuse. Mostly we assumed he had decided he just didn't want to get married, regardless."

Jerry gives a different version of events—but one that doesn't necessarily contradict the stand-up's recollections. "Turning thirty just blind-sided me, and I thought I had better hurry up and do the things I needed to do, so I got engaged." Then, he said, "I realized I didn't want to start a family—what I wanted was to be out on the road."

"It was his decision to end it; he knew it wasn't right," adds his sister, Carolyn. "I had just given birth to my son, and he [Jerry] was out of his twenties, and I think he felt it was time to get on with life. And I think he would have gone through with it to not upset her and her family, but as time went on, he realized it wasn't right. It was very difficult for him to end it, very difficult."

After that, Jerry kept his romances more at an emotional arm's length—even those that on the surface seemed relatively serious, such as his on-and-off relationship with L.A. publicist Stacey Effron. The couple met through her father, who happened to be Jerry's dentist, and dated for five years, between 1986 and 1991. After Effron, Jerry seemed to go from one comfortable dating relationship to another, never getting *too* serious. This was partly because, at least according to Jerry, he had no choice.

While professional success had given Jerry more confidence personally ("I do feel confident enough now to make the first move"), ironically his increased fame seemed to shrink his dating opportunities. "Fame has changed romance but hasn't really improved it," Jerry explained. "In some ways, women are actually put off by it. They assume I'm dating millions of women and that they won't be special. They think I'll take them for granted. But the truth is, I'm not dating a million women."

Because of the time he was putting into *Seinfeld,* Jerry said, his opportunity to date nearly vanished. "Along with the saturation there's a price. And that price is time. I can go out on a date maybe two or three times a month, ten months out of the year. That's a maximum. It's a funny situation. You get yourself to this point in life where you have a nice job, a nice car, a nice place to live, you know where the good restaurants are—and you can't go."

When he was able to date, there was now the issue of whether women were interested in Jerry the man or Seinfeld the show business titan and multimillionaire. "Jerry told some friends that one woman he took out not only ordered prime rib for herself but wanted a second one to take home to her dog," recalls an associate. "Another time he was walking with a date on Rodeo Drive when she stopped outside a Chanel store and pointed out what she wanted. She was joking, but Jerry didn't think it was funny."

Early in his career, Jerry dated almost exclusively women who were not in show business. "I go out with regular girls who have regular jobs, like a waitress, a producer, and an events planner. I'm not in the right places to meet supermodels," he said before he became a household word. In more recent years he has been linked with several well-known women in the industry, including model Kathy Ireland. Seinfeld insisted the attraction was more than physical: "She happens to have a genius-level I.Q."

Jerry's more noteworthy romances include two with women who appeared on his series. In episode 26, "The Nose Job," Tawny Kitaen played a beautiful but shallow model; TV Jerry wonders if he should continue sleeping with her even though he finds her intellectually vacant. To decide, Jerry's brain and his penis play an imaginary chess game.

Kitaen, an outgoing, very sexy redhead, is probably best known as DJ Mona Loveland on *WKRP* and for her recurring role as Hercules' dead wife on *Hercules: The Legendary Journeys.* She had already been an object of desire for Seinfeld before she ever appeared on the show.

Kitaen first got Jerry's attention when she appeared in a series of Whitesnake music videos. She married the group's lead singer, David Coverdale, in 1989, but they split just a year later. Although she had been known to date professional baseball player Chuck Finley as well as her *WKRP* co-star Michael Des Barres, she was basically unattached when she was cast for the show in fall 1991.

"Jerry knew who she was from the videos before she was hired for *Seinfeld*," said one set source. "And before they ever dated, he had kept a picture of her in his trailer. Everyone knew he already had a crush on her. When they started dating, he was completely infatuated with Tawny. He would take her to dinner and the movies, and they would take evening strolls around town. But this time it was Tawny who played it loose, and they eventually just kind of went their separate ways."

A year later, Jerry began squiring Jane Leeves, who at the time was a relatively unknown British actress, her break on *Frasier* yet to come. Her biggest claim to public fame was being the recently estranged girlfriend of *Murphy Brown* costar Grant Shaud; they had lived for about a year and at one point appeared to contemplate marrying. Leeves appeared in episodes 50 and 51, playing Jerry's virgin girlfriend who backs out of a night of romance with him after she hears about "the contest" Jerry's foursome is having to see who can refrain longest from masturbating.

Friends recall that Jerry was immediately attracted to Leeves, calling her beautiful, smart, sexy and admiring her sense of humor. The courtship began in typical Seinfeld fashion, with Jerry inviting her along with some others for coffee after work. Then he moved on to his idea of the perfect date, dinner and a movie.

Because their relationship came on the heels of Leeves's breakup with Shaud, it caught the attention of the tabloid press. The so-called Jerry-Jane-Grant love triangle gave Jerry one of his first experiences as the subject of a breathless tabloid story, about how he and Jane were breaking Shaud's lovelorn heart. However, before the tabs could work up a decent head of steam, Jerry and Jane, the couple, had faded into Jerry and Jane, just good friends.

Throughout this time, Jerry maintained that he really would like to settle down someday. He wasn't sure when, but it wouldn't be before the series was over; until then, he wouldn't be able to give the necessary have the time or attention to nurturing a committed, life-long relationship.

He admitted his resistance was beginning to wear thin with his mother, who was eager to see her son married and with a family: "My mother once got upset when, after my best friend got engaged, I said it was like being on a plane and having the person next to you get sucked out of the window. You actually feel a suction and breeze pulling you toward that hole because the person closest to you just went through it. So you must be next."

During a 1992 interview, Jerry, then thirty-eight, mused more seriously about his ability to forge a sustained relationship; "I am comfortable with intimacy. Sometimes I wonder if I've lost the knack of it, but I don't think so. No human being is immune to love and how it can change you."

Seinfeld was about to find out that his words were prophetic.

15

Finding Love in Central Park

BY HIS OWN ADMISSION, SINCE *SEINFELD* WENT ON THE AIR IN 1990, Jerry's love life had been fairly well stuck in neutral. Even though he enjoyed some extended relationships, he remained unattached, never forging a primary, serious emotional liaison that required more than cursory time and attention. He had not found the girl he would take home to mother and introduce to his friends as possibly *the* one. As he noted in one of his stand-up routines:

Why is commitment such a big problem for a man? I think that for some reason, when a man is driving down that freeway of love, the woman he's with is like an exit, but he doesn't want to get off there. He wants to keep driving.

That changed in the spring of 1993. But Jerry's romance with Shoshanna Lonstein would face familiar hurdles—the difficulties of maintaining a relationship with a flesh-and-blood lover when your career has been, and remains, a lifelong, demanding mistress.

In May 1993, Seinfeld, then thirty-nine, was in New York, enjoying the pleasures of being back in Manhattan for a while. After going for a bike ride in Central Park, he and a couple of friends went out to breakfast. One of his usual cohorts, Mario Joyner, wasn't there this particular day, so Jerry and the others thought it would be funny to go into the park, have their pictures taken with some attractive women, and then send Mario the photos.

"It was a prank," Seinfeld explains. "Mario had to be out of

172

town, and we wanted to show him pictures of all the gorgeous girls he didn't get to meet."

In an area called Sheep Meadow, Jerry and his friends crossed paths with the group of high school girls who were also idling time away in the park. Jerry was immediately taken with one of the young women, a self-possessed dark-haired beauty, who roller-bladed past him. The guys had their pictures taken with the girls, and the two groups moved on. But on an impulse, Jerry decided he didn't want to leave it there.

"After we met the first time, we went our separate ways," he recalled. "But then later, I was talking to my friends and I realized I really liked that girl and would like to talk to her again. But how was I going to find her?"

He found her by simply scouring the park until, miraculously, he spotted her and her friends. After reintroducing himself and making small talk, Seinfeld got her name—Shoshanna Lonstein—and phone number and said he would call.

According to former classmates, Shoshanna told several people the next day at school that she had met Jerry Seinfeld and that he said he would call her. Some of the other students at Manhattan's exclusive all-girl Nightingale-Bamford School doubted he would really phone and expected Shoshanna's chance meeting with Seinfeld would lead nowhere.

But Jerry did call, unable to get the person he would later call "the most wonderful girl in the world" out of his mind. Based on his brief time talking to her, Lonstein seemed to embody the qualities Jerry looked for in a woman: she was sweet, smart, and sexy, with a great body and a nice disposition.

Instead of his usual dinner and a movie, Jerry invited Shoshanna to attend a Knicks basketball playoff game. During the course of the game, Jerry was interviewed by one of the sports commentators on camera, with Shoshanna sitting quietly alongside him.

Their first public date created a bit of a stir when reporters started checking into just who exactly this girl—this *young* girl—was. Seinfeld claims he had no idea she was only seventeen. In fact, he denied she was when, shortly after their first public date, Howard Stern phoned Seinfeld and accused him on air of robbing the cradle.

"So, you sit in Central Park and have a candy bar on a string and pull it when young girls come by?" Stern asked with his incredulous, mocking tone.

"I am not, repeat, not a cradle snatcher. Shoshanna is not seven-teen. That is all I'm going to say about it. Case closed," Jerry stated.

But Jerry later had to eat crow when an article appeared in the June 15, 1993, issue of the *Globe* tabloid about him and Shoshanna. "I met this girl; she was very sweet and very pretty," Seinfeld says. "I knew she wasn't forty, but I didn't know how old she was. It wasn't until after the article came out that she told me. By then, I was in a tabloid rocket to the moon. I guess I hadn't adjusted to celebrity yet because it was hard for me to believe that anyone gave a damn who the hell I went out with or what I did."

Once her age was made public, Seinfeld seemed to shy away from Shoshanna, at least in interviews. "I didn't realize she was so young," he said at the time. "This is the only girl I ever went out with who was that young. I wasn't dating her. We went to a basket-ball game and went to a restaurant and that was the whole thing. She's a very sweet girl, very bright, but I have to go back to L.A."

If he had been worried about any potential fan backlash, his con-cerns were quickly alleviated. "I actually couldn't believe how nice the article was. My manager couldn't, either. He told me I was bulletproof even in the tabloids, which were saying, 'I don't see anything wrong with that. If they like each other. . . .' They had every chance to stick the knife in, they could have made up anything, but they didn't do it."

Not all of Seinfeld's friends, however, were as carefree or ac-cepting of the prospect of Jerry dating a minor. "The reaction from my friends ran the gamut from horrified to pride that they know me," Jerry admits. "Guys I hadn't heard from in years called to congratulate me; women I knew wouldn't even call me back. My assistant punched me, she was so mad.

"Some of my women friends didn't like it and were really hostile. So the relationship was reviled by women—and Jay Leno. He was terrified at the suggestion of an appearance of impropriety. He was scared and concerned for me as a friend."

Although he was respectful of others' opinions, to Jerry it was really very simple. He liked Shoshanna, "and the fact is, I don't meet that many women I like, period. So when I like someone, I don't discriminate. I don't care about her race or creed or national origin. And if she's eighteen and intelligent, that's fine too."

Even so, Jerry made it clear at the time that his relationship with Shoshanna was very casual (read: not sexually intimate) and that he was dating another unnamed woman his own age. But it was a case of the man protesting too much. Jerry paid for Shoshanna to fly out to California, where she spent two weeks in L.A. with Jerry prior to the start of her first semester of college at George Washington University in Washington, D.C. Suddenly the anonymous thirty-nine-year-old was nowhere to be seen, and Shoshanna seemed to be the only woman in Jerry's life.

Likewise, in the early days of their courtship, Shoshanna continued dating another casual boyfriend, but as she started spending more time with Jerry, she eventually stopped seeing anyone else. It was obvious to everyone who know the couple that something serious was going on here.

Whereas Jerry had earlier deflected questions about their twenty-one-year age difference, he now dealt with any lingering criticisms head-on. "We're very well suited because I'm so immature and she's so mature that we meet in the middle," he once joked. "The thing is, my own age isn't really real to me. I look in the mirror and I just don't feel my age. And I don't feel any different than I did at twenty-three. I don't even look that much different, so it's weird. But I'm not an idiot. Shoshanna is a person, not an age. She's extremely bright. She's funny, sharp, and very alert. We just get along. You can hear the click."

Jerry refused to be made to feel that he was doing something untoward or unseemly. "When I wasn't involved with Shoshanna and was seeing several women, *then* it was awkward. You go out with one girl and the other sees you with her in the paper. *That* was uncomfortable. Now I'm not doing anything I'm uncomfortable with. My interest in her is very proper."

At the same time, Seinfeld was realizing the truth about love. "Two people like each other. That's not much of a story—it happens all the time. Which is why I think, 'How stupid am I, thinking this is special? It happens to everybody.'"

But it was special, and Jerry the observational comic was struck by how much of life is pure chance. "When you're writing a scene, you put characters into a situation and play it out. And if it doesn't work, you can go back and start over. But you can't do that in your life. I can't go, 'What if I never met this person?' I was just walking through the park. I was on a path, she was on a path, and you bump into each other and start talking. I mean, if you spent a little more time that morning brushing your teeth, it doesn't happen. How random is that?"

After Shoshanna started her first term at George Washington University, Jerry visited her, causing several heads to turn and stare as they walked hand in hand on the campus. Almost from the moment she got to school, Lonstein seemed less than enthusiastic about attending college in D.C. First, she complained that she didn't like the dorm and its inherent lack of privacy, so her father rented her an off-campus apartment, but she still didn't feel at ease.

Although she had been very active in extracurricular activities in high school—she played varsity basketball and soccer and was president of the Film Club—Shoshanna participated in any hardly college clubs or groups. She didn't get very involved in the social scene either. On weekends, she would either go home to Manhattan or fly to Los Angeles to spend time with Jerry.

When Jerry was in New York, his limousine became a regular sight on the wealthy Upper East Side street where Shoshanna lived with her parents. Zachary Lonstein, the owner of a very successful computer hardware business, and his wife, Betty, both approved of Jerry from the beginning.

"We love Jerry," said Betty Lonstein when asked about her daughter's famous boyfriend. "We think he's the nicest person in the world. We are not worried. He's nicer than the average person you meet anywhere, and we love his show. It's the funniest show on television, and we watch it every week."

"Shoshanna is very mature, and Jerry is a thoughtful, good person," added a family friend. "The family have nothing but positive feelings about the two of them together. Everybody respects the relationship."

When they were together in Los Angeles, their lifestyle was more casual. They would have breakfasts of eggs and cheesecake at Jerry's Famous Deli in Studio City with friends like comic Larry Miller, then go shoot basketball in a nearby park. Wherever they were, Jerry and Shoshanna would spend a lot of time shopping, in either the boutiques of Beverly Hills or the sophisticated shops of New York's Madison Avenue.

Seinfeld's longtime friend George Wallace could only sing praises about his friend's new love interest. "She's good for him. I've never seen him happier. She's beautiful and mature. I think it's serious between them."

Michael Richards had an interesting take on why Jerry and Shoshanna seemed so in tune with each other. "They know how to play together. That's their secret. They can get out and have fun and do that for each other. That's very, very important in a relationship, if two people are able to play with each other. When that goes— certainly, when the sex goes—usually everything else is moving away too. Jerry needs that playfulness. He needs somebody who can keep things light."

Seinfeld didn't disagree and, in a 1993 interview, talked about one of the key ingredients necessary for him to even contemplate marriage. "One day my sister asked me, 'Do you think you'll ever get married?' I told her sure I would, but I was having too much fun right now. She said, 'Great. Really healthy, Jerry. You view marriage as the end of fun. Like, do you take this woman and promise to stop having fun?'

"Actually, I'd like to settle down. But for me, the fun factor is essential in a mate. That ability to be kid-like, to be a playmate, I have yet to find in a woman to the extent you build a life on it."

However, Shoshanna seemed to fill that imperative, as reflected by the obvious pleasure he would take in talking about their mutual love of basketball. "We play basketball and she just knocks me down. She doesn't care."

Even in those early days, though, Jerry and especially Shoshanna were forced to deal with pressures that would haunt the relationship throughout their time together. "We don't get to spend as much time together as we'd like," Jerry commented, referring to his work schedule.

For Shoshanna, it was a challenge to learn how to live under the constant spotlight of media attention. "I would like my life to be normal and just go about being a student. But," she added, "these daily obstacles don't take away from our relationship."

As the new year approached, Seinfeld decided it was time to take her to meet his mother. Shoshanna accompanied Jerry to his 1993 New Year's Eve performance at the Sunrise Musical Theater in Fort Lauderdale, Florida, and stayed with Jerry's mom in nearby Delray Beach. By all accounts, Betty Seinfeld very much approved of Shoshanna.

"Actually, my mother was *thrilled*," Seinfeld reported, "because Shoshanna is part Syrian and so is my mother. All my aunts and uncles on the Syrian side were fine about the age difference too. In

Syria, girls are married off when they are fifteen and sixteen, so to them it was like, 'Eighteen? She's a little over the hill, but if you like her. . . .'"

In May 1994, some of Shoshanna's friends indicated she was considering dropping out of college to pursue a career in television production but had allegedly met heavy resistance from Jerry. "At first, Shoshanna didn't care about Hollywood stuff," said one friend. "She just liked being with Jerry. But after having been around him for a while, she's seen a whole new world she'd like to fit into. She has a really good head on her shoulders, and Jerry knows there are a lot of jobs she'd be very capable for."

In any event, Shoshanna decided to continue with her college education, but not at George Washington University. Constant commuting can wear anyone down, no matter how young and vibrant, and it just didn't make sense for her to stay in Washington D.C. At first, she considered transferring to NYU because it would be close to her parents and because Jerry flew to New York regularly, but in the end she chose to continue her education in Los Angeles.

Shoshanna spent part of the summer of 1994 traveling with Jerry during his now annual hiatus comedy tour. She also attended classes at UCLA, to which she had transferred as a history/art history major. If there had been any doubt that Jerry and Shoshanna's relationship had passed into the serious phase, it was dispelled when she made the move west, leaving behind all her friends and family in order to be with Jerry full time.

Although he tended to be circumspect when talking about Shoshanna, seldom even calling her directly by name, Jerry did admit this was not just another romance: "I have gone through freelance periods over the years, but generally I have been involved. But I definitely prefer my current situation to anything I've been in before. After a couple of months I realized this is not your average individual."

Of course, being in Los Angeles meant that Shoshanna was in the media spotlight more often. It wasn't just the tabs that seemed fixated on their relationship. In *Esquire,* under the title "Jerry's Kid," a writer wrote a column that basically was only about Shoshanna's breasts:

"Ah, the pleasures of an immature relationship! You can stay up all night talking, drinking, staring at her breasts. Ah, Lord. To be sixteen and have those breasts within your hands. Later, you grow up, of course, and want different, more mature things from a woman. Unless you are very, very lucky.

"Give 'em hell, Jerry."

"That's aggravating, when you're dealing with intelligent, supposedly sophisticated people and they treat you that way," Seinfeld said shortly after the article appeared.

Jerry also said Lonstein understood how to handle media attention. She was flattered when *Playboy* offered her $100,000 to pose for a nude pictorial, and when rudely asked if her figure was cosmetically enhanced, she answered calmly, "I'm very proud of the fact that I've never had plastic surgery, and I have no plans to do so in the future."

"Of course it got crazy," Seinfeld said. "But luckily I was with someone who was very grounded about it. And so am I. Otherwise, we would not be able to deal with it. I suppose it would have bothered me more if I were uncomfortable with things I did, but I'm not. It's just people talking in a bathroom. Just part of being a celebrity."

Seinfeld and Lonstein seemed to attract attention wherever they went, even just walking down the street. "Yes, I have the sense that people are very curious about our relationship," Seinfeld noted. "But I don't consider that outside the bounds of doing this for a living."

Even so, sometimes he was amazed at how indiscreet people could be. "One day we were on the street and kissed. There was a woman nearby who was just staring and watching, and I caught her eye. It wasn't like it was another human being she was staring at. To her, it was just like she was watching television. And the demeanor of the woman was so unself-conscious, as if there was nothing wrong with just staring at these two people."

Everything seemed so idyllic between Jerry and his young love that it was jarring to learn that the couple had broken up. In November 1994, Lonstein's father, Zachary, told the tabloid TV show *American Journal* that indeed his daughter's romance with Seinfeld was over. "It's just another couple breaking up. It's not a big deal," he said. He blamed the twin pressures of Jerry's career and Shoshanna's schooling and denied reports that the breach came because Shoshanna had refused to sign a prenuptial agreement.

Although none of Jerry's friends were talking, several of Shoshanna's did. Basically, they said Shoshanna needed to spread her wings a bit so that she and Jerry decided to take a break and start dating others. Within weeks, she was linked to L.A. business-man Guy Starkman, who, ironically, happened to run Jerry's Famous Deli, Seinfeld's favorite hangout spot.

Naturally, the tabloids had a field day. SEINFELD'S A MAMA'S BOY— BLASTS HIS TEEN LOVE, one headline blared. The thrust of the article was that Jerry and Shoshanna's interests were a generation apart; it painted her as a young woman who wanted to go out and party and have fun, and Jerry as a cranky stick-in-the-mud whose interests ran more toward art galleries and museums.

Even though the stories were speculating on a relationship obviously very dear to Jerry, he was still able to keep things in perspective. "I'd pick up the tabs and was able to find out what I was up to that week," he joked. "Sometimes it was completely true, other times entirely fabricated. I kind of wanted it all to be true, because I love the tabs."

Even the most scrupulous journalist would have had trouble accurately reporting on the relationship. Not only did Jerry himself not talk much about his private life, he maintained a completely professional demeanor and attitude on his set, so one of the primary avenues by which entertainment and tabloid journalists find out information about TV stars was closed.

It's not unusual for television actors to bring their personal problems to work; if for no other reason, that's where they spend most of their time. Burt Reynolds's irregular behavior on the set of *Evening Shade,* which included throwing a chair at other cast members, and Brett Butler's tirades on *Grace Under Fire* quickly became public knowledge because they took place in front of a large group of people. But when Jerry was on the set, he worked, leaving his private life somewhere else.

In Shoshanna's case, she was three thousand miles away from her closest friends, so they seldom knew where things stood. Consequently, many reporters relied on pure conjecture and speculation.

Whatever the exact reasons for the split, it didn't last long. Within a few months, Shoshanna and Jerry were back in public, arm in arm, looking as happy together as they ever had been. They were the king and queen of the entertainment columns, which climbed all over each other to report when Seinfeld's purchase of a $10,000 gold, diamond, and opal necklace for her.

Surprisingly, it was Lonstein's family who seemed to talk to the press most regularly. Younger brother David unabashedly made it clear what he would like to see happen. "My whole family loves Jerry and we're hoping he's going to be a member of the family soon. He'll make a fantastic brother-in-law."

Indeed, even to the casual observer it seemed that Jerry had finally discovered the woman he had waited all his life to find.

When Shoshanna turned twenty-one in the summer of 1996, what began as a buzz of speculation over whether or not she and Seinfeld were finally engaged became a roar of unconfirmed confirmation. Although the couple themselves weren't talking, several news organizations reported that Jerry and Shoshanna were planning to get married at some point after she graduated from UCLA.

The bad news for *Seinfeld* fans was the caveat that Jerry would also make the 1996–97 season his last on the show. That would allow him to concentrate on his relationship with Shoshanna and move back with her to New York, where they would make their home.

As it was, many were surprised Seinfeld had opted to proceed with the 1996–97 season at all. He had always indicated he wanted to go out when the show was at a peak, not in the waning days of creativity. Early on, Jerry and Larry had made an unofficial pact that they would leave the show together, but that hadn't happened. Instead, when Larry decided not to return for the 1996–97 season, Jerry announced he would assume Larry's role. It meant even more work for Jerry, which translated into even less personal time to devote to his private life. But then, Shoshanna was still in school, so it was assumed they had agreed to fulfill their respective commitments before concentrating more fully on each other.

That Jerry and Shoshanna were indeed engaged became more credible when she began wearing a $200,000, four-carat emerald-cut diamond ring Jerry bought at Harry Winston's in Beverly Hills. The ring also boasted two rare pink diamonds. Back in July, 1995, it was reported that Jerry and Shoshanna had taken her parents out to dinner and told them of their intention to get married.

Even if people didn't know the details of their plans, one thing seemed obvious: Jerry's love for Shoshanna was genuine. "Those two are pretty much in love with each other," Michael Richards offered. "They don't get to see a lot of each other right now. Jerry's working so many hours on the show, and Shoshanna's finishing up her undergraduate work at UCLA. But I think they're going to do a little traveling together. They need more time to see what keeps them together."

It was a perceptive observation. Even though Jerry dismissed the age difference, the fact remains that people born more than twenty years apart have different perspectives on life based, if nothing else, simply on experience. No matter how mature Shoshanna was, she still hadn't *lived* as many years as Jerry. While there can be a meeting of the mind and heart, there's no way to adjust experience, which has to come from simply *doing*. The real question was whether Jerry would be willing and able to give Shoshanna the freedom she needed to experience parts of life he had already lived.

As people get older, they also develop, however slightly, a "been there, done that" attitude about certain things. For example, clubs catering to young adults tend to be more frenzied places than clubs with a more mature clientele, which are usually more laid-back and less fueled by the pent-up sexual energy of youth.

Although he was by no means a stranger to clubs, Jerry made it no secret that he craved normalcy and simple pleasures, while Shoshanna, born and raised in New York City, loved the nightlife. That was not lost on the roving paparazzi who kept close tabs on Lonstein's social calendar when she was in New York away from Jerry.

Jerry had warned Shoshanna that any time she met up with an old boyfriend, the tabloids would turn the encounter into screaming headlines. In as early as 1994, for instance, an article alleged she had been all over old flame Jake Spitz. "She was parading Jake around like a trophy," the story claimed. "They were hugging and dancing. She's already told Jerry she's too young to consider marriage and intends to finish her education. Going out with other guys is one sure way to send a message."

The *National Enquirer* even tried to hint at a romance between Lonstein and Fabio, who in fact did know each other. In 1990, when Shoshanna was fifteen, she and her parents vacationed at a Club Med in the Caribbean, where they met Fabio. Back in New York, the pair had hung out together for about six months, working out at the Vertical Club gym. Although the article was careful not to suggest that Fabio had an intimate contact with the then-underage Shoshanna, the implication was clear that they had been more than just friends.

Then, in December 1996, the *New York Post* ran an item about

Shoshanna and Steve Ehrenkranz, whom she dated in high school. They had recently been photographed together at Creation, a club in Manhattan's Chelsea neighborhood. The paper quoted an onlooker at the club as saying, "One night she was sitting on his lap making out with him." The *Globe* picked up the story and headlined it SEINFELD TELLS YOUNG GALPAL: STAY AWAY FROM HIGH SCHOOL HUNK.

Although she flew back to L.A. and attended the *Hamlet* premiere with Jerry at the Academy Theater, stories began appearing hinting at trouble in the relationship. Somewhat uncharacteristically, Seinfeld's representative took the time to deny the rumors: "It's absolutely untrue they are having any troubles. They are perfectly happy."

But the stories wouldn't go away. Week after week, unnamed friends of Shoshanna would claim that she and Jerry were having problems over her desire to have more fun and his single-minded focus on work.

A July article in the *Star* wondered, IS IT GOODBYE SHOSHANNA?

Still, Jerry and Shoshanna seemed to maintain their equilibrium— and sense of humor. Once, when they realized they were being videotaped by a paparazzo, Jerry and Shoshanna jokingly staged a fake argument for the lensman, making clear they were not the least bit perturbed by the intrusion by making fun of it.

However, occasionally the cameras did intrude on decidedly less lighthearted moments. In 1996, for instance, Jerry and Shoshanna had been photographed on 84th Street in New York during a tear-laden discussion. The pictures are uncomfortable to look at because the emotion was so obvious and so real and so familiar to anyone trying to overcome a relationship hurdle. This wasn't like watching television. These were real people trying to deal with real issues.

Suddenly, the stories took on a different tone, one that simply felt more accurate. Named sources began recounting seeing Jerry out and about without Shoshanna, as on the evening he spent at the Beverly Club in Los Angeles with a mystery blonde. The couple that used to be observed regularly out shopping or at Jerry's Famous Deli abruptly dropped out of sight. Finally, in the spring of 1997, it was revealed that Jerry and Shoshanna had indeed once again separated.

The breakup had actually occurred in February. They had kept it quiet because, according to a spokesman, "it's not something they felt they should have to comment on. There was no nasty scene. They both agreed it was time for a break."

Once again, neither Jerry nor Shoshanna commented on their private relationship, but others did. "She said it was fun but Hollywood was just too much a pain, being in the press all the time," said Steven Santagati, who once dated Lonstein. "She really wants to see what she can do, live a little before she gets married."

Betty Lonstein revealed that her daughter planned to move back to New York as soon as she graduated from UCLA in June. "She's evaluating different offers here," said her mother. "She's missed New York. This is her home. All her friends are here."

Very few of Seinfeld's associates were willing to comment, except to say, "The only reason they broke up was because Seinfeld couldn't focus on both Shoshanna and the series at the same time."

The breakup only served to pique the interest of the entertainment newsmagazine shows and the tabloids. Pictures appeared of Jerry squiring around an unidentified blonde in one of his Porsches and of the couple lounging at an outdoor cafe. Shoshanna was photographed passionately kissing Jay Anston, a member of a prominent New York family well known on the social "A" list.

Interestingly, few who know either Jerry or Shoshanna seem convinced the relationship has truly run its course. Some have suggested that the reason Seinfeld abruptly decided not to return for a tenth season was based in large part on his desire to try again with Lonstein, the one woman he ever said he loved. One friend who requested anonymity seemed to sum up everybody's sentiment: "They've broken up before. Who knows what's going to happen?"

Jerry himself seems convinced the relationship is indeed over, and he acknowledges he and Shoshanna don't even speak anymore. "I know everyone looked at that relationship as here's this rich TV guy and here's this young, hot girl, but it wasn't like that at all," he says seriously. "We were very much in love, but the timing wasn't quite right. I almost got married to Shoshanna, but it didn't feel like our lives were dovetailing. She was starting out in life, and I was finishing up a big chapter. She's the type of person who needed to do things. She will accomplish a great deal. The timing wasn't quite right. But it was wonderful."

16

A Little Older, a Little Wiser, and a Little Staler

"THE OPPOSITE" WAS THE 1993–94 SEASON FINALE, MARKING THE END OF the official fifth season. In the episode, Kramer appears on *Live With Regis & Kathie Lee* to promote his new coffee-table book about coffee tables.

The idea of having Philbin and Gifford on the show came up after Jerry told Barbara Walters during a television interview that he found the morning talk show hosts fascinating because they did nothing. "You can't do less than they do and make a living," he said. "And I for one couldn't be more impressed—to do little more than dent a seat cushion in a chair and make a zillion dollars."

Proving he meant no malice by his remarks, Seinfeld invited them to appear as themselves, an offer the pair readily accepted. They thus proved to be better sports than, say, the folks at *Entertainment Tonight,* who in 1992 had refused to grant *Seinfeld* use of the news-magazine's theme song for an episode in which Kramer has seizures every time he hears the voice of the show's news anchor, Mary Hart.

"I knew it would be well done and we wouldn't be the object of ridicule," said Gifford, explaining why she had no qualms about the show. "I knew we would be in on the joke, not *be* the joke. This was not the least bit mean-spirited. It was just perfect. It captured us. Boy, they've got us down to a T."

Then Gifford added, "Hey, we were nothing before they were

nothing, and you can quote me on that. We own nothingness. Let's give credit where it's due."

During the 1994 hiatus, Jerry returned to the road while Larry recuperated and relaxed by working on some movie scripts. The other cast members either reacquainted themselves with family and friends or squeezed in some outside acting work; they weren't required to return to work until production was scheduled to resume. For Seinfeld and David, though, the spring-summer hiatus was much shorter. They went back to work when the writers convened to begin developing ideas for the next season.

While most of the staff looked forward to returning to work, it was always a painful process for Larry David. Occasionally he seemed as anxious for the series to end as he had been for it to be a success. Although Seinfeld talked frequently about not wanting to overstay his primetime welcome, it was obvious that he was having fun, and the odds were that as long as he felt good about the show, he would keep doing it.

With Larry, the parameters for staying were different. Although both Seinfeld and David oversaw every aspect of the show, the creative vision was still skewed toward Larry. Because of his nature, each episode was an exercise in emotional bloodletting that wore him down as the season progressed. By the end of the shooting year in March, Larry was depleted, both mentally and physically. So gearing back up for another season took a monumental effort of will as the seasons passed.

Consequently, every year, network and Castle Rock executives convened for what Glenn Padnick, one of the company's founders, called the "Annual Convince Larry to Stay Lunch." Padnick explained, "It's where David maintains he's running out of ideas and everyone else assures him he's not,"

"And it ends," joked NBC executive vice president Rick Ludwin, "with a Brink's truck backing up to David's house."

In March 1993, David's salary was nearly doubled—to $125,000 per episode, almost $3 million for the season—to induce him to return for 1993–94. To the network and the production company, he was worth every penny, because the sixth season would be a milestone for *Seinfeld* and everyone who had been associated with it since its inception.

*   *   *

SOMETIME in early 1995, the one hundredth episode would be filmed and aired, meaning that the sitcom had reached the magic, arbitrary number set by the industry for syndication, wherein the production company sells the show for what is referred to as off-network show-ings—in other words, reruns seen on local affiliates. It was believed Castle Rock would earn nearly $3 million *per episode,* making *Seinfeld* one of the most profitable comedies in syndicated television history.

Because Jerry and Larry were the creators of the show, they also shared in the syndication package revenues. Typically, the other cast members were not entitled to participate in the off-network prof-its—a situation that would become a major issue a few years down the road.

The hundredth-episode celebration gave NBC the opportunity to trumpet *Seinfeld*'s achievements and spotlight the show as the net-work's comedic crown jewel. Considering the often winding, not to mention bleak, road the series had taken on its way to success, the hundredth episode offered Jerry and the others a chance to reflect on where they had been, how far they had come, and how the show and its characters had evolved—and also what the show was not.

Although *Seinfeld* was now universally referred to as the "show about nothing," Julia Louis-Dreyfus offered this perspective: "Clearly, the show is *not* about nothing. But also, it *is* about noth-ing, because thirty minutes after you've seen it, you can't really re-member what you saw."

"Nothing and everything are really the same thing," Jerry com-mented. "We are on screen talking for twenty-two minutes, so obvi-ously something is happening. Whether that is a large event or a small event depends on how you look at life. To some people, little things are little things. To us, the little things *are* the big things. What I'm saying is that the show is all about perspective. Our prem-ise in starting the show was to look at the mini-events in life, the kinds of things that comprise most of life for most people.

"This is not a show about being on television, like Gary Shandling's," Seinfeld explained, referring to Shandling's television verité cable series, *The Larry Sanders Show.* "This is a show about being a human being. Or, in my case, about being in a comedian, which is almost the same thing."

"I'm surprised that NBC actually allows any of these shows on the air," David added, with his typical dry outlook, "because they don't sound anything like normal network shows, but I think it works because the more personal it is, the more universal it is. You would think the opposite is true, but it's not. For example, usually they say, 'Okay, we'll have a guy and a girl and people will relate.' But they *don't* relate. What they do relate to is saying the wrong thing to somebody, so we make a show out of *that*."

Jason Alexander was struck by the difference in audience reaction compared to the early days. "Doing the show has become a lot easier, but that can be both good and bad, because you can get lazy. I know there are certain things that I can draw a laugh on. The audience now *presumes* it will be funny, so they react to it before we even get there."

The occasion also afforded an opportunity to give *Seinfeld* a State of the Sitcom review, revisiting the question of just why this show had become so popular. "We always had a strong following, you know," said Jerry, indulging in a bit of revisionist series history. "Everyone who works on the show knows this is a broad-based hit. But the *perception* was, it was a narrow demographic hit, when in actuality, there were all kinds of people watching the show."

"Imagine if all you had to do was hang out with your friends and had frequent romantic encounters which really don't hurt and work is only sporadically dealt with except when it's interesting or exciting," noted Louis-Dreyfus. "There's nothing really likable about them except they remind you of yourself. That's their only redeeming quality."

Many credited not only Jerry's comic vision but also his willingness to share the stage and the laughs. "Jerry has made himself the straight man just like Mary Tyler Moore," said one comic. "Rhoda and Sue Ann got more laughs and zippy one-liners than Mary Richards ever did. Ted Danson did the same thing on *Cheers*. And they all borrow from Jack Benny's classic show—make the central character the straight man and let the other people be the funny ones."

Seinfeld felt he had improved as an actor each year, though his approach was simply to enjoy the experience and to be loose. "The acting has become a lot of fun because I love the people I work with. It's like putting on a show with your brothers and sisters. Or, thought of in another way, I am Superman on the show. George is Perry White, Elaine is Lois Lane, and Kramer is Jimmy Olsen."

The fact that Seinfeld and the others still thought of themselves as both friends and family—through wondering if there would be a next week, much less a next season, then through suddenly being touted at one of the greatest things ever to hit television—was perhaps the most remarkable achievement over the course of the first hundred episodes.

"It's a survival thing," Seinfeld pointed out. "Fame is like perfume—you smell it, you don't eat it. We've all kept our heads together. Nobody's become weird or difficult as a result of all the success we've had. The chemistry we have is the heart and soul of this show. I've never been on another show, but I hear stories about people who don't talk anymore. All these petty ego games. When we're not shooting, we sit around the set and talk. We know it's not going to last forever, so we're enjoying it.

"That's what I work hardest at. One day we'll look back and say, 'This will never happen again.' The whole cast knows this will never happen again in our careers, not only comedically, but personally."

But even as they reveled in the moment, there was an understanding that some things had already begun to change, simply because the cast members were growing as people outside the walls of the soundstage. "Every year we have more fun with each other," Jason Alexander agreed, then added, "but these days, we also want to get home a little sooner. I remember when the four of us would never rehearse; we would just clown and clown and clown. We didn't care if we ever got home. But now, you see Julia and me going, 'Hmmm, the store closes soon, and the baby goes to bed at seven. . . .' "

Although the actors may have been maturing and moving forward with their personal lives, the rest of America seemed to just be catching up to what they had spent the last five years working on professionally. The January 19, 1995, episode earned the series' highest rating ever, a 35 share, meaning that 35 percent of people watching television were tuned in to *Seinfeld*. The previous high had been set just one week before. *Seinfeld* had seemingly started to take on a life of its own. It was almost unheard of for a show to increase its performance consistently so far into the life of its run.

"I feel that it's only very recently that we've become a hit," said Louis-Dreyfus. "So when you consider we've done this for five years, it means a lot of the audience hasn't seen a lot of the shows."

"It wasn't until last year that I felt we had a hit," added Castle Rock's Padnick. "It's an odd thing to be in the middle of the sixth season and only now be a bona fide hit. As we began our fifth season, there were still incredible question marks about the show's long-term health. I remember during the 1993 TV critics tour some-one asked, 'Aren't you concerned whether Seinfeld is a hit?' I was annoyed, yet I could understand the question."

"It's good to be famous, I can tell you that," quipped Seinfeld. And how could he tell that? "You just leave a trail of turned heads."

For Larry David, the essence of success was more subtle: "The only change I can really see is that I don't have to shop for pants in stores anymore. I can just call up and they'll bring the pants right over. That's no small thing. Trying on pants is one of the most humiliating things a man can suffer that doesn't involve a woman."

On a more serious note, Jerry acknowledged that the show's cur-rent success—not only that they had made it to one hundred epi-sodes but that the series was considered to be of the highest qual-ity—vindicated him as a comic. "When you're a comedian, you don't feel like you're in show business. It's like you're selling belts on the street. It's not a real job. Anything with a camera is legitimate show business. With this show, I'll have exorcised that demon. It's my Mount Olympus.

"I no longer have that 'Am I really any good?' monkey on my back, which everyone in show business deals with on some level," he said. "It's what drives you; it also drives you nuts. But if you do one good thing, you can always say, 'At least I did that one great thing in my life.' That's deeply satisfying to say.

"I've always had a lot of confidence. But I wanted more. As a comedian, you're never as good as you want to be. To me that means being strong enough to take your time with an audience. Most comedians work onstage at a breathless pace, and that's out of fear. I do it too. But when you can slow down and hold people, that's being good enough.

"Comedy strength is slowness. Jack Benny is a perfect example. He would come onstage and not say anything. He would just stand there and people would start to laugh. I mean, that is comic strength."

Spurred by the ever-increasing interest in the show, NBC milked the occasion of *Seinfeld*'s hundredth episode for as much, and for as long, as it could. On February 2, 1995, a special one-hour retrospec-tive celebration was aired. It had George and Jerry at their local diner reminiscing about the past and included scenes from nearly seventy episodes.

"We've crammed as much of the classics as we could into an

hour," noted Seinfeld. "We're emphasizing past shows because the newer shows have just been seen. After our regular stand-up opening, it's one big bobsled down memory lane."

On February 9, "The Beard" was broadcast. It was actually the 101st episode; the hundredth filmed show was "The Kiss Hello," which finally aired February 16. After its filming, the cast and crew threw themselves a party, although the celebration was short-lived: Seinfeld and David were back at work as always early the next day.

"It was business as usual," reported Carol Leifer. "They just take it in stride."

Still, they were not unaware, or unappreciative, of the fact that they had beaten not only the odds but nearly every convention of television sitcoms as well. "We've really managed to have an awful lot of success for having so little in the way of conventional comedy," Jerry noted. "But whatever it is we do, it's still working. Audiences don't laugh on reputation alone. It's an involuntary response. The success we've had with this is beyond anything I ever imagined I could do. If I stopped and thought about it, I'm sure it would overwhelm me. That's why I never do. Every once in a while, I'll see SEINFELD stenciled on a prop or chair and it's just amazing. '*Seinfeld*' isn't *my* name anymore. It's a brand name."

The idea of being a product in the control of others made Jerry uneasy, however. "For ninety-eight percent of my career I have been completely at the wheel. All my performances, my level, my work load, was under my control. Now I'm just hanging onto this thing. My career has now developed a life and a power of its own, and I am just a passenger.

"I don't like peaks. I always wanted to have a plateau kind of career. I shudder when I see these people skyrocket and then flame out in a second. I'm more interested in having a body of work, to say I created all this material and I did these shows."

Because of the unique situation the series found itself in, peaking five years into a run, many predicted it could have a very strong life for another five years—or seven years, or even longer. *M*A*S*H* had lasted eleven years and was still popular and creatively strong when the producers decided to end it. Even a noninnovative and creatively mediocre show like *Coach* spent seven and a half years on the air.

Jerry quickly jumped in to stop the speculation of a comedic dynasty: "It's a matter of how much life you think the thing has. You don't want to be onstage too long. You want to get off at the right moment and send people home feeling like they had a good experience. We really haven't decided when that will be, but I can guarantee you we're not going to break any records here."

Before *Seinfeld* became a Top Ten hit series, it played to a smaller but rabidly loyal audience. While it didn't get all that much attention, neither did it get much criticism. With the spotlight now shining on it at full beam, the show was suddenly subjected to scrutiny of the most meticulous kind. Fans and critics alike would dissect each episode and applaud signs of continued creativity—and reprove any perceived signs of slippage.

Ironically, after the series went into syndication, Jerry would find that he was competing against himself in a way, judged by his own high standards. Fans would compare the early episodes with those currently being produced, and in the opinion of many, the later episodes weren't as consistently fresh and funny as shows from the second, third, and fourth seasons.

Seinfeld shrugged off the criticism: "It's hitting a baseball. You do the best you can. Comedy will only work a certain percentage of the time. If you have a high average, you're one of the lucky ones. I would put our batting average up against anybody's. We do very few weak shows. If you watch the show, chances are you are going to laugh a few times. To me, that's the real success of the show. We just hit the ball."

IN THE spring of 1995, reports began surfacing of a rift between Jerry and Larry. Although creative disagreements are a daily occurrence in Hollywood, special attention was paid to the Seinfeld-David rupture because of its implications. It was no secret that Larry David was vitally important to the series, and many wondered if Jerry could manage the show on his own.

The argument stemmed from Jerry and Larry's original pact: they would not only go out together but would make sure the show went out at its peak. With that criterion in mind, during 1993 Seinfeld had frequently commented that he thought the 1994–95 season would be the show's last. But in November 1994, he had a change of heart.

"Maybe we *will* do one more year," he said at the time. "I just want to make sure I complete it in the right way. This is a very good season for us. I've loved the shows."

From Jerry's point of view, they were having too much fun to stop. For Larry, it was a matter of being able to keep reaching the almost impossibly high bar they had set for themselves. Simply put, Larry insisted *Seinfeld*'s 1995–96 season be its last; Jerry wanted to continue through 1996–97. In the end, Seinfeld told NBC it could count on him for a two-year commitment.

Larry was so upset by what he considered a betrayal that he initially said he would resign rather than continue for *any* more shows. However, after some cajoling on Jerry's part and some additional financial incentives, he agreed to come back—but for only one more season.

Although he had capitulated and unresigned, Larry's relationship with Jerry remained strained for a while. For the first time, there was personal tension behind the scenes at *Seinfeld*.

"With Larry," said one set source at the time, "it's one day at a time."

Many of the NBC brass assumed that David's pronouncement that this was absolutely his last season was his way of saving face and were confident he would remain with the show throughout its entire run. Even if some were concerned, all they cared about was the upcoming season. They would worry about the 1996–97 season next year.

"The important thing," said NBC Entertainment president Warren Littlefield, "is that Jerry is back. As far as I'm concerned, I don't want anything changed."

Others who knew Larry firmly believed he would leave the show once filming for the seventh season wrapped in March of 1996. Few could imagine doing the show without him.

Even Michael Richards was prompted to say, "I think we'll go one more year. I've been wrong. I didn't think the show would go as long as it's gone. But at this point, we're thinking one more year."

Part of the reason emotions ran so high for both Jerry and Larry was likely the criticisms being leveled at *Seinfeld*. In the spring of 1995, at the end of its official sixth season, both critics and fans started to express disappointment over the show. It was one thing to be ignored as they had been in the early days, quite another to be told that the show "just wasn't as funny anymore." That was the ultimate stab through the heart for Larry and one reason he felt they should pack it in. He had worked too hard to let the show slide into mediocrity—or even the perception of it—just to fatten people's bank accounts and help NBC's ratings.

Also, it was no secret that Larry wanted to work in films, but any such opportunity would have to wait until he was no longer involved with *Seinfeld*, because he was so consumed with the series. Although Jerry, too, was in great demand to star in movies, he was more interested in maintaining close ties with his stand-up roots, which he was able to do during hiatus.

The question of whether *Seinfeld* was losing its much-touted edge was a nagging little gnat that kept buzzing around their ears, becoming more and more annoying the longer it droned on. They heard it from all sides.

Mournful-sounding fans posted their opinions on *Seinfeld* bulletin boards and in chat areas on the Internet:

"They need new material."

"Nothing this season can match 'The Puffy Shirt.' "

"I can't believe I'm saying it, but the writing is lacking its luster."

"Kramer is overused and not funny."

"The show has not been consistently funny for about a year now."

Jerry was unconcerned. "I don't concern myself with what people think, because I can't change human nature. There's a point where people go, 'Okay, that's enough,' and I'm very comfortable with people saying that."

Soon several mainstream publications echoed what was showing up with regularity on the Net: the show had lost . . . *something*. Critics asked, 'What's wrong with Seinfeld?' Some speculated that the writing was simply better in the early years because the ideas were the first ones drawn from the new *Seinfeld* well. After six seasons, perhaps the well had started to run dry. Others blamed the crop of so-called *Seinfeld* imitators or the fact that the cast members were being overexposed through their numerous commercial endorsements.

Some involved with the show harbored the same concerns. One former writer, requesting anonymity, said bluntly, "Last season, the shows were painful to watch."

Even Jason Alexander candidly admitted the show's tenor was subtly changing: "In the fifth and sixth seasons, the show went in a different direction that I wasn't personally interested in. It went from being about the little things that happen to everybody, the minutiae of life, the funny examination of that stuff, to very broad, very wacky story lines."

Jerry, however, refused to admit there was anything amiss. Rather uncharacteristically, he took an adversarial position with the media who questioned the show's direction. "The critics who try to be the first to say *Seinfeld* is not what it used to be are very amusing to me. That's just funny, because it's the natural tendency. Each is trying to be the first to announce it, but it hasn't happened yet. The show is still as good as it's always been. Maybe it was time for people to think it's not as fresh and new. But I understand the press has to have an angle."

When the critical articles continued, the normally unflappable Seinfeld seemed to be losing his famous cool, even if just a little. "It's ridiculous, these people," he said. "We're on top of every page of every episode. There's no way in the world the show is slipping. It's just the nature of the cycle. People get used to it. They've seen Kramer, they've seen George, they've seen me. They get used to it. If you went back to see *Schindler's List* every week for six months, you'd think it was slipping.

"It's normal for people to get used to a show, and I think that's what has happened to us. That is unfortunately the nature of television or anything people have a lot of. That is why any TV series has a rise, a peak, and a fall. Critics generally want to be the first one to say it's bad. So go ahead. But obviously *we* would know. I know we're not hitting the wall. But at the same time, that's why I'm probably not going to do the show that much longer. It's inevitable. You can't change the basic situation or the basic characters. And after a while, you've seen it.

"I think even the best TV series has a healthy life of five years to maybe eight years tops. You can go longer, based on your ratings, but that's just milking it."

That, apparently, is exactly what Larry David had worried was happening. Jerry remained confident, at least outwardly, that the show's creative edge was still very much honed and that reports of *Seinfeld*'s death were premature. "We have not started to dip, believe me, and," he promised, "we'll be gone before we do."

However, the series *had* undergone a change—and one of great significance, although few in the viewing audience would be aware of it unless they took the time to read the opening credits carefully. After they had wrapped their fifth season a year earlier, in April of

1994, Larry and Jerry shocked the writing staff when they announced they were replacing Tom Cherones—who had directed all but two of the episodes up to that point—as well as line producer Joan Van Horn. In addition to that bloodletting, Larry Charles was leaving on his own volition because of a series deal he had made with NBC Productions.

While it is in the nature of the television business for writers such as Larry Charles to work their way up the promotion ladder to a writer-producer credit, then leave for their own development deal, the dumping of Cherones—and, to a lesser extent, Van Horn—took most everyone by surprise. Cherones was the man primarily credited with helping Jerry make a relatively smooth transition from stand-up to actor; he was a Directors Guild of America Award winner; most significant, he had just signed a new contract in November 1993, which would force the show to pay him in the neighborhood of $1 million to *not* direct the sixth season.

The housecleaning was seen by some as a sign that there was indeed some strong concern that the series might be stagnating. There was also speculation floating around Hollywood that Larry David was looking to take over the directing duties, on top of everything he was already doing. The truth, however, was that Jerry and Larry, sensing the show was perhaps starting to settle into itself, had decided they needed to shake things up *before* slippage set in.

Replacing Cherones was a tricky proposition because, although they wanted a fresh outlook, they also needed to keep some sense of continuity and find someone who understood that *Seinfeld* was not like any other sitcom. They considered several top television directors—all of whom were salivating at the thought of taking over *Seinfeld*—and ultimately chose Andy Ackerman, whose credits included *Cheers* and *Wings,* two of the more sophisticated comedies in recent years.

The new director had a slightly broader hand with characters, concerned, encouraging bigger reactions from the actors. So the changes noticed by fans in many cases weren't merely figments of their imaginations.

There were also other factors involved, as Seinfeld had correctly pointed out. Now in its sixth season, *Seinfeld* simply wasn't new anymore; still, viewers expected it to be groundbreaking, not merely good. If a given episode didn't grab them with a "Not that there's anything wrong with that" or "sponge-worthy," many fans came away slightly disappointed.

The writers were ever more mindful that the four characters had to have equal time. Although still funny, some of the writing was veering away from reality-based minutiae to stories that required more suspension of disbelief, even tiptoeing to the edge of slapstick. For example, sixth-season episodes would include "The Jimmy," in which Kramer is mistaken for a mentally handicapped person because he's feeling the effects of Novocain, and "The Diplomat's Club," in which Elaine gets fired because they think she's trying to kill her boss, Mr. Pitt.

One New York critic accused the show of resorting to a "predictable, paint-by-number quality. This season's attempts at nothing have been as graceful as shoving a bowling ball into a sock. In the last two seasons, the *Seinfeld* writing team has turned to taking their ideas from actual events. For example, a recent episode had Elaine hosting a marathon runner who lost (true story) his chance at an Olympic gold medal because he overslept on the day of his race. These ripped-from-the-headlines plots may succeed on *Law & Order,* but on *Seinfeld,* they just don't work.

"One of the more disturbing trends is the overabundance of subplots crammed into a single episode. The first half of almost every show is devoted to annoyingly short scenes of exposition, which are eventually intended to tie together at the conclusion. More often than not, though, the endings fall flat and if you miss the first five minutes, you're screwed."

Seinfeld stood by his decision to shake up his staff and doggedly resisted the suggestion that any strain on the creative process was beginning to show: "I know in my heart that we are every bit as funny as we always have been. There are episodes from this season that I'd put up against anything we've ever done. For now, people are still laughing. We have nothing else to worry about."

17

Goodbye, Larry

TWICE A YEAR, FOR TWO WEEKS IN JANUARY AND THREE WEEKS IN JULY, television critics from all over the country converge on Los Angeles for what is known as the Television Critics Press Tour. During the press tour, broadcast and cable networks present their new series and promote upcoming specials and sweeps programming via panels that include actors, producers, and directors. The network heads also make an appearance to give a State of the Network address to the assembled critics and journalists.

Although NBC had a relatively large lead over ABC and CBS, the truth was, it was only because of Thursday night. The rating numbers for Thursday were so high that they made up for the network's sometimes glaring problems on other nights. While it was true that *Friends* had developed into a solid lead-in for the night, the cornerstone was still believed to be the one-two punch provided by the respective comedy and drama powerhouses of all television, *Seinfeld* and *ER*.

During the NBC portion of the January 1996 press tour, held at the Ritz Carlton in Pasadena, California, NBC's Warren Littlefield was one happy television executive. Not only was NBC basking in the glory of being the top-rated network, he was confident it could do so for at least another year, because the network had been informed over the recent holidays that Jerry had decided to return for another season.

"We usually vote around Christmastime," Jerry explained later. "I pretend it's a democracy."

But everyone knew as Jerry went, so went the show. The day he decided it was over, it would not matter what anyone else thought, because Seinfeld simply could not be replaced.

The importance of *Seinfeld*'s return could not be overstated, either financially or strategically. To show just how thrilled the network was about it, NBC graced the critics with a surprise visit from the man himself. Walking out from the wings of the ballroom in which the presentation was being held, Seinfeld had his game face on, the lone comic ready to win over the expectant crowd. Most of the journalists in the crowd knew what his presence meant; networks don't bring on stars to make specially trumpeted announcements about leaving. Jerry was obviously there to spread the news that his show would be returning for an eighth season.

"We went into this season thinking it was our last," Seinfeld began his remarks. "But as the season went on, we were laughing so much and enjoying each other's company so much—like we did in the beginning when we were a bomb—that we found it was too enjoyable not to continue the show next season."

Despite all of his protestations the previous year, Seinfeld finally admitted that the sixth season had been a bit of a struggle. "At the end of the 1994–95 season, we all felt like we were crawling and felt we'd be lucky to get through this year. But the wind caught the sails this season. We have new writers who injected fresh ideas and fresh energy. I have to give them credit for the show having more life at this stage of the game."

Even with that admission, he still took issue with critics who dared say *Seinfeld* was back, because he didn't believe they had ever been away. Just because getting through the season was tougher didn't mean the product itself was in any way inferior or less funny. It had just been harder to maintain the level of quality.

For whatever reason, the cast members now felt newly invigorated by the work and, apparently, each other. "The core experience of the four main cast members performing the show has remained enjoyable," Jerry said. "To enjoy the people you're doing a show with this much, that's rare. So we want to stay together.

"It's really just like when you're sitting at a dinner table with friends, having a good time. You have the coffee, have the dessert, you're all just kind of sitting there, and then there is that moment when somebody goes, 'Okay, let's go.' And everybody just gets up and leaves. But I guess we're at the point where the waitress comes over and asks if anyone wants more coffee and you say, 'Yeah.'

"The show is at such a nice place right now, because all the battles are behind us. Will we ever be a hit? Will we ever win any awards? Will the public like us? Now we can just have fun with it. It's the greatest position to be in, and everyone wanted to enjoy that feeling a little more."

Well, not exactly *everyone*.

What both Seinfeld and the network neglected to mention was that Larry David had held true to his word and had informed Jerry, Castle Rock, and NBC that he would not be returning for the eighth season. Not everyone believed him; not everybody *wanted* to believe him.

When confronted with this rather important bit of news, Warren Littlefield shrugged and said, "Well, you know Larry."

But this time, there wasn't a Brink's truck big enough to change his mind. "I've wanted to leave since the show began," David said. "I set the bar very high for myself. I couldn't live with bad shows. The time is coming when I should be doing something else. I would have preferred if we had ended this year. I'm the sort of guy who's always shirked responsibility. I had a lot of responsibility for a long time and I wanted to shirk."

In dealing with Larry's desire to leave the show after the sixth season, 1994–95, he and Jerry had agreed at the time that the 1995–96 campaign would definitely be the last. To many, it seemed inconceivable that *Seinfeld* would—or could—go on without the Jerry-Larry symbiosis. Even Seinfeld had seemed to believe that.

In 1992, Jerry had gone on the record saying, "Our senses of humor dovetail in such a way that the words sound right coming out of my mouth, but most of the time they're his words. I'd say ninety percent of the show comes from Larry. When one of us quits, the other will have to go, too, because this show is *us*."

Jerry's decision to stay on after Larry's departure actually made sense, given Seinfeld's finely honed sense of ambition. Always one to rise to new challenges, Jerry was suddenly faced with the prospect of losing the person everyone, including himself, had dubbed the creative soul of the series. The easy thing to do would be to quit with Larry and go on to something else.

But it was probably precisely the assumption that *Seinfeld* wouldn't be able to maintain its quality that spurred Jerry to stay, in addition to the fact that he was still having fun and the others wanted to keep the show going. He would have the chance to prove that the show could be just as good without Larry—different in tone, perhaps, but just as funny.

If Larry appreciated this subtext, it didn't show. "I keep trying to get Jerry to quit with me, but he won't. I can't stop them from doing the show, but I probably won't watch it," he admitted. "When the shows finish filming at the end of March, I'll go back to being a fuck-off."

Actually, he would finally have the time to try his hand at writing and directing feature films, which he had been forced to put off until freed of *Seinfeld*'s constant demands. With his typical pessimistic public outlook, Larry was skeptical about his chances of becoming the next Woody Allen, but of one thing he was certain: "After I fail at movies, I'll go back to stand-up. I'll never do another television show. It's just too hard."

THE 1996 season finale was classic Larry David, a fitting swan song for the man whose darkly skewed humor had given the show its distinctive edge. Throughout the season, David had written scripts dealing with George's pending wedding to his dogged fiancée, Susan, played by Heidi Swedberg.

Swedberg first joined the series as a recurring character in 1992 and over the next three and a half years would play the one woman George first couldn't get past, then couldn't get rid of. Viewers were introduced to Susan in the fourth-season episode "The Pitch," in which Kramer throws up on her.

Over the course of an eight-show story arc, Susan's relationship with George and his friends results in her father's cabin being burned down, the revelation her father was once John Cheever's secret lover, and Susan getting fired from her job as an NBC executive after George kisses her during a staff meeting. After she leaves George, Susan returns in a later episode, which reveals she now has a lesbian lover—whom she loses after the girlfriend falls for Kramer.

A year and a half later, Larry David called on Swedberg again. In the seventh-season opener, George and Jerry agree to change their lives and settle down. Jerry changes his mind and breaks up with his girlfriend, but George has already proposed to Susan and suddenly finds himself stuck in an engagement he really didn't want.

For Swedberg, being cast in *Seinfeld* was her biggest career break to date. Born in Honolulu, Hawaii, and raised in Albuquerque, New Mexico, Heidi began performing in community theater while she was still in high school. After studying acting for three years at the University of New Mexico, she dropped out in 1987 to work in professional theater. That same year, she made her movie debut as a pregnant teenager in the Bruce Willis vehicle *In Country*. She soon moved to Los Angeles, finding work in television with guest spots on both comedies and dramas.

"I look like the girl next door," Swedberg says. "That makes it easier to stick me in things. One day I'm a doctor, the next day I'm a prostitute."

For the classically trained actress, television work isn't always a joy to behold. "You start off with Shakespeare and end up on *Who's the Boss?*— and that's when you know you've made it? But *Seinfeld* is different. It wasn't like doing television. I didn't feel embarrassed to tell people about it."

In person, Swedberg exudes a quirky sense of humor, which explains why Jerry and Larry cast her. Ironically, the character of Susan was anything but quirky. "Susan is the straight man," Heidi pointed out. "Susan is *so* stiff, she's got uptightness on tap."

Susan also is determined to marry George at any cost, it seems, and patiently puts up with all his machinations of trying to extricate himself from the engagement, as well as a brief infatuation with actress Marisa Tomei.

Larry played with the fans all season. Will George really get married? If he does, how will that affect the chemistry and balance of the show? Several times, the wedding date is postponed, giving George another reprieve and another chance to scheme his way out of marriage. Finally, it seems he has run out of time. The wedding is set.

The final episode of the season, "The Invitations," was built up to be one of NBC's premier "must-see" events of the season. The marriage is on, and it's time to send out the invitations. Adhering to his philosophy of not spending more money than necessary, George buys the cheapest invitations possible, which he leaves for Susan to mail out.

In a surprisingly dark turn of events, Susan collapses while licking the envelopes and is rushed to the hospital, where she dies from having ingested too much of the toxic glue that had been used on the cheap invitation envelopes. In the final scene, after a brief pause to absorb the news of Susan's death, Jerry and the others shrug off the tragedy and go out for coffee.

To some critics Larry's script was too black, and there was some spirited criticism leveled at the show. Julia Louis-Dreyfus, for one, thought those who were upset or who thought the characters were portrayed as too dehumanized missed the point.

"Absolutely they were dehumanized, and that's why it was funny," she explained. "I mean, let's face it, if you look at them realistically, these four characters aren't really nice or kind people. They haven't been for years, so I don't think that should be a surprise to anyone. Personally, I loved the episode. I know that it was very black comedy, but I think that's in keeping with the style of *Seinfeld*. I thought it was fabulous."

Larry David left *Seinfeld* the same way he had started—unapologetic, unafraid to push the limits of sitcom humor, uncompromised, and with his comedic integrity intact. He bowed out on his own terms, and he had changed the face of television sitcoms forever.

"I wish Larry would have stayed, but the show was very difficult for him," Jerry said after the seventh season ended. "He labored over every detail. Sometimes that's a personal asset, and sometimes it's a liability when it becomes so difficult you can't work anymore. He was worn out, and the show was running on its own momentum in terms of the writers. I wish him nothing but success and happiness."

Without Larry there to go painstakingly over every line of dialogue written by the staff, Jerry wouldn't have the time to write the weekly monologues that had bracketed the beginning and end of the show. "I'm going to develop a little different style of writing the show," Seinfeld said. "I'm not going to do any stand-up. . . . With Larry gone, it's a one-parent family now. I have more responsibility and more writing to do. I won't be doing anything next season I haven't already been doing, but without Larry there, I have more of it to do."

REGARDLESS of the changes made to accommodate Larry's departure, there was no replacing his creative input or his knack for guiding the development and use of secondary characters. One of the strengths of the show had always been the unique portraits it painted of the peripheral characters and the *Seinfeld* universe in which they lived, much of which came from Larry's comic palette. Even nonfictional characters got his distinctive treatment. Among them was such as his play on Yankees owner George Steinbrenner, for whom Larry supplied the voice when George's character worked for the baseball organization.

"I grew up in Sheepshead Bay in Brooklyn, and I've always loved the Yankees and was a huge Mickey Mantle fan," Larry says. "It was a kid's fantasy that if you couldn't play center field for the Yankees, maybe you could work for them in some capacity.

"I don't know the man, but from seeing him interviewed on television and seeing his quotes in newspaper stories, I came up with this version of the way he speaks, going on and on from one topic to another almost without stopping to take a breath."

Other than Jerry's apartment, the characters' main place to meet, hang out, and converse is the fictional restaurant Monk's. The coffee-shop venue was with the series from almost the beginning, primarily because that's the kind of place Larry hung out in with friends during his struggling comic days.

The inspiration for Monk's is an Upper West Side eatery called Tom's Restaurant, located a few blocks south of Columbia University and easily identifiable by its distinctive neon sign. Known for its chicken gyros and shish kebabs, Tom's has been made famous in song as well. Suzanne Vega is said to have been so inspired by the place that she wrote the song "Tom's Diner" in its honor.

The employees have occasionally expressed displeasure that *Seinfeld* wasn't so direct in its homage; by not using the name, the show deprived restaurant of invaluable free publicity. As it is, though, enough people are aware of Tom's history to make it a tourist destination for many *Seinfeld* fans visiting Manhattan.

Throughout its run, *Seinfeld* developed a stable of one-time and recurring characters quite unlike any found in other series. The Bubble Boy, Crazy Joe Davola, David Puddy, Mickey Abbott, J. Peterman, and Bania each added a unique and specific flavor to the *Seinfeld*ian casserole.

Often overlooked but pivotal in many episodes and to the overall development of the George and Jerry characters are their parents. The Costanzas were played by Estelle Harris and Jerry Stiller, while Liz Sheridan and Barney Martin assumed the roles of the more sedate Seinfelds.

Harris and Stiller painted the Costanzas—mother from hell, cloying father—in broad strokes, but grounded reality enough in to remind many people of their own parents. Off camera, Stiller and Harris often kept up the blustery banter for the benefit of others, but the bickering was strictly for show. "We like each other," Harris said of her relationship with Stiller. "We enjoy working together—although it seems everybody loves to see us screaming."

Outgoing, seemingly bursting with energy, and possessing a distinctive voice, which she used to shrieking proportions on the show, Estelle Harris relished being recognized as the mother of television's most notable neurotic. "At the supermarket, people will come up and say, 'Are you George's mother?' Then when I open my mouth, they know. People remember my shows and quote back stuff to me all the time."

Harris tried to explain the source of George's parents' constant mania. "Here's what I think. She married the first man who asked her, and they're not well-suited at all, which is why they're always shouting at one another. She would like to brag about George, but he hasn't given her much to brag about. Even when he gets a good job, she knows he's going to fuck it up eventually."

Jerry Stiller, whose longtime comedy partner and wife is Anne Meara, said he saw some of himself in his television son. "I was very much like George when I was his age. I had no balance. When you think about George, this is a guy who had a mission. He's not Generation X, he's generation Why? My father probably behaved toward me the same way Frank behaves toward George, giving him plenty of leeway."

The fictional Seinfeld parents are the opposite of the Costanzas, loving parents who let their son live his own life without much interference. Martin's Morty Seinfeld is a bit of a bumbler who still worries about his son's earning potential. Helen is particularly pragmatic, often assuming the voice of reason.

"I remember the first time I met Jerry's real mom, Betty," Sheridan said. "We got along wonderfully. I told her she had raised a wonderful son and that she should be proud."

Off camera, she noted, Jerry was fascinated by her youthful romance with James Dean. "One day out of the blue, Jerry came over and said, 'So, you were a friend of James Dean, huh?' Every once in a while, he'll ask me if I have any good stories about Dean."

Indeed she does. Enough to fill a book, which she is currently writing. In it, she plans to recount the romance she had with the idol when they were both struggling actors in 1952. "It was the first love for both of us, so it was very magical," says the actress, who worked on Broadway for years before coming west and becoming a mainstay on television, in series such as *Alf* and *Melrose Place*. They later lived together, but the relationship eventually drifted apart as work took him to Los Angeles. "He was being hauled away into this career, and I couldn't follow him."

Sheridan enjoyed working on *Seinfeld*. Her only complaint: "I wish I had more to do on it. The parents are only peripheral characters so you never know how much you'll work in the course of the year. But it's nice to be associated with a show like this."

Of all of the characters presented on *Seinfeld*, surely none touched more nerves than the restaurateur introduced in *"The Soup Nazi."* The character was based on Al Yeganeh, who runs the very popular and well known Soup Kitchen International on West 55th Street in Manhattan.

The Kitchen—which is strictly takeout—rated number fourteen in the 1998 Zagat New York City Restaurant Survey. It specializes in homemade soups that sell for $6 to $13. However, Yeganeh is also famous for his brusque manner and impatience with indecisive customers, which results in his dismissive call of "No soup for you!" In the episode, "The Soup Nazi," played by Larry Thomas, terrorizes Elaine for not being able to decide quickly enough which soup she wants.

The episode proved such a success that several articles appeared after the fact about Yeganeh and his soups. The soup maker was not pleased. "I never look at who is good or bad. I just do my work," he said.

Yeganeh also claimed the notoriety hurt his business, because the time he had to spend dealing with all the media attention affected the quality of his soup making. "Soup is holy," he said in complete earnestness. "I'm like a heart surgeon. I'm a pilot. My conscience has to be as clean as any doctor or any surgeon who has your life in their hands."

Yeganeh also gave several interviews denouncing the use of the word "Nazi," declaring the word "is never funny." Although Seinfeld has said on many occasions that comedy should take no prisoners, he broke with his own practice and sought out Yeganeh to apologize for offending him by using "Nazi" to describe the character. The soup maker reported, "For three minutes he just kept saying 'I'm sorry,' and I just kept cursing him."

Wayne Knight, who played the ever-annoying Newman, is the perfect example of a classic character actor: he works constantly, is never the leading man, doesn't get the girl, and dies before the movie is over. Although he's a familiar face, the majority of people don't know his real name.

But after Knight joined *Seinfeld* in the third season as Jerry's snarky postal nemesis, they certainly knew what to call him. These days when he strolls down the street, he's still likely to be greeted by a steady, and slightly hostile, chorus of "Hellooo, *New*man" from otherwise smiling strangers. "People don't recognize me. They recognize Newman. Don't get me wrong. I like playing Newman. I just don't like *being* Newman," Knight commented while the show was in production.

"When people see me, they feel like they can come over and say, 'Hello, Newman,' because everyone knows somebody like Newman. And as long as they don't get *too* loud, I don't mind. Actually, it makes me feel like I must do a pretty good job, because they all seem to really hate me. The only time I do mind it is when my mother does it. She'll say, 'And this is my son . . . Newman,'" he laughed.

Although Newman, whose first name was never revealed, is Wayne's signature role, the forty-one-year-old actor has a career that ranges far beyond the world of *Seinfeld,* including roles in *Jurassic Park* as the dastardly dinosaur-egg stealing Nedry, in *Space Jam* with Michael Jordan, opposite Nicole Kidman in *To Die For,* and as the voice of Tantor, the elephant in Disney's upcoming animated version of *Tarzan.*

Little did Knight's mother know that what started as impressions of Huntley and Brinkley and John F. Kennedy in the living room would eventually lead to a steady career, fame, and fortune. Although born in New York City, Wayne grew up in the small town of Cartersville, Georgia (pop. 12,000) after his parents, who worked in women's apparel, were relocated.

Knight has a tendency to deflect personal questions with a quip. When asked what it was like growing up in the rural South, he answers with typical comic flippancy, "It was always hard to tell my friends that my dad was in ladies' underwear."

As the only child of two working parents, Wayne necessarily spent a lot of time on his own. As it had been for Jerry, television became his constant companion and primary source of entertainment. "I was so into TV, I would just soak it up," he told an interviewer. "And by the time I was in kindergarten, I had already gotten the bug to act. So I started doing impressions of people I saw on TV and would perform for my parents and their friends. I had a good five minutes that I would do for the cocktail hour."

However, Wayne sensed that his desire to be an actor would not be well received in Cartersville's conservative, rural community, so he kept those ambitions a closely guarded secret until he was in high school. "I prepared for acting by failing at all high school athletics," he says dryly. "Then, finally, I was cast in a play at the local community theater. I remember the first time I went backstage because there were all these people making out with each other and I thought, 'This life is for me!' "

Wayne attended college at the University of Georgia, majoring, he says, in "theater and beer." After doing enough regional theater to earn his Equity card, he moved to New York. Within a year he had landed his first Broadway show, Albert Innaurato's comedy *Gemini,* one of the longest-running plays in Broadway history with 1,788 performances.

"I played a socially retarded kid with a fifty-four-inch padded waist and a fascination for subway transfers," Knight recalls. "I did that for three years, because once a young actor gets on Broadway, you don't want to leave. And doing that play for eight shows a week, year after year, is where I really learned to act."

Despite having been showcased in a popular play, Knight hit a career lull after the show closed. He found work, but it wasn't steady enough to make a living. Rather than go on unemployment between acting jobs, Knight instead moonlighted as a private investigator, a profession much less glamorous than movies and fiction would have us believe.

"It was not an exciting line of work," he says with pointed understatement. "The agency where I worked did background investigations on people, and I did a lot of surveillance stuff, but I never carried a gun or anything."

When he wasn't tracking down vendors selling fake Rolexes on the streets of New York, Knight was building up his resumé on projects like *Salted Nuts,* a series he shot in London opposite Emma Thompson, who remains one of his closest friends. When each acting job ended, he went back to being a gumshoe, a cycle that continued for five long years.

"I remember standing outside this woman's apartment one Saturday night in Brooklyn at three in the morning, while the rain came down on me, and a three-legged dog hopped by," he recalls. "I thought to myself, 'I gotta get out of this!' "

The owner of the detective agency agreed; tired of Knight's frequent absences, he fired him. With his career as a PI finally over, Knight moved to California, where he quickly found work, including roles in *Dirty Dancing, Born on the Fourth of July, JFK,* and *Basic Instinct,* in which he played one of the San Francisco cops mesmerized by Sharon Stone's famous leg-crossing in the interrogation scene. "In truth, Sharon wasn't there when they filmed the reaction shots," Knight admits. "She was having a cup of coffee someplace, so I was sitting there using my fabulous sense-memory."

Then came *Seinfeld.* Originally Knight was supposed to appear in a single episode, but producers liked using his abrasive Newman characterization as a foil for Jerry. They kept inviting him back until he became a permanent part of the series' universe, albeit one carefully meted out in small doses. "I don't think anyone could stomach the character on a full-time basis or even for a full episode, because a little Newman goes a long way," Knight said. "It would be like having a steady diet of jalapeño peppers."

While he was obviously grateful for the exposure the series gave him, there was also a surprising downside to his *Seinfeld* association. Knight says it has become harder for him to get jobs in feature films because producers worry he's now *too* recognizable as Newman. Television executives, though, have no such concerns. Beginning last season, Knight became a recurring character on another NBC series, *3rd Rock From the Sun,* playing Officer Don, making him the only actor currently appearing on two different Top Twenty shows.

In May 1996, Wayne married Paula Sutor, a makeup artist he had met three years earlier while both were working on the movie *The Second Half.* The ceremony was held at Michael Richards's Italian villa–style home in Pacific Palisades, California, in front of ninety family members and friends, including his *Seinfeld* castmates, who gave him a standing ovation as he kissed the bride.

Marriage apparently agrees with Knight. Since the nuptials, his career has been on an upswing, and he's also lost close to fifty pounds on a serious diet he started shortly before the wedding. "I've had food obsessions my entire life," he recently told a reporter. "I was the only child of an Italian mother who cooked for a family of eight even though I was the only one at home. I've been trying to lose weight for twenty-five years. I'd lose a few pounds and then suddenly get amnesia and pack it all back on. I always seemed to be at my biggest waistline whenever I was in a big movie. But when I was bigger than my dinosaur costars in *Jurassic Park,* I made weight loss a real priority."

Knight was also aware that his portly size had significantly limited his career. "When you get typed as a fat, funny guy, you also become the killer—a gluttonous, murderous guy. You play either end of the spectrum, so what you have to do is work your way to the middle. I'll still be the schleppy character guy, though, and that's okay."

But a *wealthy* schleppy character guy. In 1997, Knight signed a three-year, $2 million television deal with Carsey-Werner Productions to develop his own series. In addition, he appeared in nine episodes in *Seinfeld*'s ninth season—at a reported $60,000 per show.

Interestingly, though his moment to shine has arrived, Knight seems increasingly ambivalent over the prospect of being prime time's newest leading man. NBC publicist, Melissa Herald, explains that Wayne genuinely dislikes too much attention shone in his direction. "If Wayne thinks something is going to make too big a deal about him, he doesn't want any part of it and shies away. He the one celebrity who really doesn't like talking about himself. He's always been that way."

"I enjoy being just the third suit to the left," he admits. "I find being a character actor a great thing, in that I have never had a desire to hear people say, 'There goes Wayne Knight.' Right now I'm in the best place. People recognize me, they like me, they say, 'Hey, Newman' or now even sometimes 'Hello, Wayne' but don't bother me."

NOW THAT he was the sole chief cook in the *Seinfeld* kitchen, it was Jerry's turn to blend together these disparate characters who resided in the series' world and use them as skillfully as Larry had—as accents and flavoring, not the main course. It would prove to be a trickier recipe than Jerry might have anticipated.

18

Alone at the Top

ALTHOUGH LARRY DAVID HAD MOVED ON, HE HADN'T COMPLETELY LEFT *Seinfeld*. According to people familiar with the production, Larry had left behind story outlines and ideas for scripts that he had never gotten around to developing, so the eighth season still carried a remnant of the David sensibility. The only problem was, nobody could develop a Larry David idea like Larry David.

Some of the episodes showed signs of flair, such as "The Little Kicks," in which Elaine's terrible dancing is revealed, or "The Bizarro Jerry," in which Elaine makes friends with three guys who are the exact opposite of Jerry, George, and Kramer. While not particularly groundbreaking, the shows were still funny and the performances crisp and expertly defined. But there was a noticeable difference in the tone; *Seinfeld* seemed to have lost a certain edge, a certain comic darkness.

Kenny Kramer thought the reason was fairly obvious. "Look, Larry is dark," he explained. "Insidious depravity is the human element he loves to examine, the worst parts of nice people. That's what guided the show when he was there. Jerry is not really a dark guy. It's just not him. So what's being experienced now on the show is a different comic sensibility. It's not that one is funnier than the other, they're just grounded differently."

In fact, few viewers seemed to notice the difference, or if they did, they didn't care. *Seinfeld* continued to be the highest-rated comedy, even if it wasn't necessarily the most honored. Kelsey Grammer's

Frasier was suddenly the comedy of choice for Emmy voters, but *Seinfeld* didn't need awards, because it had reputation, expectation, and the hallowed Thursday night time slot going for it.

To the casual viewer, *Seinfeld* looked and felt the same as it always had. To Jerry, proving he could carry on without missing any of Larry David's beats was a source of satisfaction. The first months of the 1996–97 season ran so smoothly, and Seinfeld was so enjoying his new single-parent role, that he decided to continue with the show for at least another year. Nobody was more surprised than his costars.

Prior to the season, Julia Louis-Dreyfus had been particularly adamant: "Let me say it now. No ninth season. Next year I will finally feel like a high school senior, and that's exciting. It's a great job, believe me. But I have a lot on my plate from a family point of view, and I don't know how I'm going to pull it off this season. I'm actually very nervous about it."

After the announcement, Michael Richards admitted he, too, had thought the eighth season would be the last. "We were all set to end the show this year; we were folding up. But when we were around our eighteenth show, Jerry sat down with us and said, 'NBC wants to know what we want to do. What do you think?' I was amazed that all of us said basically the same thing, which was 'We're having a great time, we don't see any cracks in the hull, so let's keep going.' "

NBC was so grateful that it said thank you to Seinfeld with a *really* big check. The fabled Brink's truck backed up to Jerry's house and unloaded an astonishing contract that called for him to make $1 million per episode for the 1997–98 season. (The year after *Seinfeld* won the Emmy for Best Comedy Series, Larry David had held out for the 1993–94 season in order to *double* his salary to $125,000 an episode.)

The network's opening the vault so wide confirmed just how valuable the show was to NBC—and anybody else with profit participation, a fact not lost on Jerry's three costars. *Seinfeld* went into syndication in the summer of 1995 and immediately turned Larry David and Jerry into mega millionaires. Although its $3 million per episode fee fell short of the all-time record set by *The Cosby Show*'s $4.7 million, that was still enough to eventually fetch Jerry, as a creator of the show, an estimated extra $40 million out of the $1 billion in overall syndication revenues the series stood to earn.

Columbia TriStar Television Distribution President Barry Thurston noted, "From an advertiser side, *Seinfeld* is probably the most sought-after show which has ever hit the syndication market."

The almost unimaginable sums of money being generated by *Seinfeld* naturally made the other cast members feel a bit short-changed. "It's a bone of contention," Alexander admitted in 1996, "but that's how the deal was done."

Being cut out of the syndication profits was a bitter pill, but one that could be justified considering that Jerry and Larry had created the and molded it from its inception. However, when word leaked out that Seinfeld's actor's salary alone would double to $1 million per episode in the 1996–97 season, money suddenly became a major issue. The dissatisfaction felt by Louis-Dreyfus, Alexander, and Richards over what they felt were unfair contracts would soon become a potential series-buster.

There had always been a discrepancy between Jerry's acting salary and those of his costars, which in itself was not unusual; stars get paid more than costars. However, in the case of *Seinfeld,* the costars were uniquely important to the series. Additionally, as the years went by, the salary disparity seemed to increase.

An NBC document dated May 1991 listed these salaries for the cast and principal members of the production team per episode for the 1991–92 season:

Jerry Seinfeld	$41,667
Jason Alexander	$30,250
Julia Louis-Dreyfus	$30,000
Michael Richards	$16,500
Larry David	$35,000
Larry Charles	$10,000
Tom Cherones	$17,500

In 1994, *Seinfeld*'s costars agreed to negotiate their contracts collectively under what is called a "favored nation" basis, which simply means that what one got, they all got. Obviously, the person who gained the most from this arrangement was Michael Richards, who had been the lowest paid because he didn't have the credits that Alexander and Louis-Dreyfus had when they joined the show.

A 1995 deal memo from Castle Rock to NBC shows that Jerry was to be paid $4.2 million as an actor for twenty-two episodes, roughly $200,000 a show, in the 1995–96 season. (He was also paid a bonus of $5 million, which was due May 28, 1996.) Each of the three costars was to be paid $125,000 per episode for the same season. The memo also notes that Alexander, Richards, and Louis-Dreyfus were locked into a salary of $150,000 per episode for the 1996–97 season, should there be one.

So when NBC made Seinfeld, for the moment, the highest-paid performer on television (until Tim Allen one-upped him by negotiating a $1.25 million per episode deal with ABC to return for his eighth season, up from $750,000), his costars balked and decided to play hardball.

The ultimatum came just days after reports of Jerry's new $1 million an episode contract for the ninth season was leaked to the press. NBC was thrown into shock when the united front of Louis-Dreyfus, Alexander, and Richards made a very simple, straightforward demand: pay *us* $1 million per episode or *we* won't be back for a ninth season.

At that point, each of the three actors was contracted to be paid approximately $150,000 per episode, a respectable $3.6 million a year—but it couldn't compare to Jerry's $1 million per episode, not to mention his percentage of syndication profits. Jerry's costars also knew that the time to make up some of that salary discrepancy was running out: most industry insiders felt that the show had perhaps two seasons left before Jerry would walk away.

While asking for $1 million an episode might have smacked of pure avarice to some, for the performers it was security against an uncertain future and compensation for being part of a uniquely successful show. "I sometimes worry that this is just a magical illusion and that it will all go up one day in a puff of smoke," Jason Alexander once explained. "I'm convinced in the great Jewish Guilt way that this will all end. The series will go off the air, nobody will hire me, we'll run out of money, and I'll spend my last years wandering around morosely asking, 'Do you remember . . . ?'

"It's happened to other people. Think of Carroll O'Connor when he was the star of *All in the Family*, which was the *Seinfeld* of its day. He was phenomenally good on it, but when the show ended he became, as far as I can see, a pariah for years. Why? Because to the world he was Archie Bunker and they wouldn't accept him as anything else. He had to wait a generation for that image to be cleared out of everybody's heads before he could get on with his life. When you're in a show that makes that much of an impression, you never know what'll happen to you next."

The *Seinfeld* salary dispute came in the wake of another closely watched financial mutiny. Prior to the start of the previous season, the cast of *Friends* had decided they didn't like the terms of their five-year contracts—which they had willingly enough agreed to sign when cast in the series—and demanded new ones. After a couple of tense months, during which they maintained a united front, the actors successfully cowed NBC into paying them each $75,000 per episode instead of the originally contracted $40,000.

Of course, not every holdout works. Television is full of examples of actors overplaying their cards. Consider Suzanne Somers, who demanded a huge raise during her *Three's Company* heyday only to find herself relegated to a cameo appearance at the end of each episode.

On the heels of the *Friends* negotiations, *New York Undercover* stars Malik Yoba and Michael DeLorenzo refused to show up for work and demanded raises to $75,000 per episode, more creative input, a gym, star trailers, and better food. The show's producer, Dick Wolf, responded by ordering his casting people to audition other actors to replace Yoba and DeLorenzo and filing a breach of contract suit against the pair. The actors were back to work within a week, given no choice but to honor the contract they had signed.

Wolf, who also produces NBC's *Law & Order,* was adamant that producers must stop capitulating to actors. "Deals *have* to stop being done this way," he said at the time. "It's going to destroy the industry."

Others, like Andy Kaplan, vice president of Sony Television Entertainment, which distributes the *Seinfeld* reruns, saw the *Seinfeld* situation as unique and not comparable to the circumstances of *Friends* or *New York Undercover.* "When a show becomes successful in syndication, actor renegotiations become fairly normal," Kaplan pointed out. "And *Seinfeld* is the number one comedy show on television. I don't think there will be an enormous ripple effect, because there isn't another number one show. It starts with network performance and network ad revenue. NBC makes a lot of money on the series, so it stands to reason that the talent will get whatever they want."

It was true: *Seinfeld* was a veritable cash cow, and the amount of money it was responsible for pouring into NBC's coffers was substantial. According to trade estimates, the network earned $150 million in advertising revenue each season from *Seinfeld,* meaning that even if NBC acquiesced and agreed to give everyone $1 million an episode, it would still turn a profit of $120 million.

There was another side of the argument, however, as illustrated by an article in *Daily Variety* discussing the vagrancy of network advertising revenue: "In the battle to keep the stars who bring in the viewers, the networks have been paying out huge sums of money to the casts of hit shows. Jerry Seinfeld, who, courtesy of NBC, now finds himself sixth on the *Forbes* money list of megabuck entertainers, turned nothing into a $98 million income last year.

"When they made pay-to-stay deals with stars like Seinfeld, the networks believed they could get the money back by upping ad rates. But Madison Avenue is balking at the plan, refusing to ante up big bucks for shows that have actually lost ratings.

"No show is immune. *Seinfeld,* still the top-earning show, saw its Nielsens drop 3 percent last season. This year, a thirty-second spot is a bargain at $525,000, compared to $550,000 a year ago. *ER,* down 4 percent, had ad rates falling to $475,000 down from $500,000, and *Friends,* whose high salaries are now guaranteed through the end of the century, dropped 10 percent in only its third season, reducing its rates drastically from $475,000 to $350,000. *3rd Rock From the Sun* only gets $200,000 a pop."

Even so, most industry analysts believed the negotiations would be settled fairly quickly because, as one television executive said, "I don't think NBC can afford to lose the show." But the salary demand put NBC in a bind beyond any immediate financial concerns. Once a salary door is opened, it is nearly impossible to shut it again anytime soon.

The network resisted for what to many was a good reason: to give in to the demand would be to set a potentially disastrous precedent—especially considering that lead actors such as David Duchovny of *The X-Files* and George Clooney of *ER* were making a scant, by comparison, $100,000 per episode. In the film industry, Jim Carrey's $20 million deal for the movie *Cable Guy* had proven that the bandwagon effect was real; the ink had barely dried on the contract before Arnold, Sylvester, Bruce, Tom, and all the other big-name movie stars announced they wouldn't work for one penny less than $20 million per picture. If the network brass opened their collective wallet for *Seinfeld,* many believed, it would inevitably lead other costars to line up wanting to make up their lack of syndication money to demand huge salary increases.

Another complicating factor was the behind-the-scenes politics involved. Castle Rock is owned by Time Warner, which also owns Warner Brothers Television, which at the time produced *Friends* and *ER*, two other major components of NBC's all-important Thursday night. Some at the network felt it was dangerous to give any one production company too much leverage. On the other hand, losing *Seinfeld* the series would be a disaster, both financially and in terms of public relations.

Initially, NBC offered the trio $250,000 each per episode which was flatly and quickly rejected, as was $300,000 per week. For several months, there was a tense standoff, as the network pondered its options and the actors dug their heels in. To the surprise of many, the stalemate lingered on.

When asked about the negotiations, Warren Littlefield stated the obvious but offered no insight: *"Seinfeld* has clearly established that it is *extremely* valuable to us and to the people who own the negatives."

By the time May came, the situation was critical. NBC needed to announce its fall lineup by May 12, and the network affiliates were anxious to know that *Seinfeld* would be back on their schedules. For the first time, the prospect of the show not returning began to seem shockingly possible, even to the actors. Although Louis-Dreyfus and Alexander consistently refused to comment, Richards finally vented.

"When it was reported that the cast members were demanding a million dollars per episode to return, I was worried that people were going to look at us as nothing more than a bunch of greedy pigs who were trying to hold everybody up and didn't care whether the show came back or not," he said. "And that wasn't the case at all. It's just that, in view of how successful the show has become, we needed to be a part of that. It's the same as with sports salaries. You see these great players making so much money and go, 'How can they be worth that?' Then when you start to think of what these teams generate in revenue, you begin to understand. Well, we're the Chicago Bulls of television.

"Besides, it's been a long haul, and there have been a lot of times when there wasn't much money coming in at all during my career. I never came into this for the money; that's always been the icing on the cake. Still, this is a lot of icing.

"But money *is* an issue. And I say that because I'm worth every penny for what I've brought to the show. I've worked hard for eight years. If they want to go another year, I need some compensation. I'm not on the syndication side of the show. I don't own. I don't have points. I don't have anything. And while I've invested eight years of my time, everyone has gotten enormously wealthy from the show. And I haven't—not to the point where I could let five or six years go by and go off and work at the Steppenwolf Theater [in Chicago; alumnae include Laurie Metcalf, John Mahoney, and John Malkovich, among other notables] for two or three years. The money buys time for an artist, and I'd like to have some of that time."

Richard kept his sharpest comments for the network. "NBC has kept everybody dangling. They should say yea or nay, tell us what they want to do or don't want to do. I'm stalled right now, in a position where I don't know whether I should go ahead and commit to certain things or not. I'm sitting here waiting, and I don't like that. Why couldn't the network at least have the common decency, after everything we've done, to just let us know?"

At one point, NBC considered giving Seinfeld a huge chunk of stock in General Electric, the network's parent company, so that he could turn around and give it to his costars. That idea was eventually dismissed as unworkable.

With May 12 approaching, the situation was so uncertain that NBC was forced to draw up two schedules, one with *Seinfeld* and one without. The plan was to move *Frasier* to *Seinfeld*'s time slot if an agreement with the cast could not be reached.

Even other networks began to believe the unthinkable might actually happen. When NBC Entertainment President Warren Littlefield said dryly, "Our peers said, 'We'd pay them a million,' " he wasn't kidding.

Bill Burke, president of the TBS Superstation, admitted that his cable network was ready to offer the cast of *Seinfeld* $1 million per episode each in the hope of getting Seinfeld to agree to let his show air on cable for a season. "We were able to find room in our budget to accommodate *Seinfeld*," he acknowledged later. "With a show like that, the audience that we expected to move from NBC to a cable network was significant, and it was something that we were very interested in pursuing."

What most surprised the so-called experts was the costars' apparent determination to walk away from the $300,000 offer. The consensus of belief within the industry was that their salaries would plummet after they left *Seinfeld* and that none of them would be likely of them to receive more than $75,000 per episode to star in a new TV show.

According to sources familiar with the negotiations, the most obstinate holdout was Julia Louis-Dreyfus, with Jason Alexander running a close second. When the next offer, of $400,000, was refused the week before the lineup was announced, it was time for the network brass to do some serious soul-searching, led by NBC president Robert Wright and General Electric chairman Jack Welch. "We were close to burying this show," said the source.

Finally, just days before the May 12 deadline, Richards, Alexander, and Louis-Dreyfus struck an agreement with NBC to return for $600,000 each per episode, which worked out to $13.2 million each for the season. For the money, NBC got a two-year contract extension from each of the three actors.

"We're extremely pleased that *Seinfeld,* the show about nothing that means everything to viewers nationwide, will be with NBC for another year," crowed a visibly relieved Littlefield. "With the cooperation of Castle Rock Entertainment, and all the other profit participants on the show, we were able to construct an agreement that was financially acceptable to all parties and would allow the show to remain on our primetime schedule."

The $13 million–plus annual salary was greeted with both support and shock. Everybody seemed to have an opinion. House Speaker Newt Gingrich said that if NBC could afford to pay the *Seinfeld* costars collectively close to $50 million a year, the networks could afford to air antidrug commercials for free: "We need to go to the networks and say, 'No, we're not going to buy advertising. Donate it.' When the networks can give $600,000 a show to three stars in the same half hour, the networks can give every single ad we need to communicate with our kids, and they ought to do it as citizens, because Americans have been pretty darn good to the networks."

The reaction from other members of the *Seinfeld* cast was more supportive. "I would be more concerned about the many more actors who make only $2,000 a year than the few who rise to the top of their profession," commented Jerry Stiller, who said he was satisfied with the money he was earning. "I'm making more money doing three shows than Joe DiMaggio made in a year. I get what I deserve.

I'm very fortunate at this point in my life to find myself on the tail of a comet, as this show is. I asked for a fair amount of money and they gave it to me."

Estelle Harris also supported their stance. "I've been given raises, too, but only if we ask and fight for them. I don't know anybody who's ever happy with what they're getting, unless they're getting $600,000 per episode."

Not surprisingly, the *Seinfeld* agreement seemed to make other stars of shows start reevaluating their own perceived worth. Drew Carey, Della Reese, and Suzanne Somers (this time for *Step by Step)* all demanded significant salary increases to stay with their respective shows. Even though Carey is cocreator of his series and thereby entitled to profit participation, he said he expected a new deal to be negotiated after his original five-year contract was up—or else: "I'm not going back for the deal I have now. They'll have to back up the money truck for me to stay or I'll be on the first bus back to Cleveland."

Those negotiations, however, were someone else's problems. For Jerry and his costars, it was time to put the salary dispute behind them and go back to work. The only concern felt by anyone involved with the show was that there might be a temporary viewer backlash, fueled by the massive amounts of money that had been argued over.

But as the 1997–98 season began, *Seinfeld*'s ratings were as strong as ever and NBC looked certain to finish as the number one network again, based solely on its huge ratings advantage on Thursday nights.

In September, *Seinfeld* got some welcome free publicity from a very unexpected source—the medical journal *Catheterization and Cardiovascular Diagnosis*. According to a letter written to the journal by a trio of neurologists, doctors had linked a condition involving a drop in blood pressure and fainting with people watching *Seinfeld*. They dubbed it the *"Seinfeld* Syncope," ("syncope" refers to fainting.)

The physicians claimed they first noticed the phenomenon in a sixty-two-year-old man who would pass out while laughing at *Seinfeld*. Once, the man blacked out face down in his dinner plate and had to be rescued by his wife. According to Dr. Andrew Eisenhauer, the man experienced *Seinfeld* Syncope "almost uniformly after hysterical laughter." The primary object of his hysteria was the character of George.

Actually, the man's spells resulted from diminished blood flow to the brain caused by several blocked arteries, but the association with the sitcom made the story newsworthy. When told his show now had a medical condition named after it, Jerry said he was both flattered and amused. He indicated they would try to incorporate *Seinfeld* Syncope into an episode somehow.

One interesting caveat was largely overlooked in the media coverage. Dr. Eisenhauer commented that his patient hadn't fainted once while watching the new ninth-season episodes. "Either we fixed him," quipped the doctor, "or the show's no longer funny."

For many fans and critics, the doctor's comment was no joke. Although the question of whether the series was losing its comic edge had been asked before, this time the buzz turned into a roar. *Los Angeles Times* Pulitzer Prize–winning television critic Howard Rosenberg—a longtime devoted *Seinfeld* fan—commented in a November 1997 column that the show had served up "four consecutive bummers. The cheap one-liners are more frequent, the comedy broader."

His assessment merely gave voice to a growing sentiment that the show was settling into being just another sitcom. The criticism was further fueled by a reader's poll conducted by the *New York Post*. IS SEINFELD STILL GREAT? the paper breathlessly asked, while noting that "even followers are expressing disappointment in this season." In response to the poll, a majority of fans thought the show was losing its edge; 52 percent expressed mild displeasure, although the other 48 percent thought the show remained brilliant.

Surprisingly, Seinfeld felt compelled to respond. He not only defended the show but asked viewers not to judge an entire season on the basis of the first few episodes—perhaps a tacit admission that the shows aired so far had not lived up to his own expectations. "I've done seven episodes already, but only four have aired. I think four episodes this season doesn't seem like a fair sampling out of a twenty-four-episode season. I think most television seasons go that way. It takes a few weeks to get back on track, get back into it. I am extremely proud of every episode we have done this season.

"With the next three coming out, I feel like we've really taken off. They're so totally unique and original. There's no accounting for personal taste, but the next few episodes are all different, and that's what makes this show work. Every week you have no idea what you're in for. Most shows have a certain formula, but we try to keep it unexpected.

"I have to be honest with you, I was so flattered that the show is even worthy of a poll. That we are still able to provoke such strong reactions from the press and our audience is amazing. That people actually think about *Seinfeld* or give enough of a damn to actually answer a question like that is the highest compliment to me."

Predictably, NBC's Warren Littlefield dismissed the notion that the general viewer was displeased with the show: "We listen to the audience, not to what critics have written. The show goes where no one else dares. If they continued exactly as in year five, we wouldn't be in year nine."

The reality was, however, that the series had again suffered the loss of some important behind-the-scenes personnel. After season eight, consulting producers Tom Gammill and Max Pross left to pursue their own development deal, and co–executive producer Peter Mehlmen (formerly a writer) accepted his own development deal at DreamWorks SKG.

Mehlmen downplayed his importance to the show. "Larry David was the only person who was basically irreplaceable," he said, then defended *Seinfeld* against the criticism being leveled at it. "I don't see *any* other show held to the same kind of standard."

But the criticism had obviously touched a nerve with the most important person involved. Never before had Jerry been confronted with evidence that fans of the show saw it as slipping, as becoming *ordinary*. It obviously gave him pause. "I don't know about these shows that become little businesses," he mused. "You will definitely not see us trying to wring out one last year from this thing. Watching these others decline is horrible. It's like cancer. I'd rather just get a heart attack and go."

One critic rather lyrically expressed a heartfelt desire to see the show go out strong: "Maybe the rise and fall of *Seinfeld* is the natural order of things. An original voice is heard singing in a crowd. This voice is lifted up, influencing those around it, and then disappears again. When *Seinfeld* does make its final exit, it should be remembered as one of the most innovative and hysterical sitcoms ever. Hopefully, its producers will also be remembered for knowing when to say, 'Enough is enough.' "

Jerry was obviously thinking along those same lines. Although it had become traditional for Seinfeld to hem and haw over whether or not he'd be returning for one more year, in late 1997 those musings carried an unmistakable tone of finality: "The decision is made in December. It's a very philosophical question. I just don't know what I'm going to do yet. Just because you're going well doesn't mean you should continue. I want to go out feeling this way. It's important for me to go out in full blazing color. Most shows don't time it right. Almost any show you can name has waited too long. . . .

"If people are not terribly upset when we go off," he said, "I will have judged it wrong."

19

Sayonara, Jerry

JERRY'S DECISION WASN'T SUPPOSED TO BE MADE PUBLIC UNTIL JANUARY, BUT on Christmas Day 1997, the *New York Times* broke the blockbuster news: Jerry was quitting and taking *Seinfeld* with him. The current season, the show's ninth, would be its last. And that was final.

Judging from the way journalists were scrambling to find out more details, one would have thought the government had been overthrown. The ballyhoo was intensified by the timing of the announcement: because the Christmas–New Year's week is a traditionally a very slow one for news, there wasn't much else for magazines and newspaper to talk about. That was evidenced by *People* magazine's cover headline, SAY IT AIN'T SO!

Of course, that was exactly the mood in the plush suites of corporate NBC. Besides being extremely unhappy about Jerry's decision, the network executives were also upset that the story had been leaked so soon. There were some who naively believed that they might have changed Jerry's mind given more time, but now that the word was out, he'd never capitulate.

In reality, nobody could have changed his mind. "I hate petering out," Jerry explained. "When I first started my career, I would watch *The Tonight Show,* and the first shot a comedian would have would be this huge, electrifying thing. And then, two or three appearances later, they would run out of material and start to peter out. I just hated watching that happen. It was just a slow withering of inspiration. It was always my ambition not to do that."

Although he had often talked about pulling the plug in the past, it had become clear in recent months that the possibility that he'd follow through was greater than it ever had been. For one thing, he seemed to be getting worn down emotionally.

"I don't really live here," he said, referring to his house. "I get home at ten. I'm asleep by ten-thirty. I get up at six, have a little exercise, then I'm back at the office. I'm not out in the world. I missed the whole nineties. I don't know what happened. I have no life. This show has overwhelmed my life completely. It's not healthy. Having a show named after you, and you're the star, is supposed to be this great thing, but I have trouble handling it at times. I wake up in the morning with a start and go, 'Ohmigod.' It's always been like that. It's a lot of weight."

NBC was acutely aware of this and was waging a no-holds-barred campaign to woo Jerry back for just one more season. There were sound business reasons to do whatever it would take. The first was purely financial: NBC made an estimated $500 million in 1997, and *Seinfeld* contributed some 40 percent of that total. Another reason was that having the number-one-rated comedy brought prestige to the network. Finally, *Seinfeld* was gold when it came to helping new comedies get a ratings foothold. Many of the sitcoms currently on the network's primetime schedule had been nurtured in the time slot following *Seinfeld*.

NBC knew *Seinfeld* would end eventually, but it wanted to squeeze one more season out of Jerry if it could. Not all of their appeals set well with Jerry: "It was suggested to me by some executives, 'What if we did a survey of the public and asked them their opinion?' And I said, 'No, that's my job.' If you're the pilot of the plane, you don't ask the passengers what you should do next. The audience wants to feel that someone's in control.

"The whole system of television market research is ridiculous. That's your job. That's what being a creative person is. And if they don't like it, fine. But you don't try and hedge your bet. That's why primetime television stinks."

Although Jerry had always discussed the future of the show with his costars in their annual pre-Christmas powwow prior to the last taping in the calendar year, the only person's opinion that mattered in the end was Seinfeld's. When he decided it was time to go, the show was over.

"This was between me and the show," Jerry said. "I just know from being onstage for years and years and years, there's one moment where you have to feel the audience is still having a great time, and if you get off right there, they walk out of the theater excited. And yet, if you wait a little bit longer and try to give them more for their money, they walk out feeling not as good. If I get off now I have a chance at a standing ovation. That's what you go for. I felt the Moment. That's the only way I can describe it."

On December 17, he sat in his dressing room on the soundstage where *Seinfeld* was filmed and let Julia Louis-Dreyfus, Jason Alexander, and Michael Richards in on his decision. Jerry admits it was a difficult thing to tell them. One of the issues he'd had to weigh was the financial ramifications for his costars, but money was apparently not a deciding factor.

"They just started making good money last year, but they were generous enough to respect the timing of the curve," he said. Then he added, "Not that they could have talked me out of it, I don't think."

"There was no question in anybody's mind when the four of us sat down that it was time to go," agreed Alexander.

Michael Richards would later talk about how the sheer work load was beginning to be a factor. "I've been taking note of how everyone was working and the difficulties of maintaining the show each week. It was becoming work, real work, and we were losing our sense of play. After twelve episodes, Jerry was weary. To think about coming back and doing another year—he doubted he could. And he never wanted that weariness to affect the show. That was his greatest fear."

It was by all accounts an emotional discussion, but a positive one as well. "It was pretty heavy, pretty wild," Louis-Dreyfus recalled. "There were no tears shed, but there was a lot of heart-thumping."

Even though Jerry's mind was made up, he agreed to listen to NBC's last-ditch appeals. On the Sunday before Christmas, Seinfeld and his longtime managers, Howard West and George Shapiro, got together in New York City with Robert Wright, president and CEO of NBC, and Jack Welch, chairman and CEO of General Electric, NBC's parent company.

The meeting went on for two hours at Wright's apartment, and Seinfeld later admitted he was torn: "What made me want to come back was how much they believed in me. That was the sum and substance of our meetings. Because they know that's all I care about, the quality of the show. Jack Welch told me this was one of the products GE is most proud of. That affects me. I like that the people who own the show take pride in it."

At the end of the meeting, Jerry refrained from giving Wright and Wells a definite yes or no. He and his managers walked the streets of *Seinfeld*'s Upper West Side neighborhood while Jerry talked out his feelings. The three returned to L.A. that same evening without Seinfeld having made a final decision.

In the end, he would make his choice based on what was best for the show and its legacy. Hence NBC's reported offer of a mind-boggling $5 million per episode for a tenth season was never really a consideration—especially considering that his estimated 1997 earnings were in the neighborhood of $66 million.

"I don't really care about the money," Jerry has said repeatedly. "In my business, the only way you get as much money as I have is if you don't care about money and you care about comedy; then somehow you end up with money. I'm not the kind of person who could do a show and think, 'Well, we've kind of run out of gas here, but the money's great and the ratings are still good, so let's keep grinding them out.' It would break my heart."

On Christmas Eve, two days after his meeting with the executives, Seinfeld personally phoned Wright and told him there would be no tenth season. The news sent a palpable shock wave through the homes of the NBC executives who were subsequently called with the news. When the *New York Times* broke the news to the public at large, it also caught many of the *Seinfeld* cast, crew, and writing team completely off guard.

"The way I heard the show was ending was on the news, along with the rest of America," admitted Liz Sheridan. "It was a bit of a shock, but not a great one."

On the morning of December 26, 1997, NBC released a statement regarding Jerry's decision to bring his series to an end: "It's been an incredible nine years, and even now the show continues to break ratings records as viewers have made Thursday nights at 9:00 P.M. truly appointment television. To keep a show of this caliber at its peak is a great undertaking, and we respect Jerry's decision that at the end of this season, it's time to move on."

FOR MANY of the fans, and probably even some in the entertainment industry, it was inconceivable to end a series that still seemed creatively solid. Even if the show lacked the zing and bite of earlier seasons, it was still good television. Jerry understood the confusion many of the viewers felt: "If I was at home, watching the show as a fan, I would think, 'Why would he want to stop doing that? That looks like fun! So easy. Just lean against the kitchen counter, say a joke, and everyone laughs.'

"But there's a tremendous amount of paddling beneath the surface that you don't see. At this level, the amounts of money are huge—huge!—for everyone involved, and that translates into strong feelings. Because people gauge themselves by money. So you're dealing with primal forces of human nature, and the bigger the money, the bigger the forces. That's the stuff nobody knows about.

"I know the whole game. I know the agent's game, the network game, the producing game, the awards game, the negotiating game. I know what everybody's agenda is. I've had a seat at every table in the whole world of television."

Because of that knowledge, Jerry knew there would be a scramble in his wake. In financial terms, the end of *Seinfeld* would cost NBC an estimated $200 million annually in advertising revenue. It would also leave a huge programming hole to fill on Thursday nights. When *Cheers* went off the air, NBC gambled, and won, with the decision to replace it with upstart *Seinfeld*. Now, in the age of five hundred channels, it was even more important to find the right show to keep the network's all-important primetime Thursday juggernaut from slipping.

The leading candidates to replace *Seinfeld* were *Frasier, Friends, 3rd Rock From the Sun, Mad About You,* and newcomer *Just Shoot Me.* NBC would wait until May to make its decision, but in the end Warren Littlefield and his programming brain trust went for age and experience over young and fresh, naming *Frasier* the official *Seinfeld* heir apparent.

Some had thought that the network might rush a spinoff into production, but that was never a serious possibility, primarily because it would have to be approved by Seinfeld himself and the other executive producers. Beyond that, Louis-Dreyfus, Alexander, and Richards had all denied they would be interested, for both personal and professional reasons.

Alexander had already set up a TV production deal with Universal and was itching to get back to doing theater work, where he was out of the television public's eye. "Jason thinks it's important to take a few years out of the spotlight," a friend, TV writer Michael Markowitz, confirmed.

Richards wanted to concentrate on movies and on getting to play some non-Kramer characters.

Louis-Dreyfus was finally getting her wish to be an at-home mom to her two sons, Henry, five, and Charles, one. "While she enjoys acting," her half-sister Lauren Bowles said, "if she had to choose to do just one thing in her life, it would be motherhood."

Jerry's emotions would remain mixed throughout the remaining months of the show's life. "I'll miss these guys," he said in an interview, referring to his writing staff. "It's one of the things I'm sad about. But it's time to leave. My life is out of balance. I just want to have fun for a few years. In my imagination, my life after the show is so fantastic I don't even like to think about it."

"I couldn't tell you what motivates Jerry, what drives him," said Jason Alexander. "I think Jerry is very driven about this project because it's so much a part of him. His name has become a noun and a verb. It's so much a defining instrument of what he thinks is funny, what he thinks is important, what he wants to focus on. But if somebody said to me, 'Stand up and tell us what Jerry would do here, what Jerry would say here,' I couldn't do that. Because I don't know."

To Seinfeld, it was all about the luxury of freedom from work and responsibility. "I'm looking forward to saying things like, 'It's Sunday, I go for a drive on Sunday.' Or 'It's Sunday, I read the paper on Sunday.' It's so tantalizing that if I think about it I can't face going to work tomorrow. After I leave, I'm going into paradise. My life will begin again."

BEFORE he could start that new life, he had to play out his TV life. Now the most important thing was to come up with a fitting end to the series. For Jerry, that meant only one thing—to get Larry David back to write the series finale.

Of course, everybody had an opinion on how it should end, including Julia Louis-Dreyfus, who said if she had her way, the show would end with the grisly accidental deaths of all four main characters. "I don't think that's going to happen, but I can guarantee that we won't be hugging and misting up in the last episode."

Larry David concurred in that last thought. "The show's managed to survive for nine years without anybody hugging," he said. "The characters that we're writing never express any emotion, except probably anger. So I don't know how worked up we're gonna get."

"It's not a big thing," Seinfeld claimed. "It's the shoelace that comes undone in the men's room and touches the floor."

Not to NBC. It was going to milk the end of the series for every drop of promotion it could squeeze out. Between the network hype and the fan frenzy, in the months leading up to the May 14 final episode even a showman like P. T. Barnum would have blushed at the audaciousness of it all.

NBC began the *Seinfeld* countdown in March. Distraught Net-surfing fans commiserated with each other in overflowing chat rooms and on message boards dedicated solely to what the end of *Seinfeld* meant to the greater cosmos. There were auctions of *Seinfeld* memorabilia; *Seinfeld* viewing parties were being organized; nearly every newspaper and magazine in the country was honoring the series with near-reverential praise. People claimed to be suffering from depression at the thought of having no more original episodes.

NBC commandeered $2 million for one thirty-second block of commercial time during the final episode from Disney, while Budweiser, Coors, Fuji, and MasterCard each paid $1.9 million for its own thirty-second segments.

The cable network TV Land announced that in honor of the final episode of *Seinfeld* it would broadcast "nothing" between 9:00 and 10:00 P.M. on the night of May 14. "Nothing is more important than the last episode of *Seinfeld*," said the network's general manager, Larry Jones. "We think airing nothing is a fitting salute to a show about nothing. As *Seinfeld* is one of the greatest shows ever to air on television, TV Land is honored to preempt an hour of programming for this historic and monumental occasion."

Even Columbia-TriStar television got into the act, conducting a poll to learn the Top Ten episodes, which the company would then air in syndication, starting the week before the May 14 finale. The results:

10. "The Outing"
 9. "The Parking Garage"
 8. "The Marine Biologist"
 7. "The Opposite"
 6. "The Bubble Boy"
 5. "The Hamptons"

4. "The Pick"
3. "The Junior Mint"
2. "The Soup Nazi"
1. "The Contest"

Nothing was too over-the-top or overblown for NBC. Its analysts predicted that the final episode would be the most watched television event in history, outpacing the 60 share garnered by the final episode of *M*A*S*H*. Ironically, only Jerry seemed to care about the dangers of overpromotion and overexposure: "There are certain movies where the promotion is so well-coordinated and so pervasive that, before the movie comes out, I hate it, just because they're so good at telling me about it. They've done such a complete job of selling that it breeds resentment."

And that's exactly what the hype and hoopla surrounding the end of *Seinfeld* did. As the media feeding frenzy surged out of control fans expressed outrage at the mayor of New York's refusal to shut down traffic around Times Square for a *Seinfeld* viewing party, a few brave voices began to speak up.

Joss Whedon, creator of *Buffy the Vampire Slayer,* offered his thoughts: "It's the coldest show on TV. I understand that it is witty. But I never feel compelled to turn it on, because I don't care about these people. If I'm making the emotional connection to the person in the story, the person in the story could be an amoeba. The show is about disenfranchisement, the people nobody takes seriously."

"The closer the fateful date gets, the less tragic and traumatic it seems," said *Washington Post* TV critic Tom Shales. "Is it really going to be that hard to live without? To quote a frequent *Seinfeld* expression, '*I don't think so.*'"

Ron Rosenbaum, a TV columnist for the *New York Observer,* suggested starting a Can't Stand *Seinfeld* Society. "There is a vast, or at least substantial, minority of Americans, and not just New Yorkers, who find the insipid, overrated, timid, smug, insular, and self-satisfied sitcom just sets their teeth on edge. We get it, we just can't stand it," he wrote.

Even the comic strips got involved in the fray. In *Doonesbury,* the character B.D. said, "If there's anything our generation should have learned, it's that middle age and adolescence don't mix. It's no longer hip to be some whiny Boomer who never manages to get his life together! In fact, it's just plain pathetic!"

It's a sentiment Louis-Dreyfus could relate to: "I can guarantee that none of these characters, no matter how long we go on, will ever have any satisfaction in their lives, and if they do, it will be fleeting. You can bet that at sixty-five Elaine would be a bitter old drunk, hanging out in Jerry's apartment with the same furniture. Except maybe there'll be plastic on it."

As the shooting date for the final episode neared, speculation over what its final story line would be turned into obsession. All anyone knew was that the code name for the final episode was "A Tough Nut to Crack." Bogus scripts turned up on the Internet, reporters tried to bribe crew people, actors on the series were besieged with questions—all in vain.

Staff writer Jennifer Crittenden denied that the writers had any idea what Larry was planning: "We don't know what's going on."

"I know nothing about the finale," concurred Wayne Knight. "It's a bigger trade secret than anything I've ever seen. Larry David says he's very excited about it. I think it ties together every human being who's ever had anything to do with the show."

Seinfeld himself was spotted wearing a badge that said DON'T ASK ME. I DON'T KNOW.

Nobody but Larry David knew, and he wasn't talking. In fact, the collective mania typically annoyed David, who viewed who fell victim to it as "a lot of mental cases with time on their hands who feel that to know the ending is to be in the 'in' crowd, and they want to be in too. But they should know that if I know, it can't be an 'in' crowd, since I'm rarely in an 'in' crowd."

That the show's end should be given such disproportionate attention astounded him. "Every now and then Jerry and I would look at each other and say, 'What the hell happened?' You've got to understand, we're the same people we were at the beginning of the series. We were just in this room writing this thing. We have no idea how this success happened."

Kenny Kramer thought knowing would spoil the fun: "It would be really sad if it got out what the show was about, because it would spoil all the surprises. There's going to be no moral message and no reason to bring handkerchiefs to the TV set. It's just going to be these four despicable people being more despicable than ever before."

The series and cast were also being honored left and right with viewer and industry awards. Julia Louis-Dreyfus won her fifth

American Comedy Award for Funniest Supporting Female Performer. She also won the Screen Actors Guild Award for Best Actress in a Comedy Series.

Backstage, the usually unflappable actress got surprisingly sentimental about the show's last days. "It's been a fabulous job," she said. "If I thought anything other than that, I'd be a moron. I do feel melancholy about this. I'm going to miss these boys more than I can tell you."

At the Fiftieth Annual Writers Guild of America Awards, the *Seinfeld* episode "The Fatigues," written by Gregg Kavet and Andy Robin, won for best episodic comedy. The Directors Guild of America honored Andy Ackerman for his work on "The Betrayal."

However, there were some defeats too. When *Seinfeld* lost out at the Golden Globes to newcomer series *Ally McBeal,* the entire *Seinfeld* cast, who were sitting near the stage, reportedly got up abruptly and left. Considering all the other attention they and their show were receiving, it seemed to convey an uncharacteristic degree of pique. Still, Jerry had already proven to be sensitive to any suggestion that his show had slipped, and being upstaged by a freshman hit probably didn't sit very well with him.

Finally, the last taping day arrived. Despite their best efforts, everyone on the set couldn't help but feel the emotion of the event.

"I was being made up," Estelle Harris recalled, "and Julia Louis-Dreyfus had just finished being made up. She leaned down and said how thrilled she was I had been a part of the show. It just made me cry."

Although he's earned the reputation of being unflappable and in control of his feelings, even Seinfeld couldn't ignore the sentiment around him: "It is starting to feel a little unreal today. Like it's hard to concentrate, you know? Like something's going on. It's like a storm brewing. I'm feeling that now.

"I was sad the last few days. I saw an old *Odd Couple* rerun, and it was all yellow. You know those old shows—why are they all yellow? And then I thought, 'This is what my show is now—a rerun. It's not going to be a living thing anymore.' But," he added, "I'm more sure of my decision now than when I made it."

The audience for the final episode was made up of 250 invited guests, each of whom was required to sign a confidentiality agreement. Outside the Studio City studio where the show was filmed, dozens of news vans and teams of reporters kept vigil as the audience members filed in. What they saw, and what the television audience would see on May 14, was in many ways a fitting end to the series. Although at least half the viewers were disappointed, the reality was that the expectations had been so high, it would have been impossible to live up to them. But Jerry and Larry were pleased, and that, in the end as in the beginning, was all that mattered.

The plot was quintessential David. A new NBC president revives Jerry's long-forgotten pilot and gives the show a half-season order. To celebrate, Jerry, Elaine, George, and Kramer decide to fly to Paris on the network's corporate jet. The jet develops mechanical difficulties, and the four soon find themselves stranded in Massachusetts, where they witness an obese man being carjacked. Instead of intervening on his behalf, they stand around watching and making jokes, unaware of the state's new Good Samaritan law, which makes it a crime not to assist crime victims.

The four are arrested and put on trial in front of Judge Art Vandelay who sentences them each to a year in jail. But first, during the trial sequence, all the people they have done wrong over the years reappear to testify, from the Bubble Boy to Mulva to Keith Hernandez. In the end, Jerry ends the show with a monologue—but instead of performing in a club, he's in prison clothes entertaining his fellow inmates.

Because the show was an hour long, it wasn't until 2:30 A.M., after five and a half hours of filming, that Jerry Seinfeld looked around and announced, "It's a wrap."

The very last scene would be shot without an audience three days later, but for all intents and purposes, the series was over. According to the show's warmup comic, Jeff Bye, when the cast took curtain calls, "Jerry was near tears."

At the wrap party a few days later, when Jason Alexander stood in front of everyone and said, "I don't know if I ever thanked Jerry," Seinfeld would lose it again. This time he would cry openly.

IN spring 1998, Jerry went on an early-June working vacation in Australia, which he followed by a European tour.

In August, Jerry spent a week doing stand-up on Broadway in New York City. The show, titled *I'm Telling You for the Last Time*, featured all of his old routines—for the final time. HBO aired the last night of the show on August 9 as a special. The proceeds of the entire week of performances were donated to New York City's public schools.

Seinfeld, who calls stand-up the noblest profession, retired his old material in order to force himself to start over, in a sense. He wanted to add more resonance to his act, to have what that long-ago reviewer saw he lacked: depth.

"I would like to be considered a great comedian," Jerry said. "I don't think I'm there yet. I haven't gotten personal enough yet to be considered great by my definition. That's what being great is, doing material only you could do and no one else. It's about getting to my truer inner feelings about things."

Seinfeld, who sold his house even before the series had finished, is moving back to New York full time and into his dream home. In February, he paid $4.35 million—in cash—to buy a terraced co-op in the exclusive Beresford, which is also home to Beverly Sills and John McEnroe.

According to *People Magazine,* the unit is a three-bedroom, 3,900-square-foot duplex on the nineteenth and twentieth floors with a library, maid's quarters, and a wood-burning fireplace; it previously belonged to violinist Isaac Stern. Jerry plans to put the front door from his *Seinfeld* apartment in the living room.

"Jerry is like a kid with this apartment," says Lois Peerce, his real estate broker. "He's having it totally redone."

What does tomorrow hold for Jerry Seinfeld? He plans to start a production company and, of course, hone a new stand-up act. Otherwise, Jerry seems unconcerned about future work projects.

"I don't even know what my position in the industry is at this point," he says. "Until you're available, you don't know where you rate or the way people see you. I haven't been a salable commodity for nine years. I know there'll be something. But I don't know what. I'm sure Jackie Gleason never thought that *The Honeymooners* was going to be *it* for him, but it really was. I think about that a lot. But I don't worry about it, because I feel like the glow of the show is going to stay with me for quite a while after it's over."

His friend Larry Miller says he teases Jerry by suggesting, "Just go sit on an island, the kind of island off a European country where the guy who brings you the drinks is always angry. Or just go fishing."

To which Seinfeld replies: "I don't want to go fishing. Who's ever been fishing?"

He has at various times said he might like to dabble in films, but only if he's in control. He might reinvent the talk show the way he did the television sitcom. Or he may do what he claims he wants to do: simply enjoy his new home and play.

Except—he would be playing alone. While Seinfeld might be the master of his professional domain, his personal domain seems a much emptier place. For all his wealth, for all his success, and for all his achievement, Jerry Seinfeld seems to lack a real life. Although he is Jewish, he has no apparent ties to his religion. His most serious relationship, with Shoshanna Lonstein, ended sooner than he would have liked. He sits atop a business empire worth untold billions and yet for solace and companionship, he turns to two airport hangars full of expensive cars. He's the emperor ruling over an empty kingdom.

"The show has been Jerry's life," says Julia Louis-Dreyfus. "He was always thinking about the next episode. This has been it for him. You know, he doesn't go home to a wife and kids. He goes home to a blank piece of paper."

The biggest challenge for Seinfeld, it would seem, will be to find a way to translate his professional success into personal growth and fulfillment. Whatever shape future real-Seinfeld episodes take, there will, Jerry is sure, be plenty of them. And he'll always have his comedy to keep him warm.

"I will have longevity," he says confidently. "Just like George Burns, I'd like to play the London Palladium when I'm a hundred." Then, after a moment's thought: "No—make that a hundred and ten."

EPISODE GUIDE

PILOT The Seinfeld Chronicles
(July 5, 1989)

SUMMARY Jerry doesn't know what to expect when a woman he met on the road says that she is coming into town.

OF SPECIAL NOTE The pilot was later aired as the episode "Good News, Bad News." Jerry calls Michael Richards's character Kessler, although in the *TV Guide* he is listed as Hoffman.

TRIVIA Jerry lives in apartment 311.

DIRECTOR Art Wolff
TELEPLAY Larry David and Jerry Seinfeld
GUEST CAST Pamela Brull (Laura); Lee Garlington (Claire)

SEASON ONE

2. "The Stakeout"
(May 31, 1990)

SUMMARY Jerry goes to a birthday party for a friend of Elaine's, where he meets a woman he is attracted to. On his father's advice, Jerry and George stake out the lobby of the building she works in.

INTRODUCING Julia Louis-Dreyfus as Elaine Benes; George's fictional alter ego, Art Vandelay.

OF SPECIAL NOTE Phil Bruns will later be replaced by Barney Martin in the role of Jerry's father. However, in syndication, Bruns can still be seen in this episode because the producers decided against refilming Bruns's scenes with Martin.

Starting with this episode, the series was retitled *Seinfeld*.

DIRECTOR Tom Cherones
TELEPLAY Larry David and Jerry Seinfeld
GUEST CAST Phil Bruns (Morty Seinfeld); Lynn Clark (Vanessa); William Fair (Roger); Joe George (Uncle Mac); Ellen Gerstein (Carol); Janet Rotblatt (Woman); Ron Steelman (Artie Levine); Maud Winchester (Pamela)
RECURRING CAST Liz Sheridan (Helen Seinfeld)

3. "The Robbery"
(June 7, 1990)

SUMMARY While Jerry is out of town, his apartment gets robbed after Kramer leaves the door open. This makes Jerry want to move. George finds him a great apartment, then realizes he also wants it. Whoever gets it, Elaine wants his old apartment. Of course, neither gets the new place.
FOR FUTURE REFERENCE Jerry tells Elaine to use the bathtub if she wants to have sex while apartment-sitting. In episode 151, "The English Patient," Elaine comments that sex in a bathtub doesn't work.

DIRECTOR Tom Cherones
TELEPLAY Matt Goldman
GUEST CAST Anita Wise (Waitress), James F. Dean (Larry), Kimberley Kates (Diane), Bradford English (Cop), David Blackwood (Man #1), George Simms (Man #2)

4. "Male Unbonding"
(June 14, 1990)

SUMMARY Jerry tries to break off his friendship with a clinging and obnoxious childhood friend. George has trouble with his latest relationship. Kramer has the idea of opening a chain of make-your-own-pizza parlors and is looking for investors.

DIRECTOR Tom Cherones
TELEPLAY Larry David and Jerry Seinfeld
GUEST CAST Kevin Dunn (Joel); Kimberley LaMarque (Teller); Frank Piazza (Customer); Anita Wise (Waitress)

5. "The Stock Tip"
(June 21, 1990)

SUMMARY George convinces Jerry to invest in the stock market, where he loses money, much to Kramer's delight. Jerry takes his girlfriend to Vermont for the weekend and has a bad time. Elaine is allergic to her boy-friend's cats, so he dumps her.

DIRECTOR Tom Cherones
TELEPLAY Larry David and Jerry Seinfeld
GUEST CAST Lynn Clark (Vanessa); Ted Davis (Dry Cleaner); Jill C. Klein (Waitress); Benjamin Lum (Stock Boy)

SEASON TWO

6. "The Ex-Girlfriend"
(January 23, 1991)

SUMMARY After George breaks up with his girlfriend, Jerry starts dating her. Elaine is obsessed over why a guy in her building has stopped saying hello to her. Kramer becomes fixated on fresh fruit. Jerry loses his girl-friend after she sees his act.

DIRECTOR Tom Cherones
TELEPLAY Larry David and Jerry Seinfeld
GUEST CAST Karen Barcus (Receptionist); Tracy Kolis (Marlene)

7. "The Pony Remark"
(January 30, 1991)

SUMMARY Jerry's parents come to town for a fiftieth anniversary party, dur-ing which Jerry inadvertently offends one of his relatives by saying immi-grants shouldn't have ponies. After she suddenly dies, Jerry is torn be-tween going to her funeral and playing in his championship softball game. Kramer decides to put levels in his apartment. Elaine is interested in the deceased relative's apartment. George wonders if he'll ever be able to have sex again.
CATCHPHRASE These peas are bursting with country-fresh flavor.

DIRECTOR Tom Cherones
TELEPLAY Larry David and Jerry Seinfeld
GUEST CAST Earl Boen (Eulogist); David Fresco (Isaac); Rozsika Halmos (Manya); Scott N. Stevens (Intern)
RECURRING CAST Len Lesser (Uncle Leo); Barney Martin (Morty Seinfeld); Liz Sheridan (Helen Seinfeld)

8. "The Jacket"
(February 6, 1991)

SUMMARY Jerry buys a very expensive suede jacket with a colorful inner lining, which he wears to meet Elaine's father—and gets ruined when it starts to snow. George can't get a song from *Les Misérables* out of his mind.

DIRECTOR Tom Cherones
TELEPLAY Larry David and Jerry Seinfeld
GUEST CAST Harry Hart-Browne (Manager); Susanne Spoke (Customer); Lawrence Tierney (Alton Benes); Frantz Turner (Salesman)

9. "The Phone Message"
(February 13, 1991)

SUMMARY After a misunderstanding, George leaves a series of nasty messages on his girlfriend's answering machine. When he realizes his mistake, he plots with Jerry to retrieve the messages before she can hear them. Jerry and his girlfriend have a disagreement about a TV commercial for Dockers pants.

DIRECTOR Tom Cherones
TELEPLAY Larry David and Jerry Seinfeld
GUEST CAST Gretchen German (Donna); Tory Polone (Carol)

10. "The Apartment"
(April 4, 1991)

SUMMARY Kramer tries mousse in his hair. Jerry tries to help Elaine rent the apartment one floor above his, then changes his mind when he considers the possible implications. George dons a wedding band, believing women will suddenly find him more attractive if he's "unavailable."
CATCHPHRASE: You're all winners!

DIRECTOR Tom Cherones
TELEPLAY Peter Mehlman
GUEST CAST David Blackwood (Stan); Jeanine Jackson (Roxanne); Leslie Neale (Rita); Tony Plana (Manny); Theresa Randle (Janice); Melody Ryane (Joanne); Glenn Shadix (Harold); Patricia Amaye Thomson (Susie)

11. "The Statue"
(April 11, 1991)

SUMMARY Jerry finds a statue in a box left him by his grandfather. George wants to give it to his parents to replace a similar one he broke as a child. The statue turns up missing after Jerry has his apartment cleaned by the boyfriend of an author Elaine is working with. Later, Elaine and Jerry see the statue at the author's apartment. Elaine is torn between risking her chance to work as an editor and helping George, whose parents are now expecting the statue.

DIRECTOR Tom Cherones
TELEPLAY Larry Charles
GUEST CAST Michael D. Conway (Ray), Nurit Koppel (Rava)

12. "The Revenge"
(April 18, 1991)

SUMMARY George quits his job in a snit after being demoted to the regular bathroom instead of the private executive "lounge." When the boss won't take him back, George hatches a plan to slip the guy a mickey. Kramer pours a bag of concrete into the washing machine of Jerry's laundryman after $1,500 he had stashed in his laundry bag turns up missing.

FOR FUTURE REFERENCE While mulling over possible career opportunities, George mentions he might get a job working for a sports team; in a later episode, he will be hired by the Yankees.

OF SPECIAL NOTE For the syndicated rerun, Wayne Knight supplies the voice of the never-seen Newman, but when the episode was originally aired, the voice was Larry David's. Also, Newman is said to be unemployed, but in his next episode, he's working at the post office.

DIRECTOR Tom Cherones
TELEPLAY Larry David
GUEST CAST Fred Applegate (Levitan); Teri Austin (Ava); John Capodice (Vic); Patrika Darbo (Glenda), Marcus Smythe (Dan); Larry David (Voice of Newman, uncredited)

13. "The Heart Attack"
(April 25, 1991)

SUMMARY George thinks he's had a heart attack; in fact, he needs to have his tonsils taken out. Elaine begins dating the doctor, who is interested in her tongue. Kramer takes George to a holistic healer, but the treatment turns George purple.

DIRECTOR Tom Cherones
TELEPLAY Larry Charles
GUEST CAST John Fleck (Attendant); Pat Hazell (Man in Other Bed); Heather James (Waitress); Sharon McKnight (Nurse); John Posey (Dr. Fein); Stephen Tobolowsky (Tor); Thomas Wagner (Cook); Jimmy Woodward (Driver)

14. "The Deal"
  (May 2, 1991)

SUMMARY Jerry and Elaine are watching TV late at night. While channel-surfing, they come across a show featuring naked people, which leads to a discussion of whether or not they could have a sexual relationship without jeopardizing their friendship. They try, but the system they devise falls apart after Jerry gives Elaine cash for her birthday.

DIRECTOR Tom Cherones
TELEPLAY Larry David
GUEST CAST Norman Brenner (Clerk); Siobhan Fallon (Tina)

15. "The Baby Shower"
  (May 16, 1991)

SUMMARY Elaine uses Jerry's apartment to hold a baby shower for a woman who once dated George. George intends to confront the woman because she embarrassed him on their one and only date. Kramer sells Jerry on the idea of getting an illegal cable hookup. Jerry is confronted by a woman he said he'd call but never did.

DIRECTOR Tom Cherones
TELEPLAY Larry Charles
GUEST CAST Christine Dunford (Leslie); Audrey Frantz (Party Guest); Marla Fries (Stewardess); James Lashly (Assistant); Kate Mulligan (Party Guest); Don Perry (Passenger); Vic Polizos (Tabachnik); Margaret Reed (Mary); George C. Simms (FBI Man)

16. "The Chinese Restaurant"
  (May 23, 1991)

SUMMARY Jerry, Elaine, and George stop for a quick Chinese dinner before a showing of *Plan 9 From Outer Space* on the big screen but are kept waiting forever. While waiting, Jerry sees a woman whose name he can't recall; George needs to use the phone, but it's tied up; Elaine needs food.

DIRECTOR Tom Cherones

TELEPLAY Larry David and Jerry Seinfeld

GUEST CAST Kate Benton (Woman on Phone); James Hong (Bruce); Judy Kain (Lorraine); David Tress (Mr. Cohen); Kendall McCarthy (Man); Michael Mitz (Phone Guy)

17. "The Busboy"
(June 26, 1991)

SUMMARY George inadvertently gets a busboy fired. When he tries to make it up to the guy by watching his apartment, he loses the busboy's cat. Elaine can't get rid of an unwanted houseguest.

DIRECTOR Tom Cherones

TELEPLAY Larry David and Jerry Seinfeld

GUEST CAST Doug Ballard (Eddie); David Labiosa (Antonio); John Del Regno (Manager)

SEASON THREE

18. "The Note"
(September 18, 1991)

SUMMARY Jerry, George, and Elaine have a dentist friend, Roy, write notes so that insurance will cover massages for them all; As a result, Roy may lose his license in an insurance-fraud investigation. George is worried, thinking he may have been aroused during a massage given to him by a man. Kramer thinks he has seen Joe DiMaggio in Dinky Donuts.

CATCHPHRASE I think it moved.

DIRECTOR Tom Cherones

TELEPLAY Larry David

GUEST CAST Ralph Bruneau (Lloyd); Flo Di Re (Receptionist); Liz Georges (Pam); Terri Hanauer (Julianna); Jeff Lester (Raymond); Dale Raoul (Dental Patient); Paul Rogers (Man in Waiting Room); Joshua Liebling (Billy)

19. "The Truth"
(September 25, 1991)

SUMMARY Jerry is getting audited, so he gives his records to George's girl-friend, a former IRS agent. But after George dumps her, she checks into a mental hospital and throws away Jerry's records. Kramer, who is dating Elaine's roommate, sees Elaine naked.

FOR FUTURE REFERENCE George confesses he's driven women to lesbianism—something that will happen again in episode 61, when he sees former girlfriend and future fiancée Susan holding hands with another woman.

DIRECTOR David Steinberg
TELEPLAY Elaine Pope
GUEST CAST Valerie Mahaffey (Patrice); Siobhan Fallon (Tina)

20. "The Pen"
(October 2, 1991)

SUMMARY Elaine accompanies Jerry on a nightmare trip to Florida to visit his parents, where they end up sleeping on a bad sofabed. Jerry causes a stir when he accepts an astronaut pen from Jack Klompus.

OF SPECIAL NOTE Jerry based this episode on his mother's sofabed at her Delray Beach retirement community condo. "He takes the cushions off the pullout and puts them on the floor when he stays with me," confirms Betty Seinfeld.

DIRECTOR Tom Cherones
TELEPLAY Larry David
GUEST CAST Ann Morgan Guilbert (Evelyn); Magda Harout (Stella); Annie Korzen (Doris Klompus); Roger Nolan (Chiropractor); Tucker Smallwood (Photographer)

21. "The Dog"
(October 9, 1991)

SUMMARY Jerry gets stuck taking care of a dog owned by a drunk he met on an airplane who ends up in the hospital. After the drunk gets released, Jerry can't find him. When Jerry can't go to a movie, George and Elaine go alone and find they have nothing to talk about except Jerry. Kramer tries to break up with his girlfriend.

TRIVIA The dog's name is Farfel.

DIRECTOR Tom Cherones

TELEPLAY Larry David

GUEST CAST Joseph Maher (Gavin); Kelly Wellman (Attendant #2); Tom Williams (Bark of the Dog); Marvin Wright-Bey (Attendant #1)

22. "The Library"
(October 16, 1991)

SUMMARY A librarian calls and asks Jerry about a book, *Tropic of Capricorn*, he checked out in 1971 and never returned. Jerry remembers he gave it to George. George blames not returning the book on his former high school gym teacher. Kramer has his eye on a librarian. Elaine's boss hates her recommendations.

BLOOPER Marion mentions that Mr. Bookman has been working at the library for twenty-five years. Later it's revealed that he started the job in 1971, which would mean he'd been working there twenty years, not twenty-five.

OF SPECIAL NOTE In this episode, Mr. Lippman is played by Harris Shore. In future episodes, Richard Fancy takes over.

DIRECTOR Joshua White

TELEPLAY Larry Charles

GUEST CAST Marie Barrientos (Receptionist); Ashley Gardener (Marion); Philip Baker Hall (Lt. Bookman); Neal Lerner (Shusher); Harris Shore (Mr. Lippman); Cynthia Szigeti (Sandy); Biff Yeager (Heyman)

23. "The Parking Garage"
(October 30, 1991)

SUMMARY The foursome splits up to locate the car in a huge parking garage. Jerry and George get arrested for urinating in a public place. Elaine's fish die. Kramer has to lug around an air conditioner, which he puts down and then can't find.

DIRECTOR Tom Cherones

TELEPLAY Larry David

GUEST CAST Gregory Daniel (Man in Corvette); David Dunard (Security Guard); Cynthia Ettinger (Michele); Ron Evans (Bodybuilder); Joe Farago (Man With Woman); Carlyle King (Mother); Tucker Smallwood (Man in Mercedes); Adam Wylie (Kid)

24. "The Cafe"
(November 6, 1991)

SUMMARY Jerry tries helping Baboo, the owner of a small restaurant, attract customers. Elaine performs poorly on an IQ test she takes for George and gets caught when they try the scheme a second time. Kramer tries to keep his mother's ex-boyfriend's jacket because it helps him meet women.

OF SPECIAL NOTE The jacket will be a recurring "character" in the next two episodes.

DIRECTOR Tom Cherones
TELEPLAY Tom Leopold
GUEST CAST Dawn Arnemann (Monica); Brian George (Babu Bhatt)

25. "The Tape"
(November 13, 1991)

SUMMARY George is excited about a new baldness cure discovered in China. A mysterious woman leaves an erotic message on Jerry's tape recorder. When George finds out it was Elaine, he falls in love with her. Kramer searches for the jacket.

DIRECTOR David Steinberg
TELEPLAY Larry David, Bob Shaw, and Don McEnery
GUEST CAST John Apicella (Repairman); Norman Brenner (Beder); Ping Wu (Delivery Boy)

26. "The Nose Job"
(November 20, 1991)

SUMMARY Jerry's brain and penis play chess against one another to determine whether he should keep dating a beautiful but shallow model. George is dating a woman with a big nose; Kramer tells her to get a nose job. Kramer uses Elaine to get the jacket back from his mom's boyfriend.

DIRECTOR Tom Cherones
TELEPLAY Peter Mehlman
GUEST CAST David Blackwood (Interviewer); Roy Brocksmith (Landlord); Susan Diol (Audrey); Tawny Kitaen (Isabel); Joseph V. Perry (Newsstand Owner)

27. "The Stranded"
(November 27, 1991)

SUMMARY Jerry and Elaine go to a party with George, who abandons them to take a coworker home. George feels cheated by a drugstore and gets caught stealing in revenge. The party host visits Jerry and parties with Kramer and a lady of the evening. Jerry is arrested for solicitation.

OF SPECIAL NOTE This episode was filmed during the second season. NBC ran a lead-in broadcast in which Jerry acknowledged that it was being shown out of sequence, which is why George still has his job.

DIRECTOR Tom Cherones

TELEPLAY Larry David, Jerry Seinfeld, and Matt Goldman

GUEST CAST Teri Austin (Ava); Michael Chiklis (Steve); Marcia Firesten (Jenny); Dwayne Kennedy (Frank); Bobbi Jo Lathan (Patti); Michael Milhoan (Security Guard); Frank Piazza (Cop); John Putch (Roy); Ellen Ratner (Ellen); Gwen Shepherd (Cashier); Melissa Weil (Gwen)

28. "The Alternate Side"
(December 4, 1991)

SUMMARY Jerry's car is stolen. George's decision to take a job moving cars from one side of the street to the other turns into a disaster. Kramer gets a chance to say a line in a Woody Allen film. Elaine gets tired of her sixty-six-year-old boyfriend, but he has a stroke before she can dump him.

CATCHPHRASE These pretzels are making me thirsty.

TRIVIA Jerry's car phone number in this episode is 555-8383, the same number used in a later episode as his home number.

DIRECTOR Tom Cherones

TELEPLAY Larry David and Bill Masters

GUEST CAST Jeff Barton (Paramedic); Jay Brooks (Sid); Edward Penn (Owen March); Janet Zarish (Rental Car Agent)

29. "The Red Dot"
(December 11, 1991)

SUMMARY Jerry accidentally causes Elaine's alcoholic boyfriend to drink. Elaine gets George a job, so he buys her a cashmere sweater, which is marked down because it has an imperfection—a little red dot. George gets fired for having sex with the cleaning lady on his desk at work.

DIRECTOR Tom Cherones

TELEPLAY Larry David

GUEST CAST Rachel Davies (Saleswoman); David Naughton (Dick); Bridget Sienna (Cleaning Woman)

RECURRING CAST Richard Fancy (Lippman)

30. "The Subway"
(January 8, 1992)

SUMMARY Everyone has an experience on the subway. George blows off a job interview after meeting a beautiful woman, who robs him in her hotel room. Jerry falls asleep and ends up going to Coney Island with a naked man. Elaine's train gets stuck, so she misses being the best man at a lesbian wedding. Kramer overhears a hot tip on a horse on his way to pay $600 in traffic violations and almost gets robbed of his winnings.

DIRECTOR Tom Cherones
TELEPLAY Larry Charles
GUEST CAST Christopher Collins (Thug); Rhoda Gemignani (Woman With Elaine); Chet Nelson (Kid); Mark Boone Junior (OTB Patron); Joe Restivo (Player #2); Daryl Roach (Violinist/Cop); Ernie Sabella (Naked Man); Barbara Stock (Scam Woman); Barry Vigon (Player #1)

31. "The Pez Dispenser"
(January 15, 1992)

SUMMARY Kramer joins the Polar Bear Club. Jerry makes Elaine laugh during George's girlfriend's piano recital. George gets the upper hand by breaking up with her as a preemptive strike. Kramer has an idea for a cologne that smells like the beach. The Pez dispenser plays a part in a drug intervention.

SEINFELD-ESE Hand—control; what George says one must maintain in a relationship, as in "You gotta have hand."

DIRECTOR Tom Cherones
TELEPLAY Larry David
GUEST CAST Bill Applebaum (D'Giff); Chris Barnes (Richie); Kate Benton (Roberta); Allen Bloomfield (Polar Bear); Steve Kehela (Intervenor); Elizabeth Morehead (Noel); Fred Sanders (John)

32. "The Suicide"
(January 29, 1992)

SUMMARY Elaine needs to fast before getting an X ray but begins to hallucinate from hunger. After his neighbor tries suicide, Jerry starts dating the man's girlfriend. A psychic warns George to cancel his dream vacation to the Cayman Islands, so he lets Kramer go instead.

OF SPECIAL NOTE George mentions he has a brother.

TRIVIA Jason Alexander's mother has a cameo appearance in this episode, sitting on a bench next to Elaine.

DIRECTOR Tom Cherones
TELEPLAY Tom Leopold
GUEST CAST Aimee Aro (Faithy); Gina Gallego (Gina); C. E. Grimes (Martin); Mimi Lieber (Rula); Peggy Lane O'Rourke (Nurse); Howard Schecter (Doctor)
RECURRING CAST Wayne Knight (Newman)

33. "The Fix-up"
(February 5, 1991)

SUMMARY Jerry and Elaine talk Elaine's friend and George into going on a blind date. George thinks he may have gotten her pregnant, because his condom was defective.
CATCHPHRASE My boys can swim!

DIRECTOR Tom Cherones
TELEPLAY Elaine Pope and Larry Charles
GUEST CAST Maggie Jakobson (Cynthia)

34. "The Boyfriend"
(February 12, 1992)

SUMMARY Jerry meets Keith Hernandez and acts like the two of them are dating. George tries to get an extension on his unemployment benefits. Kramer and Newman hate Hernandez, believing he once spit on them. Jerry supports the "second-spitter" theory. Keith is attracted to Elaine and breaks a "date" with Jerry to take her out.
OF SPECIAL NOTE This was the first hour-long episode of *Seinfeld* aired; in syndication, it is shown as two separate episodes.
George uses the faux name Vandelay again, this time as the name of a company.

DIRECTOR Tom Cherones
TELEPLAY Larry David and Larry Levin
GUEST CAST Rae Allen (Mrs. Lenore Sokol); Richard Assad (Cabbie); Keith Hernandez (Himself)
RECURRING CAST Wayne Knight (Newman)

35. "Of Mastodons and Men"
(February 12, 1992)

SUMMARY Kramer gets Jerry to accompany him to see a former neighbor's new baby. Jerry breaks it off with Keith when the ballplayer asks him for help moving. Elaine breaks it off with Keith when she finds out he smokes.

CATCHPHRASE: You've got to see the baby.

DIRECTOR Tom Cherones
TELEPLAY Larry David and Larry Levin
GUEST CAST Rae Allen (Mrs. Sokol); Richard Assad (Cabbie); Melanie Good (Woman); Keith Hernandez (Himself); Roger McDowell (Himself); Lisa Mende (Carol); Stephen Prutting (Michael); Carol Ann Susi (Carrie)
RECURRING CAST Wayne Knight (Newman)

36. "The Limo"
(February 26, 1992)

SUMMARY Jerry and George take a limo designated for a passenger who, Jerry knows, didn't make it onto the plane. They call Elaine and Kramer to join them for an event at Madison Square Garden, where they are mistaken for leaders of the Aryan Union.

DIRECTOR Tom Cherones
TELEPLAY Larry Charles; story: Marc Jaffe
GUEST CAST Jodi Baskerville (Herself); Norman Brenner (Man at Airport); Ray Glanzmann (Protester #2); I. M. Hobson (Businessman); Aaron Kanarek (Protester #1); Peter Krause (Tim); Adam Leslie (Man at Protest); Jeremy Roberts (Chauffeur); Suzanne Snyder (Eva); Harley Venton (Dan)

37. "The Good Samaritan"
(March 4, 1992)

SUMMARY Jerry tracks down a hit-and-run driver and starts dating her. Then he discovers the victim is someone he's even more interested in dating. George has an affair with Elaine's friend. Kramer has violent reactions to Mary Hart's voice.

DIRECTOR Jason Alexander
TELEPLAY Peter Mehlman
GUEST CAST Joseph Malone (Michael); Melinda McGraw (Angela); Helen Slater (Becky Gelke); Ann Talman (Robin)

38. "The Letter"
(March 25, 1992)

SUMMARY Kramer poses for a painting. George feels obligated to buy something when he accompanies Jerry to his new girlfriend's art studio. Elaine wears an Orioles baseball cap to a Yankees game and refuses to take it off. Jerry finds out his new girlfriend is a plagiarist.

FOR FUTURE REFERENCE Elaine comments that no one would want to watch a bris—which she and Jerry do in episode 69, "The Bris."

DIRECTOR Tom Cherones

TELEPLAY Larry David

GUEST CAST Shashawnee Hall (Usher); Justine Johnston (Mrs. Armstrong); Catherine Keener (Nina); Elliott Reid (Mr. Armstrong); Richard Venture (Leonard West)

RECURRING CAST Richard Fancy (Lippman)

39. "The Parking Space"
(April 22, 1992)

SUMMARY Kramer tells Jerry his friend Mike thinks Jerry is a phony. George gets into a confrontation with Mike over a parking space in front of Jerry's apartment. Everyone on the street debates parking etiquette and whether "front in" or "back in" has priority.

DIRECTOR Tom Cherones

TELEPLAY Larry David and Greg Daniels

GUEST CAST Lee Arenberg (Mike); Jay Brooks (Sid); Maryedith Burrell (Maryedith); Zachary Charles (Angry Man); Shannon Cochran (Sheila); Michael A. Costanza (Truck Driver); Steven Marcus Gibbs (Bystander #2); John Christian Graas (Matthew); Peggy Lane O'Rourke (Bystander #1); Mik Scriba (Cop #1); Stan Sellers (Cop #2)

RECURRING CAST Wayne Knight (Newman)

40. "The Keys"
(May 6, 1992)

SUMMARY Jerry takes away Kramer's spare-key privileges. Kramer gives his keys to George, then takes off for California to follow his acting dream. George takes his keys from Elaine to give to Jerry but doesn't give Jerry Elaine's keys.

DIRECTOR Tom Cherones

TELEPLAY Larry Charles

GUEST CAST Sharon Barr (Trucker); Candice Bergen (as Murphy Brown); Carissa Channing (Kramer's Girlfriend); Heather James (Waitress); Eric

Allan Kramer (Biker); Ricky Dean Logan (Hippie #1); Nina Tremblay (Jerry's Girlfriend); Maud Winchester (Hippie #2)
RECURRING CAST Wayne Knight (Newman)

SEASON FOUR

Seinfeld won the Emmy for Outstanding Comedy Series for the 1992–93 season for the body of work in the following episodes.

41. "The Trip (Part I)"
(August 12, 1992)

SUMMARY Elaine is in Europe. George goes with Jerry to LA, where Jerry is performing on *The Tonight Show,* so they can look for Kramer. George disturbs the guests at *Tonight,* and Jerry bombs. Police suspect Kramer is the Smog Strangler serial killer.

OF SPECIAL NOTE Because Julia Louis-Dreyfus was having a baby, Elaine is in Europe with her current boyfriend, who is also her psychiatrist.

DIRECTOR Tom Cherones
TELEPLAY Larry Charles
GUEST CAST Vaughn Armstrong (Lt. Coleman); Corbin Bernsen (Himself); Michael Gerard (Receptionist); Ricky Dean Logan (Freak); Manfred Melcher (Officer); Debi A. Monahan (Chelsea); Keith Morrison (Himself); Christopher Michael Moore (Studio Guard); Peter Murnik (Lt. Martel); Dyana Ortelli (Chambermaid); Fred Savage (Himself); Elmarie Wendel (Helene); George Wendt (Himself);

42. "The Trip (Part II)"
(August 19, 1992)

SUMMARY Jerry and George try to get Kramer out of jail. Before they can, another victim is found. Kramer is released but refuses to return to New York with them. Once they are back home, Kramer shows up as if nothing has happened.

FOR FUTURE REFERENCE Marty Rackham will reappear as Elaine's exclamation-point-avoiding boyfriend, Jake Jarmel, in "The Sniffing Accountant," then return as Jake in two more episodes.

DIRECTOR Tom Cherones
TELEPLAY Larry Charles
GUEST CAST Vaughn Armstrong (Lieutenant Coleman); Steve Dougherty

(Prison Guard); Steve Greenstein (Man); Clint Howard (Tobias Lehigh Nagy); Deck McKenzie (Reporter #2); Kerry Leigh Michaels (Woman); Keith Morrison (Himself); Peter Murnik (Lieutenant Martel); Peggy Lane O'Rourke (Reporter #1); Peter Parros (Officer #2); Marty Rackham (Officer #1); Elmarie Wendel (Helene)

43. "The Pitch"
(September 16, 1992)

SUMMARY Jerry is approached by NBC to develop an idea for a series. He and George pitch their idea for a show about nothing. George starts dating Susan, on whom Kramer throws up. Kramer trades Newman a radar detector for a motorcycle helmet, which saves Kramer's life when he is kicked in the head by Crazy Joe Davola.

INTRODUCING Crazy Joe Davola, a writer who goes to the same psychiatrist as Elaine. Susan, to whom George will eventually propose.

OF SPECIAL NOTE Episodes 43 and 44 were originally broadcast as one hour-long episode.

DIRECTOR Tom Cherones
TELEPLAY Larry David
GUEST CAST Peter Blood (Jay); Julie Blum (Receptionist); Stephen McHattie (Dr. Reston); Kevin Page (Stu); Ron Ross (Homeless Man); Steve Skrovan (Tommy)
RECURRING CAST Bob Balaban (Russell Dalrimple); Peter Crombie (Crazy Joe Davola); Wayne Knight (Newman); Heidi Swedberg (Susan)

44. "The Ticket"
(September 16, 1992)

SUMMARY Kramer suffers side effects from his head injury. Jerry and George take another meeting at NBC and get a go-ahead for the pilot. Jerry throws away a watch his parents gave him, which is picked out of the garbage by Uncle Leo.

DIRECTOR Tom Cherones
TELEPLAY Larry David
GUEST CAST Peter Blood (Jay); Julie Blum (Receptionist); Steve Eastin (Cop #1); Al Fann (Judge); David Graf (Cop #2); Stephen McHattie (Dr. Reston); Kevin Page (Stu)
RECURRING CAST Bob Balaban (Russell Dalrimple); Wayne Knight (Newman); Len Lesser (Uncle Leo); Heidi Swedberg (Susan)

45. "The Watch (Part I)"
(September 23, 1992)

SUMMARY Jerry's parents are in town and ask about the watch they gave him. Morty thinks someone stole his wallet at the doctor's office. George gets a box of cigars from Susan's father. Elaine returns from her trip. The deal with NBC falls through.

DIRECTOR Tom Cherones
TELEPLAY Larry David
GUEST CAST Denise Dowse (Receptionist); Susan Ilene Johnson (Nurse); Brian Leckner (Attendant); Stephen McHattie (Dr. Reston); David Sage (Dr. Dembrow)
RECURRING CAST Len Lesser (Uncle Leo); Barney Martin (Morty Seinfeld); Liz Sheridan (Helen Seinfeld); Heidi Swedberg (Susan)

46. "The Watch (Part II)"
(September 30, 1992)

SUMMARY George gets Russell Dalrimple's address and tries to get the pilot reinstated. Jerry tries to buy back the watch from Uncle Leo. Kramer acts as Elaine's boyfriend in order to help her dump the psychiatrist. Elaine meets Crazy Joe at the psychiatrist's office and starts dating him.

DIRECTOR Tom Cherones
TELEPLAY Larry David
GUEST CAST Stephen McHattie (Dr. Reston); Jessica Lundy (Naomi); Christopher Carroll (Maître d'); Lewis Dauber (Doorman); Mimi Craven (Cynthia)
RECURRING CAST Bob Balaban (Russell Dalrimple); Peter Crombie (Crazy Joe Davola); Len Lesser (Uncle Joe); Barney Martin (Morty Seinfeld); Liz Sheridan (Helen Seinfeld); Heidi Swedberg (Susan);

47. "The Bubble Boy"
(October 7, 1992)

SUMMARY Jerry asks Elaine to go with him and George and Susan to Susan's parents' to a cabin in the mountains. On their way to the cabin, Jerry agrees to visit a boy who lives in a bubble. George ends up getting into a fight with the Bubble Boy. Kramer accidentally burns down the cabin.

DIRECTOR Tom Cherones
TELEPLAY Larry David and Larry Charles

GUEST CAST Brian Doyle-Murray (Mel); George Gerdes (Man #1); Jon Hayman (Voice and Arm of Donald); O-lan Jones (Waitress); Jessica Lundy (Naomi); Carol Mansell (Mother); Tony Pappenfuss (Man #2)

RECURRING CAST Heidi Swedberg (Susan)

48. "The Cheever Letters"
(October 28, 1992)

SUMMARY Jerry and George begin to work on their pilot. George and Susan tell her father about the cabin fire. Her father turns out to have been John Cheever's gay lover. Kramer goes to the Cuban embassy in search of cigars.

DIRECTOR Tom Cherones

TELEPLAY Larry David; story: Larry David, Elaine Pope, and Tom Leopold

GUEST CAST David Blackwood (Doorman); Warren Frost (Mr. Henry Ross); Lisa Malkiewicz (Sandra); Vanessa Marquez (Receptionist); Timothy Omundson (Ricky Ross); Miguel Perez (Luis); Patricia Lee Willson (Sara Ross); Grace Zabriskie (Mrs. Ross)

RECURRING CAST Heidi Swedberg (Susan)

49. "The Opera"
(November 4, 1992)

SUMMARY Crazy Joe leaves Jerry a message saying he will put the kibosh on him. Kramer has tickets for the opera. Elaine ends her relationship with Crazy Joe, who shows up at the opera dressed as Pagliacci.

DIRECTOR Tom Cherones

TELEPLAY Larry Charles

GUEST CAST Tom Celli (Man #1); Glen Chin (Man #3); Ross Evans (Mr. Reichman); Harriet S. Miller (Mrs. Reichman); Bill Saluga (Usher); Jason Wingreen (Man #2)

RECURRING CAST Peter Crombie (Crazy Joe Davola); Heidi Swedberg (Susan)

50. "The Virgin"
(November 11, 1992)

SUMMARY Elaine upsets Jerry's virgin girlfriend and then runs into a Chinese delivery boy, Ping. George gets Susan fired when he kisses her before a meeting. George and Jerry struggle to think of an idea for their TV series. Kramer watches too much television.

OF SPECIAL NOTE After this episode aired, Michael Richards participated in a crossover with *Mad About You*, the only time any of the *Seinfeld* characters was featured on another show—although Jerry appeared as himself on an episode of *NewsRadio*, and Jerry and Larry David appeared on the December 6, 1993, episode of *Love and War* as themselves. On *Mad About You*, Paul Reiser's character was subletting his apartment to Kramer.

DIRECTOR Tom Cherones
TELEPLAY Peter Mehlman; story: Peter Mehlman, Peter Farrelly, and Bob Farrelly
GUEST CAST Peter Blood (Jay); Julie Blum (Receptionist); Leah Lail (Stacy); Jane Leeves (Marla); Kevin Page (Stu); Derya Ruggles (Woman in Bar); Anne Twomey (Rita); Dayna Winston (Carol); Ping Wu (Ping)
RECURRING CAST Heide Swedberg (Susan)

51. "The Contest"
  (November 18, 1992)

SUMMARY George is caught masturbating while leafing through an issue of *Glamour* magazine—by his mother, who falls down stunned and ends up in the hospital. After George says he'll never do it again, Jerry challenges him to a contest of self-denial. He accepts, and Elaine and Kramer want in on the bet. Elaine meets John F. Kennedy Jr. Jerry's virgin girlfriend dumps him when he tells her about the contest; she ends up with JFK Jr.
OF SPECIAL NOTE Tom Cherones won the Directors Guild of America Award for his work on this episode; Larry David won an Emmy for his writing.

DIRECTOR Tom Cherones
TELEPLAY Larry David
GUEST CAST Jane Leeves (Marla); Ilana Levine (Joyce); Andrea Parker (Nurse); Rachel Sweet (Shelly)
RECURRING CAST Estelle Harris (Estelle Costanza)

52. "The Airport"
  (November 25, 1992)

SUMMARY When their flight home gets canceled, Jerry and Elaine have to take another plane. She gets stuck in coach while Jerry lives it up in first class with a model. Waiting at the airport for Jerry and Elaine, George meets a convict, and Kramer sees a man who owes him $240.
TRIVIA Larry Charles makes a cameo appearance as the guy who uses the bathroom immediately before Elaine.

TELEPLAY Larry Charles

DIRECTOR Tom Cherones

GUEST CAST Jm J. Bullock (Attendant #1); Scott Burkholder (Prisoner); Jennifer Campbell (Tia); Maggie Egan (Ticket Clerk); Jack Graiman (Cop); Annie Korzen (Passenger #2); Mark Christopher Lawrence (Sky Cap); William Evan Masters (Driver); Deck McKenzie (Security Guard); Lenny Rose (Passenger #1); Allan Wasserman (Grossbard); Karen Denise Williams (Attendant #2)

53. "The Pick"
(December 16, 1992)

SUMMARY Elaine is humiliated when she realizes her nipple is visible on her Christmas card photo. Jerry has a date with the model from the plane, but she dumps him because she thinks she saw him he pick his nose. George returns to Susan, then tries to back out. Kramer becomes a Calvin Klein underwear model.

DIRECTOR Tom Cherones

TELEPLAY Larry David; story: Larry David and Marc Jaffe

GUEST CAST Blaire Baron (Female Executive); Jennifer Campbell (Tia); Tony Carlin (Fred); Francois Giroday (Male Executive); Gina Hecht (Dana Foley); Nicholas Hormann (Calvin); Steve Schubert (Man in Office)

RECURRING CAST Wayne Knight (Newman); Heidi Swedberg (Susan)

54. "The Movie"
(January 6, 1993)

SUMMARY Jerry tries to juggle two performances with going to the movies. In the end, everyone but Kramer misses the movie they all wanted to see.

DIRECTOR Tom Cherones

TELEPLAY Steve Skrovan, Bill Masters, and Jon Hayman

GUEST CAST Perry Anzilotti (Usher); Molly Cleator (Cashier); Barry Diamond (Buckles); Paul Eisenhauer (Man in Theatre); Montrose Hagins (Woman in Theatre); Cathy Lind Hayes (Woman Behind Elaine); Allan Kolman (Cab Driver); Tom La Grua (Kernis); Christie Mellor (Concessionaire); Jeff Norman (Man in Line); Eric Poppick (Maurice)

55. "The Visa"
(January 27, 1993)

SUMMARY George is dating the lawyer handling Ping's case against Elaine, but the lawyer is attracted to Jerry. Kramer returns early from baseball fantasy camp, where he accidentally punched Mickey Mantle. Babu is deported because his visa renewal is in Jerry's mail, which Elaine has been holding.

DIRECTOR Tom Cherones
TELEPLAY Peter Mehlman
GUEST CAST Gerry Bednob (Babu's Friend); Brian George (Babu Bhatt); John Hamelin (Babu's Brother); Maggie Han (Cheryl); Ping Wu (Ping)

56. "The Shoes"
(February 4, 1993)

SUMMARY Kramer kisses Jerry's old girlfriend. George is caught looking at the cleavage of the daughter of the NBC executive Russell Dalrimple. Elaine helps Jerry get the pilot back by showing her cleavage to Russell.

DIRECTOR Tom Cherones
TELEPLAY Larry David and Jerry Seinfeld
GUEST CAST Anita Barone (Gail Cunningham); Gina Hecht (Dana Foley); Michael Ornstein (Waiter); Denise Lee Richards (Molly)
RECURRING CAST Bob Balaban (Russell Dalrimple)

57. "The Outing"
(February 11, 1993)

SUMMARY A college reporter erroneously writes that Jerry and George are a gay couple, and the story is picked up by the *New York Post*.
CATCHPHRASE Not that there's anything wrong with that.

DIRECTOR Tom Cherones
TELEPLAY Larry Charles
GUEST CAST Kari Coleman (Allison); Charley Garrett (Man #1); David Gibbs (Man #2); Lawrence A. Mandley (Manager); Anthony Mangano (Sailor); Paula Marshall (Sharon); Deck McKenzie (Scott); Ben Reed (Male Nurse)
RECURRING CAST Estelle Harris (Mrs. Costanza); Barney Martin (Morty Seinfeld); Liz Sheridan (Helen Seinfeld)

58. "The Old Man"
(February 18, 1993)

SUMMARY Elaine talks Jerry and George into volunteering to help the elderly, which doesn't go smoothly. Jerry loses his senior citizen on the way to the dentist. Kramer and Newman try to make money by selling old records.

DIRECTOR Tom Cherones
TELEPLAY Bruce Kirschbaum; story: Larry Charles
GUEST CAST Tobin Bell (Ron); Lanei Chapman (Housekeeper); Victoria Dillard (Agency Rep); Robert Donley (Ben); Bill Erwin (Sid); Jerry Hauck (Tim)
RECURRING CAST Wayne Knight (Newman)

59. "The Implant"
(February 25, 1993)

SUMMARY Jerry dumps his girlfriend after Elaine says she has breast implants. When Elaine later discovers the breasts are real, Jerry tries to get the woman back, only to be dumped. Kramer thinks he saw Salman Rushdie at the health club. George goes to Detroit with his girlfriend for her aunt's funeral.
SEINFELD-ESE Double-dipping—sticking a chip back into the dip after taking a bite of it.

DIRECTOR Tom Cherones
TELEPLAY Peter Mehlman
GUEST CAST Tony Amendola (Rushdie); Susan Beaubian (Ticket Clerk #2); Donald Bishop (Dr. Allenwood); Teri Hatcher (Sidra); Bruce E. Morrow (Father Jessup); Megan Mullally (Betsy); Kieran Mulroney (Timmy); Peggy Stewart (Aunt May); Carol Rosenthal (Ticket Clerk #1)

60. "The Junior Mint"
(March 18, 1993)

SUMMARY Jerry can't remember his date's name—he just knows it rhymes with a female body part. Elaine visits an old boyfriend in the hospital for an operation, which Kramer talks Jerry into watching. During the surgery, Jerry accidentally drops a Junior Mint into the patient.
OF SPECIAL NOTE This episode was the centerpiece of a sexual harassment lawsuit filed in Milwaukee, Wisconsin, in which a male manager was accused of violating the civil rights of a female subordinate while discussing the episode at the office. When the woman said she didn't know what body part rhymed with "Dolores," the manager Xeroxed the page of the dictionary containing the word "clitoris." He was subsequently fired, filed a lawsuit for wrongful termination, and won.

DIRECTOR Tom Cherones
TELEPLAY Andy Robin
GUEST CAST Sherman Howard (Roy); Susan Walters (Mystery Woman); Victor Raider-Wexler (Doctor)

61. "The Smelly Car"
(April 15, 1993)

SUMMARY A parking valet leaves a permanent smell of body odor in Jerry's car; the aroma attaches itself to everyone who sits in the vehicle. Kramer has an affair with Susan's girlfriend. Jerry tries to sell the car and ultimately leaves it on the street with the key in it.

DIRECTOR Tom Cherones
TELEPLAY Larry David and Peter Mehlman
GUEST CAST Nick Bakay (Carl); Walt Beaver (Husband); Kari Coleman (Allison); Viveka Davis (Mona); Michael Des Barres (Restaurateur); Courtney Gains (Clerk); Raf Mauro (Car Washer); Taylor Negron (Hairdresser); Robert Noble (Salesman); Patricia Place (Wife)
RECURRING CAST Heidi Swedberg (Susan)

62. "The Handicap Spot"
(May 13, 1993)

SUMMARY George parks his father's car in a handicap parking spot, causing a disabled woman to be injured. An angry mob trashes his car. Kramer falls in love with the injured woman. George becomes his father's butler after his father gets arrested for parking in the spot.
OF SPECIAL NOTE After this episode was aired, Jerry Stiller took over the role of Frank Costanza from John Randolph. Prior to the series going into syndication, the scenes with Randolph were reshot using Stiller.
TRIVIA Look closely at the group of bystanders and you'll be able to see Kathy Kinney, now better known as Mimi on *The Drew Carey Show*.

DIRECTOR Tom Cherones
TELEPLAY Larry David
GUEST CAST David Blackwood (Security Guard); Marvin Braverman (Cop); Fritzi Burr (Mah-Jongg Lady #1); Elizabeth Dennehy (Allison); Donna Evans (Lula); Eric Fleeks (Kicker); Norma Janis (Mah-Jongg Lady #2); Kathy Kinney (Bystander); Nancy Lenehan (Volunteer); Rick Overton (The Drake); Ina Parker (Mah-Jongg Lady #3); Richard Portnow (Ray); John Randolph (Frank Costanza)

RECURRING CAST Estelle Harris (Estelle Costanza); Jerry Stiller (Frank Costanza) (U.S. syndicated rerun only)

63. "The Pilot (Part I)"
(May 20, 1993)

SUMMARY Auditions are held for the pilot of Jerry's sitcom. Russell Dalrimple is obsessed with Elaine. George is obsessed with a white spot on his lip. Kramer is constipated. Elaine accuses the owner of Monk's of only hiring large-breasted women.

OF SPECIAL NOTE Episodes 63 and 64 were originally shown as a one-hour special but were split into two half hours for syndication.

DIRECTOR Tom Cherones
TELEPLAY Larry David
GUEST CAST Erick Avari (Cabbie); Peter Blood (Jay); Stephen Burrows (David); Samantha Dorman (Waitress); Richard Gant (Fred); Larry Hankin (Tom Pepper—TV Kramer); Mariska Hargitay (Melissa); Gina Hecht (Dana Foley); Bruce Jarchow (Doctor); Kevin Page (Stu); Jeremy Piven (Michael Barth—TV George); Al Ruscio (Manager); Roger Rose (Mark); Bob Shaw (Paul); Anne Twomey (Rita); Laura Waterbury (Casting Director); Elena Wohl (Sandi Robbins—TV Elaine)
RECURRING CAST Bob Balaban (Russell Dalrimple); Peter Crombie (Crazy Joe Davola)

64. "The Pilot (Part II)"
(May 20, 1993)

SUMMARY Rehearsals for the pilot begin. Russell's obsession with Elaine begins to affect his work. Elaine gets an investigation started on the owner of the diner, finds Morty's wallet in Jerry's couch, and sneaks into the pilot taping, where Crazy Joe jumps out of the audience. Characters from the past season comments on the pilot as it's broadcast. *Jerry* is premiered, then canceled when Dalrimple joins Greenpeace.

DIRECTOR Tom Cherones
TELEPLAY Larry David
GUEST CAST Tony Amendola (Rushdie); Peter Blood (Jay); Brian Bradley (Butler); Jennifer Campbell (Tia); Lanei Chapman (Housekeeper); Kari Coleman (Allison); Larry David (Man on Raft); Elizabeth Dennehy (Allison); Brian Doyle-Murray (Mel); Bill Erwin (Sid); Richard Gant (Fred); Maggie Han (Cheryl); Larry Hankin (Tom Pepper—TV Kramer); Teri Hatcher (Sidra); Jon Hayman (Voice of Donald); Pat Hazell (Himself);

Nicholas Hormann (Calvin); Jane Leeves (Marla); Carol Mansell (Mother); Jeff Oetjen (Wilton); Rick Overton (Drake); Jeremy Piven (Michael Barth—TV George); Kevin Page (Stu); Al Ruscio (Manager); Bob Shaw (Paul); Deborah Swisher (1st AD); Anne Twomey (Rita); Elena Wohl (Sandi Robbins—TV Elaine); Ping Wu (Ping)

RECURRING CAST Bob Balaban (Russell Dalrimple); Peter Crombie (Crazy Joe Davola); Wayne Knight (Newman); Barney Martin (Morty Seinfeld); Liz Sheridan (Helen Seinfeld); Heidi Swedberg (Susan)

SEASON FIVE

65. "The Mango"
(September 16, 1993)

SUMMARY George battles impotence and is cured after eating some mangos. After Elaine admits she faked every orgasm, Jerry wants another chance. Kramer gets banned from his favorite fruit store and has Jerry try to buy his fruit for him.

OF SPECIAL NOTE In the original credits for the episode, a writing credit is given to "Buck Dancer." In the syndicated version, that name has been changed to Larry David; why he used a pseudonym to begin with is unclear.

DIRECTOR Tom Cherones
TELEPLAY Lawrence H. Levy and Buck Dancer; story: Lawrence H. Levy
GUEST CAST Lisa Edelstein (Karen); Veralyn Jones (Renee); Leonard Termo (Joe)

66. "The Puffy Shirt"
(September 23, 1993)

SUMMARY George is forced to move in with his parents, then is discovered as a hand model. Kramer is dating a designer who is a low-talker. Jerry unknowingly agrees to wear one of her pirate shirts on the *Today* show because he couldn't hear what she was asking him.

SEINFELD-ESE Low-talker—someone who speaks so softly that you can't understand what the person is saying.

DIRECTOR Tom Cherones
TELEPLAY Larry David
GUEST CAST David Brisbin (Client); Kim Gillingham (Assistant); Bryant Gumbel (Himself); Deborah May (Elsa); Wendel Meldrum (Leslie); Mi-

chael Mitz (Photographer); Terence Riggins (Stage Manager); Ron Ross (Homeless Man)
RECURRING CAST Estelle Harris (Estelle Costanza); Jerry Stiller (Frank Costanza)

67. "The Glasses"
(September 30, 1993)

SUMMARY George believes his glasses were stolen. Kramer gets George a discount on new ones, and he unwittingly buys women's frames. Elaine is bitten by a dog. While not wearing his glasses, George thinks he might have seen Jerry's girlfriend kissing Jerry's cousin.

DIRECTOR Tom Cherones
TELEPLAY Tom Gammill and Max Pross
GUEST CAST Anna Gunn (Amy); Rance Howard (Blind Man); Michael Saad (Doctor); Timothy Stack (Dwayne); Tom Towles (Tough Guy)
RECURRING CAST Len Lesser (Uncle Leo)

68. "The Sniffing Accountant"
(October 7, 1993)

SUMMARY Jerry thinks his accountant is on drugs. George's father gets him an interview for a job as a bra salesman. Elaine's new boyfriend is perfect—until he doesn't use an exclamation point in a message he leaves her. She breaks up with him.
OF SPECIAL NOTE Christa Miller, who would go on to costar in *The Drew Carey Show,* appeared as another character in episode 106, "The Doodle."

DIRECTOR Tom Cherones
TELEPLAY Larry David and Jerry Seinfeld
GUEST CAST Patrick Cronin (Farkus); Ralph Harris Jr. (Ralph); John Kapelos (Barry); Marty Rackham (Jake Jarmel); Christa Miller (Ellen); Marty Rackham (Jake Jarmel); Maria Stanton (Woman in Diner)
RECURRING CAST Richard Fancy (Lippman); Estelle Harris (Estelle Costanza); Wayne Knight (Newman); Jerry Stiller (Frank Costanza)

69. "The Bris"
(October 14, 1993)

SUMMARY Elaine and Jerry agree to be godparents and have to arrange the bris. Kramer is against having the infant circumcised. The bris turns into a disaster, and Jerry's finger is sliced. A suicidal man jumps off the hospital and lands on top of George's car. Kramer thinks he sees a pig man and believes he's stumbled across a genetic engineering experiment.

DIRECTOR Tom Cherones
TELEPLAY Larry Charles
GUEST CAST Jeannie Elias (Myra); John Gegenhuber (Resident); Charles Levin (Mohel); Debra Mooney (Mrs. Sweedler); Frank Noon (Patient); Tia Riebling (Woman); Tom Alan Robbins (Stan)

70. "The Lip Reader"
(October 28, 1993)

SUMMARY Kramer becomes a ball boy at the U.S. Open. Jerry is attracted to a deaf line judge. George wants Jerry's new girlfriend to read the lips of his own ex-girlfriend to find out what she is saying about him. Elaine says she is deaf to avoid talking to a chauffeur.

DIRECTOR Tom Cherones
TELEPLAY Carol Leifer
GUEST CAST Bret Anthony (Teen); Christopher Darga (Driver); Dylan Haggerty (Young Man); Veralyn Jones (Renee); Linda Kash (Gwen); Marlee Matlin (Laura); Jerry Sroka (Todd)
RECURRING CAST Wayne Knight (Newman)

71. "The Nonfat Yogurt"
(November 4, 1993)

SUMMARY Kramer invests in a nonfat yogurt shop. Jerry and Elaine have the yogurt tested after they start gaining weight. Jerry swears in front of a little boy. George is caught nudging someone to avoid talking to a childhood friend who is now the mayor's assistant.

OF SPECIAL NOTE Four versions of the ending of this episode were shot, using all the mayoral candidates. For syndication, additional footage featuring eventual winner Rudy Giuliani was added.

DIRECTOR Tom Cherones
TELEPLAY Larry David
GUEST CAST Maryedith Burrell (Maryedith); John Gabriel (Newscaster); John Christian Graas (Matthew); Lisa Houle (Cheryl); Peter Keleghan (Lloyd); Darrell Kunitomi (Lab Technician); Jed Mills (Joel); Hugh A. Rose (Doctor)

RECURRING CAST Estelle Harris (Estelle Costanza); Wayne Knight (Newman); Jerry Stiller (Frank Costanza)

72. "The Barber"
(November 11, 1993)

SUMMARY George can't decide whether he got a job or not, so he goes to work while the boss is on vacation as if he got the job. Jerry gets a bad haircut but is afraid to switch barbers and start going to his cutter's nephew. Jerry meets the nephew at the nephew's apartment for a secret haircut but is caught when the uncle stops by unexpectedly.

DIRECTOR Tom Cherones
TELEPLAY Andy Robin
GUEST CAST David Ciminello (Gino); Michael Fairman (Mr. Pensky); Peggy Maltby (Clarisse); Kenny Myles (Mike); Anthony Ponzini (Enzo); David Richardson (Customer); Jack Shearer (Mr. Tuttle)
RECURRING CAST Wayne Knight (Newman)

73. "The Masseuse"
(November 18, 1993)

SUMMARY Jerry is dating a masseuse who won't give him a massage. George is obsessed with her because she can't stand him. Elaine is dating a man with the same name as notorious killer Joel Rifkin and wants him to change it.

DIRECTOR Tom Cherones
TELEPLAY Peter Mehlman
GUEST CAST John Glen Bishop (Ticket Man); Anthony Cistaro (Joel Rifkin); Jennifer Coolidge (Jody); Lisa Edelstein (Karen); Hiram Kasten (Michael); Lisa Pescia (Lisa)

74. "The Cigar Store Indian"
(December 9, 1993)

SUMMARY Elaine takes one of Mr. Costanza's prized *TV Guide* magazines. Jerry offends a Native American friend of Elaine's, whom he is interested in dating, when he gives Elaine a cigar store Indian. Kramer gets an idea for a coffee-table book about coffee tables. George gets grounded when his parents return from vacation and find an unused condom in their bed and the missing *TV Guide*.

DIRECTOR Tom Cherones

TELEPLAY Tom Gammill and Max Pross

GUEST CAST Carissa Channing (Sylvia); Veralyn Jones (Renee); Sam Lloyd (Ricky); Benjamin Lum (Mailman); Ralph Manza (Gepetto); Irvin Mosley Jr. (Spike); Kimberly Norris (Winona); Lisa Pescia (Joanne); Al Roker (Himself)

RECURRING CAST Richard Fancy (Lippman); Estelle Harris (Estelle Costanza); Jerry Stiller (Frank Costanza)

75. "The Conversion"
(December 16, 1993)

SUMMARY George converts to Latvian Orthodox for his girlfriend, then she moves away. Jerry finds a tube of fungus cream in his girlfriend's medicine cabinet. A nun at George's new church becomes infatuated with Kramer.

DIRECTOR Tom Cherones

TELEPLAY Bruce Kirschbaum

GUEST CAST Randy Brenner (Waiter); Kimberley Campbell (Tawni); Molly Hagan (Sister Roberta); Jana Marie Hupp (Sasha); Darlene Kardon (Mrs. Lupchek); Kay E. Kuter (Older Priest); Karen Rizzo (Woman Hailing Cab); Bill Rose (Younger Priest); Tom Verica (Doctor)

RECURRING CAST Estelle Harris (Estelle Costanza); Jerry Stiller (Frank Costanza)

76. "The Stall"
(January 6, 1994)

SUMMARY Jerry's new girlfriend refuses to give Elaine a square of toilet paper ("I can't spare a square") when they are in adjacent bathroom stalls and Elaine runs out of toilet paper. Kramer thinks the new girlfriend works at a phone sex line. George has a crush on Elaine's rugged new boyfriend. While rock climbing, George causes the boyfriend to fall, and Elaine doesn't think she'll like him if his face has been damaged.

SEINFELD-ESE Mimbo—a male bimbo.

DIRECTOR Tom Cherones

TELEPLAY Larry Charles

GUEST CAST Dan Cortese (Tony); Jami Gertz (Jane)

77. "The Dinner Party"
(February 3, 1994)

SUMMARY On their way to a dinner party, Jerry and Elaine stop at a bakery to get a cake. They forget to take a number and lose the chocolate babka they wanted; the one they get has a hair on it. Kramer and George try to get the wine but can't get their $100 bill changed, then get trapped by a double-parker.

DIRECTOR Tom Cherones
TELEPLAY Larry David
GUEST CAST Sayed Badreya (Foreign Man); Langdon Bensing (Man on Street); Roger Eschbacher (Man With Cane); Mark Holton (David); S. Marc Jordan (Man in Bakery); Kathryn Kates (Counterwoman); Frank Novak (Clerk); Amjad J. Oaisen (Hussein); Fred Pinkard (Newsstand Guy); Suzy Soro (Barbara)

78. "The Marine Biologist"
(February 10, 1994)

SUMMARY Jerry tells an old college classmate that George is now a marine biologist. An infuriated Russian writer tosses Elaine's electronic organizer out of a limousine, hitting a passerby on the head. Kramer struggles with his golf swing. While walking along the beach; George is called on to use his "marine biology" skills to save a whale.

DIRECTOR Tom Cherones
TELEPLAY Ron Hague and Charlie Rubin
GUEST CAST David Blackwood (Hotel Clerk); Carol Kane (Corinne); George Murdock (Testikov); Rosalind Allen (Diane); Heather Morgan (Woman on Beach)
RECURRING CAST Richard Fancy (Lippman); Wayne Knight (Newman)

79. "The Pie"
(February 17, 1994)

SUMMARY Jerry's date refuses to take a bite of his apple pie. Then Jerry won't taste the pizza her father made because the father didn't wash his hands. Elaine wants to know why a mannequin is her double. Kramer has an itch. George gets a suit at half price, then discovers it makes a noise when he walks.

DIRECTOR Tom Cherones

TELEPLAY Tom Gammill and Max Pross

GUEST CAST Patricia Belcher (Woman #1); Mark Beltzman (Bob); Lane Davies (MacKenzie); Christine Dunford (Saleswoman); Tony Edwards (Businessman); Bernard Hocke (Guy in Diner); Robert Kino (Ricky's Boss); Sam Lloyd (Ricky); Pamela Mant (Woman #2); Paul Mantee (Health Inspector); Eamonn Roche (Waiter); Reni Santoni (Poppie); Suzanne Snyder (Audrey); Sunday Theodore (Olive)

80. "The Stand-in"
(February 24, 1994)

SUMMARY Kramer talks his stand-in friend, a little person, into getting lifts. Jerry visits a sick friend at the hospital. George is accused of not committing. Another friend of Jerry's takes "it" out on his first date with Elaine. Jerry's friend takes a turn for the worse after his first visit so he tries again.

DIRECTOR Tom Cherones

TELEPLAY Larry David

GUEST CAST Layne Beamer (Father); Jerome Betler (Director); W. Earl Brown (Al); Debbie Lee Carrington (Tammy); Thomas Dekker (Son); Joe Gieb (Johnny); Michael Rivkin (Fulton); Karla Tamburrelli (Daphne); Mark Tymchyshyn (Phil)

RECURRING CAST Danny Woodburn (Mickey Abbott)

81. "The Wife"
(March 18, 1994)

SUMMARY Jerry pretends to be married so he and his girlfriend can share a discount at the dry cleaners. George is caught peeing in the shower of his health club. Elaine is getting mixed signals from a male friend who may be interested in her. Kramer wants to impress his girlfriend's parents, so he goes to a tanning salon.

DIRECTOR Tom Cherones

TELEPLAY Peter Mehlman

GUEST CAST Courteney Cox (Meryl); Scott LaRose (Greg); Joseph Ragno (Marty); Rebecca Glenn (Paula); Nick LaTour (Grandpa); Susan Segal (Waitress); Lili Bernard (Anna); Lawrence A. Mandley (Owner)

RECURRING CAST Len Lesser (Uncle Leo); Barney Martin (Morty Seinfeld); Liz Sheridan (Helen Seinfeld)

82. "The Raincoats (Part I)"
(April 28, 1994)

SUMMARY While waiting to leave for Paris, Jerry's parents are staying with him, which prevents Jerry from spending some private time with his girlfriend. George is talked into being a Big Brother, then tries to get out of it. The Seinfelds avoid the Costanzas' dinner invitation. Elaine's latest boyfriend is a close-talker.

SEINFELD-ESE Close-talker—someone who routinely invades others' personal space.

OF SPECIAL NOTE Episodes 82 and 83 were originally aired as a one-hour special but were split for syndication.

DIRECTOR Tom Cherones
TELEPLAY Tom Gammill, Max Pross, Larry David, and Jerry Seinfeld
GUEST CAST Michael G. Hagerty (Rudy); Annie Korzen (Doris Klompus); Lisa Pescia (Joanne); Judge Reinhold (Aaron); Melanie Smith (Rachel); Dorien Wilson (Alec)
RECURRING CAST Sandy Baron (Jack Klompus); Estelle Harris (Estelle Costanza); Barney Martin (Morty Seinfeld); Liz Sheridan (Helen Seinfeld); Jerry Stiller (Frank Costanza)

83. "The Raincoats (Part II)"
(April 28, 1994)

SUMMARY Jerry is seen by Newman making out with his girlfriend during *Schindler's List*. The Seinfelds miss their flight to France. George plans to get his "little brother" back to his father. The Seinfelds manage to continue to avoid meeting the Costanzas.

DIRECTOR Tom Cherones
TELEPLAY Tom Gammill, Max Pross, Larry David, and Jerry Seinfeld
GUEST CAST Michael G. Hagerty (Rudy); Annie Korzen (Doris Klompus); Jason Manary (Joey); Stephen Pearlman (Mr. Goldstein); Judge Reinhold (Aaron); Melanie Smith (Rachel); LaRita Shelby (Tour Leader); Dorien Wilson (Alec)
RECURRING CAST Sandy Baron (Jack Klompus); Estelle Harris (Estelle Costanza); Barney Martin (Morty Seinfeld); Liz Sheridan (Helen Seinfeld); Jerry Stiller (Frank Costanza)

84. "The Fire"
(May 5, 1994)

SUMMARY Kramer is dating one of Elaine's co-workers. When he takes her to Jerry's show, she turns into a heckler. Jerry gets revenge by heckling the woman at her office. She's so upset, she runs into the street, where her toe is severed by a street sweeper. Kramer finds the toe, commandeers a bus to take it to the hospital and saves the passengers from a gunman. George panics when there is a fire at his girlfriend's apartment and acts like a coward.

DIRECTOR Tom Cherones
TELEPLAY Larry Charles
GUEST CAST Melanie Chartoff (Robin); Veanne Cox (Toby); Jon Favreau (Clown); Dom Irrera (Ronnie); Lisa Pescia (Joanne); Hiram Kasten (Michael); Lawrence LeJohn (Fireman)
RECURRING CAST Estelle Harris (Estelle Costanza); Jerry Stiller (Frank Costanza)

85. "The Hamptons"
   (May 12, 1994)

SUMMARY Everyone goes out to the Hamptons. The baby they are there to see is ugly. Everybody sees George's girlfriend topless—except George. Elaine is confused when a handsome doctor refers to her as breathtaking, then uses the same word to describe the ugly baby. Kramer finds a filled lobster trap. Jerry's girlfriend sees George naked while he's afflicted by "shrinkage."
SEINFELD-ESE Shrinkage—what happens to a certain male body part after being in very cold water.

DIRECTOR Tom Cherones
TELEPLAY Peter Mehlman and Carol Leifer
GUEST CAST Richard Burgi (Ben); Jesse D. Goins (Cop); Lisa Mende (Carol); Melanie Smith (Rachel); Mark L. Taylor (Michael); Melora Walters (Jane)

86. "The Opposite"
   (May 19, 1994)

SUMMARY George tries to do the opposite of his natural inclinations, and suddenly his luck turns around: he gets a girlfriend and a job with the Yankees and moves out of his parents' house. Elaine's luck turns bad after she buys a box of Jujyfruits. Kramer appears on *Live With Regis & Kathie Lee* to promote his coffee-table book. Jerry's luck has been even-Steven.
OF SPECIAL NOTE Larry David supplies the voice of George Steinbrenner. This was also director Tom Cherone's last episode.

TRIVIA When Larry David is not sitting in the chair posing as Steinbrenner, the part is played by Lee Bear.

DIRECTOR Tom Cherones

TELEPLAY Andy Cowan, Larry David, and Jerry Seinfeld

GUEST CAST Jeff Barton (Poker Player #3); Marvin Braverman (Poker Player #1); Siobhan Fallon (Tina); Michael Friedman (Punk #2); Kathie Lee Gifford (Herself); Paul Gleason (Cushman); Oscar Jordan (Counterperson); Hiram Kasten (Michael); Fritz Mashimo (Interpreter); Rolando Molina (Punk #1); Dedee Pfeiffer (Victoria); Regis Philbin (Himself); Marty Rackham (Jake Jarmel); Susan Segal (Waitress); Melanie Smith (Rachel); French Stewart (Manager); Ken Takemoto (Chairman); Wesley Thompson (Poker Player #2); Jeffrey Von Meyer (Poker Player #4)

RECURRING CAST Larry David (Voice of George Steinbrenner); Richard Fancy (Lippman); Estelle Harris (Estelle Costanza); Jerry Stiller (Frank Costanza)

SEASON SIX

87. "The Chaperone"
(September 22, 1994)

SUMMARY Kramer acts as chaperone on Jerry's date with Miss Rhode Island. Kramer becomes her personal coach. Elaine gets a job at Doubleday, working for an executive who likes white socks. George decides that the Yankees need to change their uniforms from polyester to cotton.

INTRODUCING Mr. Pitt, Elaine's boss at Doubleday.

OF SPECIAL NOTE Andy Ackerman took over as primary director.

DIRECTOR Andy Ackerman

TELEPLAY Larry David, Bill Masters, and Bob Shaw

GUEST CAST Marguerite MacIntyre (Karen); Buck Showalter (Himself); Gail Strickland (Landis); Danny Tartabull (Himself)

RECURRING CAST Ian Abercombie (Mr. Pitt)

88. "The Big Salad"
(September 29, 1994)

SUMMARY George buys Elaine a big salad, then gets upset when his girlfriend takes credit for it. Elaine's boss, Mr. Pitt, wants a special mechanical pencil. Jerry discovers that his current girlfriend once dated Newman.

Gednison cheats at golf and then kills the dry cleaner. Driving a white Ford Bronco, Kramer helps him evade the police.

OF SPECIAL NOTE Lauren Bowles is Julia Louis-Dreyfus's half-sister.

DIRECTOR Andy Ackerman

TELEPLAY Larry David

GUEST CAST Lauren Bowles (Waitress); Michelle Forbes (Julie); Marita Geraghty (Margaret); Dean Hallo (Gendason); Jerry Levine (Stationer); Barry Nolan (Reporter)

RECURRING CAST Wayne Knight (Newman)

89. "The Pledge Drive"
(October 6, 1994)

SUMMARY Elaine's friend Noreen is dating a high-talker, and Elaine can't tell their voices apart. Her boss eats his Snickers bar with a knife and fork, which becomes a fad. George thinks a waitress gave him the finger. Jerry gets caught throwing away a thank-you card. Jerry cashes some old birthday checks from his grandmother.

SEINFELD-ESE High-talker—a man who sounds like a woman.

DIRECTOR Andy Ackerman

TELEPLAY Tom Gammill and Max Pross

GUEST CAST Lauren Bowles (Waitress); Kelly Coffield (Noreen); Brian Reddy (Dan); James Reynolds (Banker); F. J. Rio (Street Tough); Rebecca Staab (Kristin); Danny Tartabull (Himself); Thom Vernon (Driver); Billye Ree Wallace (Nana); Tom Wright (Executive)

RECURRING CAST Ian Abercombie (Mr. Pitt); Len Lesser (Uncle Leo)

90. "The Chinese Woman"
(October 13, 194)

SUMMARY Jerry makes a date with a woman he thinks is Chinese after "meeting" her when George's phone wires get crossed. Elaine's friend Noreen is now dating a long-talker. Kramer has to give up his briefs because his sperm count is low. George's life is made miserable when his parents separate and contemplate divorce.

SEINFELD-ESE Long-talker—just what it sounds like.

DIRECTOR Andy Ackerman

TELEPLAY Peter Mehlman

GUEST CAST Kelly Coffield (Noreen); Larry David (Man With Cape); Angela

Dohrmann (Donna Chang); Lucy Lin (Hostess); Jack Tracy (Man); William Will Utay (Dr. Korval)
RECURRING CAST Estelle Harris (Estelle Harris); Jerry Stiller (Frank)

91. "The Couch"
(October 27, 1994)

SUMMARY Elaine dates Poppie, who delivered Jerry's couch. Kramer plans to start a pizza business with Poppie. George joins a book-discussion club but plans to rent the movie so he can bluff his way through the meeting without reading the book; he ends up spending the evening with the family that beat him to the video first. Elaine dumps Poppie when she finds out he's not pro-choice. Jerry and Elaine's discussion of the abortion issue causes Poppie to urinate on Jerry's new couch.

DIRECTOR Andy Ackerman
TELEPLAY Larry David
GUEST CAST Beverly C. Brown (Woman #3); Tamar Cooper (Woman #2); Denise Dowse (Mother); David James Elliott (Carl); Jessica Hecht (Marie); Robert Hooks (Joe Temple); Patton Oswalt (Clerk); Jeris Lee Poindexter (Man); Reni Santoni (Poppie); Diana Theodore (Remy); Mari Weiss (Woman #1)

92. "The Gymnast"
(November 3, 1994)

SUMMARY Jerry wants to have sex with his new girlfriend because she's a Rumanian Olympic gymnast; she wants to have sex with him because he is a comedian. Kramer passes a kidney stone. George's girlfriend's mother sees George eat something out of a trash bin. Mr. Pitt becomes obsessed with finding the image in a 3-D painting, so he sends her to represent him in a huge merger deal.

DIRECTOR Andy Ackerman
TELEPLAY Alec Berg and Jeff Schaffer
GUEST CAST David Blackwood (Beck); Maurice Godin (Misha); Jessica Hecht (Lindsay); Damian London (Party Guest); Elina Löwensohn (Katya); Lois Nettleton (Mrs. Enright); Phil Ramsey (Man in Car); James Sweeney (Aronson)
RECURRING CAST Ian Abercombie (Mr. Pitt)

93. "The Soup"
(November 10, 1994)

SUMMARY A man Elaine met in England turns out to be a moocher. Jerry gets a free suit from an obnoxious comic but has to take the guy out to dinner. George goes for a walk with a waitress from Monk's. Because of the kidney stone, Kramer decides to eat only fresh foods.

DIRECTOR Andy Ackerman
TELEPLAY Fred Stoller
GUEST CAST Daniel Gerroll (Simon); Michael Kaplan (Waiter); Tracy Kolis (Kelly); Lawrence A. Mandley (Manager); Linda Wallem (Hildy)
RECURRING CAST Steve Hytner (Bania)

94. "The Mom-and-Pop Store"
(November 14, 1994)

SUMMARY A salesman convinces George to buy a convertible he says was once owned by Jon Voight. Kramer tries to save a small shoe-repair shop by giving it all of Jerry's shoes. When it goes out of business, Jerry's shoes are sold in a garage sale. Elaine wins tickets for Mr. Pitt to Macy's Thanksgiving Day Parade, where he helps with the Woody Woodpecker balloon. Jerry crashes a party during the parade.

DIRECTOR Andy Ackerman
TELEPLAY Tom Gammill and Max Pross
GUEST CAST Pat Asanti (Electrician); Nancy Balbirer (Woman at Party); Steve Brady (Man at Party); Rick Fitts (Dentist); Dan Frischman (Guy on Phone); Matt Gallini (Tough Guy); Elsa Raven (Mom); Michael Robello (Pop); Ken Thorley (Car Salesman); Jon Voight (Himself); Tom Wright (Morgan)
RECURRING CAST Ian Abercombie (Mr. Pitt); Bryan Cranston (Whatley)

95. "The Secretary"
(December 8, 1994)

SUMMARY Jerry spots his dry cleaner wearing his jacket. George hires a secretary because she is not good-looking, then gives her a raise during sex. Kramer gets Uma Thurman's phone number and sells Bania his suit. Elaine accuses a store of having skinny mirrors.

DIRECTOR David Owen Trainor
TELEPLAY Carol Leifer and Marjorie Gross

GUEST CAST Arminae Azarian (Saleswoman); Vicki Lewis (Ada); Richard Marion (Guy); Mitzi McCall (Donna); Glynis McCants (Woman); Thomas Mills (Moviegoer); Joseph R. Sicari (Willie); Courtney Taylor (Attractive Applicant)
RECURRING CAST Steve Hytner (Bania)

96. "The Race"
(December 15, 1994)

SUMMARY Kramer gets a job as a department store Santa. Elaine is put on a blacklist for Chinese food delivery and finds out her boyfriend is a Communist. George responds to a personal ad in a Communist newspaper while at work; when George Steinbrenner hears about it, he wants to see George in his office. Jerry runs into his old rival, who wants a rematch of their high school race to prove he was faster.
TRIVIA Elaine's address is 16 West 75th Street, #2-G.

DIRECTOR Andy Ackerman
TELEPLAY Tom Gammill, Max Pross, and Larry David; story: Tom Gammill, Max Pross, Larry David, and Sam Kass
GUEST CAST Martin Chow (Lew); Claude Earl Jones (Mr. Bevilaqua); Todd Kimsey (Ned); Spencer Klein (Kid); Mark Christopher Lawrence (Boss); Vicki Lewis (Ada); Don R. McManus (Duncan); Denise Poirier (Arlene); Renee Props (Lois); Michael Sorich (Castro); Eva Svensson (Woman)
RECURRING CAST Danny Woodburn (Mickey Abbott)

97. "The Switch"
(January 5, 1995)

SUMMARY Elaine lends out Mr. Pitt's tennis racket and has trouble getting it back. George thinks his girlfriend is bulimic. Jerry's girlfriend never laughs; he meets her roommate, who does, and decides he would like to switch one for the other. George encourages Jerry to suggest a ménage à trois to turn off the girlfriend—but she's into the idea.
REVEALED Kramer's first name—Cosmo.

DIRECTOR Andy Ackerman
TELEPLAY Bruce Kirschbaum and Sam Kass
GUEST CAST Cheryl Francis Harrington (Waitress); Jacqueline M. Houston (Lorraine); Jann Karam (Sandi); Charlotte Lewis (Nina); Heather Medway (Laura); Sheree North (Babs Kramer); Clive Rosengren (Mr. Clotworthy); Tish Smiley (Woman); Gail Strickland (Landis); Terry Sweeney (Keith)
RECURRING CAST Wayne Knight (Newman)

98. "The Label Maker"
   (Janury 1, 1995)

SUMMARY Elaine and Jerry suspect a friend of being a re-gifter after he gives Jerry a label maker identical to one Elaine gave the friend. Jerry can't use his Super Bowl tickets because he's best man at a wedding taking place on Super Bowl Sunday. George dates a woman with a male roommate. Kramer and Newman play a game of Risk.

SEINFELD-ESE Re-gifter—someone who gets a gift, then turns around and gives it to someone else.

DIRECTOR Andy Ackerman
TELEPLAY Alec Berg and Jeff Schaffer
GUEST CAST Cleto Augusto (Scott); Jessica Tuck (Bonnie); Wayne Grace (Ukranian)
RECURRING CAST Wayne Knight (Newman); Bryan Cranston (Whatley)

99. "The Scofflaw"
   (Janaury 26, 1995)

SUMMARY George meets an old friend who lies about having cancer to get Jerry's sympathy. Elaine gets back at Jake Jarmel by buying the same kind of eyeglass frames he has. Kramer discovers Newman is a parking scofflaw. George gets a toupee.

TRIVIA Daniel Benzali was originally scheduled to play the part of the officer.

DIRECTOR Andy Ackerman
TELEPLAY Peter Mehlman
GUEST CAST Danny Breen (Guy With Glasses); Dale Harimoto (Reporter); Basil Hoffman (Salesman); Lillian Lehman (Judge); Jon Lovitz (Gary Fogel); Ivory Ocean (Officer Morgan); Joe Ochman (Customer); Bob Shaw (Cabbie); Elisabeth Sjoli (Woman); Marty Rackham (Jake Jarmel); Barbara Alyn Woods (Debby)
RECURRING CAST Wayne Knight (Newman); Richard Fancy (Lippman)

100. "Highlights of a Hundred (Part I)" (a.k.a. "The Clip Show")
   (February 2, 1995)

SUMMARY Jerry introduces a program of highlights from the first ninety-nine episodes of a show about nothing.

OF SPECIAL NOTE Episodes 100 and 101 originally aired as a one-hour special but were split for syndication.

DIRECTOR Andy Ackerman
TELEPLAY Peter Mehlman

101. "Highlights of a Hundred (Part II)"
(February 2, 1995)

SUMMARY Jerry introduces a program of highlights from the first ninety-nine episodes of a show about nothing.

DIRECTOR Andy Ackerman
TELEPLAY Peter Mehlman

102. "The Beard"
(February 9, 1995)

SUMMARY Elaine tries to convert a gay man to heterosexuality. Kramer sets George up with a bald woman. Kramer gives a homeless man some Chinese food and begins standing in police lineups for $50 each time. Jerry's cop girlfriend wants him to take a lie detector test to prove he's lying about *not* watching *Melrose Place*.

TRIVIA Writer Carol Leifer came up with the idea of having Kramer participate in police lineups after reading that David Caruso used to do it when he was a struggling actor. Also, she says the secret *Melrose Place* viewer on the set was Larry David.

DIRECTOR Andy Ackerman
TELEPLAY Carol Leifer
GUEST CAST Jerry Diner (Lou); Joan Elizabeth (Denise); Jonathan Gries (Homeless Man); Georgann Johnson (Mrs. Stevenson); Ken Kerman (Officer #2); Katherine LaNasa (Cathy); Robert Mailhouse (Robert); John F. O'Donohue (Gus); Mirron E. Willis (Officer #1); Ed Winter (Mr. Stevenson)

103. "The Kiss Hello"
(February 16, 1995)

SUMMARY Kramer puts tenant pictures up in the lobby. When Jerry stops kissing the women of his building hello, he becomes unpopular. George is charged for canceling an appointment with his therapist, then tries to charge her when she cancels on him in order to go skiing with Elaine. Elaine injures her shoulder carrying her equipment home.

OF SPECIAL NOTE According to a *Los Angeles Times* feature from 1995, this was actually the hundredth episode of the series filmed, after which the cast and crew had a party to celebrate the milestone. "The Beard," which aired first, was actually filmed after "The Kiss Hello."

DIRECTOR Andy Ackerman

TELEPLAY Larry David and Jerry Seinfeld

GUEST CAST Louisa Abernathy (Nurse); Belinda Barry (Stephanie); Gene Elman (Buddy); Mark Fite (Jack); C. D. LaBove (Steve); Carol Leifer (Receptionist); Wendie Malick (Wendy); Timothy McNeil (Jeff); Julio Oscar Mechoso (Julio); Rondi Reed (Mary); Mary Scheer (Joan); Billye Ree Wallace (Nana); Wendy Worthington (Louise)

RECURRING CAST Len Lesser (Uncle Leo); Barney Martin (Morty Seinfeld); Liz Sheridan (Helen)

104. "The Doorman"
(February 23, 1995)

SUMMARY Kramer robs George on the street for some German tourists. After seeing George's father shirtless, Kramer gets the idea for a male bra. Jerry is bothered by the doorman in Mr. Pitt's building. Jerry offers his soiled couch to replace the one that was stolen while Jerry was on duty.

TRIVIA Mr. Pitt's first name is Justin.

DIRECTOR Andy Ackerman

TELEPLAY Tom Gammill and Max Pross

GUEST CAST Jack Betts (Mr. Green); Patrick Cronin (Farkus); Edith Fields (Mrs. Payton); Trudi Forristal (Buxom Woman); Nigel Gibbs (Tenant #2); Nick Jameson (Horst); Deck McKenzie (Delivery Man); Larry Miller (Doorman); Barbara Pilavin (German Woman); Reni Santoni (Poppie); Toni Sawyer (Tenant #1)

RECURRING CAST Ian Abercombie (Mr. Pitt); Estelle Harris (Estelle Costanza); Jerry Stiller (Frank Costanza)

105. "The Jimmy"
(March 16, 1995)

SUMMARY The guys become acquainted with Jimmy, a man who only talks about himself in the third person. Elaine unwittingly makes a date with him. Jerry goes to the dentist's office and discovers they now provide *Penthouse* in the waiting room. Novocain causes Kramer to appear mentally handicapped, and he gets to meet Mel Tormé. Jerry thinks he might have been violated at the dentist's.

DIRECTOR Andy Ackerman

TELEPLAY Gregg Kavet and Andy Robin

GUEST CAST Alison Armitage (Cheryl); J. D. Bridges (Paramedic); Elan Carter (Receptionist); Robert Katims (Deensfrei); Anthony Starke (Jimmy); Mel Tormé (Himself)

106. "The Doodle"
(April 6, 1995)

SUMMARY Jerry has fleas, so his visiting parents stay in a fancy hotel suite that was provided for Elaine by the company she is interviewing with. Jerry is disgusted when he finds out he was eating pecans that had just been in his girlfriend's mouth. George finds a doodle that his girlfriend drew of him. Jerry figures out that Newman gave him the fleas.

DIRECTOR Andy Ackerman

TELEPLAY Alec Berg and Jeff Schaffer

GUEST CAST Norman Brenner (Passerby); Wayne C. Dvorak (Teacher); Christa Miller (Paula); Guy Siner (Mandel); Coby Turner (Judy); Billye Ree Wallace (Nana); Dana Wheeler-Nicholson (Shelly); Ellis E. Williams (Karl)

RECURRING CAST Wayne Knight (Newman); Len Lesser (Uncle Leo); Barney Martin (Morty Seinfeld); Liz Sheridan (Helen Seinfeld)

107. "The Fusilli Jerry"
(April 27, 1995)

SUMMARY Estelle is getting an eye job. Jerry lets Elaine's boyfriend in on his "move," then gets upset when he uses it. George needs a move, so he takes notes on Jerry's. Kramer accidentally gets license plates that read ASSMAN. Kramer also makes a statue of Jerry out of fusilli, and George's dad sits on it.

DIRECTOR Andy Ackerman

TELEPLAY Marjorie Gross; story: Marjorie Gross, Jonathan Gross, Ron Hague, and Charlie Rubin

GUEST CAST Yvette Cruise (Clerk); Lou Cutell (Dr. Cooperman); Marla Sucharetza (Nancy)

RECURRING CAST Estelle Harris (Estelle Costanza); Jerry Stiller (Frank Costanza); Patrick Warburton (Puddy)

108. "The Diplomat's Club"
(May 4, 1995)

SUMMARY Jerry's agent is driving him crazy. Elaine almost quits her job but then gets fired when she is suspected of trying to kill Mr. Pitt. George tries to prove to his boss that he is not a racist. While at the airport club, Kramer starts gambling again for the first time in three years.

DIRECTOR Andy Ackerman
TELEPLAY Tom Gammill and Max Pross
GUEST CAST Christine Cattell (Stewardess); O'Neal Compton (Earl); John Cothran Jr. (Man); Robert Hooks (Joe); William B. Jackson (Doctor); Debra Jo Rupp (Katie); Diana Theodore (Remy); Berta Maria Waagfjord (Bridgette); Mark Wheatle (Waiter); Ellis E. Williams (Karl the Exterminator); Tom Wright (Morgan); Kim Zimmer (Lenore)
RECURRING CAST Ian Abercombie (Mr. Pitt); Wayne Knight (Newman)

109. "The Face Painter"
(May 11, 1995)

SUMMARY George tells his girlfriend he loves her, but gets no response. Kramer gets in a fight with a monkey at the zoo, causing it to suffer depression. Elaine is dating a guy who paints his face for hockey games. Jerry gets free hockey tickets but doesn't call to say thanks.
OF SPECIAL NOTE The real Kramer, Kenny, appears in a cameo as one of the fans at the hockey game, sitting next to writer Fred Stoller.

DIRECTOR Andy Ackerman
TELEPLAY Larry David; story: Larry David and Fred Stoller
GUEST CAST Raye Birk (Mr. Pless); Mark DeCarlo (Alec Berg); Jan Eddy (Fan #3); Joe Lala (Priest); Lawrence LeJohn (Crowd Member); Pierrino Mascarino (Father Hernandez); Peggy Lane O'Rourke (Waitress); Dave Powledge (Fan #2); David Richardson (Fan #1); Katy Selverstone (Siena)
RECURRING CAST Patrick Warburton (Puddy)

110. "The Understudy"
(May 18, 1995)

SUMMARY Jerry is dating Bette Midler's understudy. George and Jerry are suspected, by the cast of Bette's show and Kramer, of deliberately injuring the star during a softball game so the girlfriend can perform in her place. Kramer becomes Bette's personal assistant. Elaine thinks the Korean manicurists are making fun of her, so she takes George's father with her to translate. She also meets the owner of a catalog, J. Peterman, and gets herself a new job.

DIRECTOR Andy Ackerman
TELEPLAY Marjorie Gross and Carol Leifer
GUEST CAST Bette Midler (Herself); William Bastiani (Vendor #2); Bok Yun Chon (Lotus); Amy Hill (Kim); June Kyoko Lu (Ruby); Adelaide Miller (Gennice); Vonnie C. Rhee (Sunny); Craig Thomas (Player #1); Michael James McDonald (Player #2); Lou DiMaggio (Stagehand); Jason Beck (Umpire); Bob Shaw (Cabbie); Johnny Silver (Vendor #1)
RECURRING CAST John O'Hurley (Jacopo "J." Peterman); Jerry Stiller (Frank Costanza)

SEASON SEVEN

111. "The Engagement"
(September 21, 1995)

SUMMARY George and Jerry agree to change their lives, so George gets engaged to Susan and Jerry plans to commit to his girlfriend. Elaine gets Kramer and Newman to help her get rid of a barking dog. Jerry breaks up with his girlfriend, leaving George trapped in his relationship with Susan.

DIRECTOR Andy Ackerman
TELEPLAY Larry David
GUEST CAST Mario Joyner (Himself); Janni Brenn (Woman #2); Mailon Rivera (Cop #1); Athena Massey (Melanie); Ron Byron (Man); Renee Phillips (Alice); Cindy Cheung (Woman #1)
RECURRING CAST Estelle Harris (Estelle Costanza); Wayne Knight (Newman); Jerry Stiller (Frank Costanza); Heidi Swedberg (Susan)

112. "The Postponement"
(September 28, 1995)

SUMMARY George gets Susan to postpone the wedding date. Elaine is jealous of George's being engaged and confides in a rabbi, who proceeds to tell everyone. Kramer and Jerry try to see *Plan 9 From Outer Space*. Kramer sneaks a café latte into the theater and spills it all over himself, burning himself. His lawyer says he has a case.

OF SPECIAL NOTE Bruce Mahler worked with Larry David on *Fridays,* where he also played a rabbi.

DIRECTOR Andy Ackerman
TELEPLAY Larry David
GUEST CAST Bruce Mahler (Rabbi Glickman); Kelly Perine (Usher); John Rubano (Man); Evie Peck (Woman)
RECURRING CAST Heidi Swedberg (Susan)

113. "The Maestro"
(October 5, 1995)

SUMMARY Kramer sues the coffee shop because the latte was too hot. Elaine dates a man who insists on being called the Maestro. George thinks a security guard who works at Elaine's uncle's store should be allowed to sit down. Jerry rents a house in Tuscany from Poppie's cousin. Kramer settles in his lawsuit against the coffee house for free coffee at any location around the world.

DIRECTOR Andy Ackerman
TELEPLAY Larry David
GUEST CAST Mark Metcalf (Maestro); Gary Yates (Security Guard); Paul Michael (Giggio); James Noah (Ned); Tim Bagley (Manager); Richard McGonagle (Mr. Star); Kenneth Ryan (Mr. Burns); Kymberley S. Newberry (Ms. Jordan); David Wendelman (Waiter)
RECURRING CAST Phil Morris (Jackie Chiles); Heidi Swedberg (Susan)

114. "The Wink"
(October 12, 1995)

SUMMARY George gets grapefruit juice squirted into his eye and can't stop winking at inappropriate times. Jerry is dating Elaine's cousin, but his vegetarian diet is incompatible with her meat-eating ways. Elaine's wake-up service goes bad when she starts dating the caller. Kramer promises a sick boy that Yankee Paul O'Neill will hit two home runs for him.

DIRECTOR Andy Ackerman
TELEPLAY Tom Gammill and Max Pross
GUEST CAST Tom Wright (Morgan); Stacey Travis (Holly); Brian McNamara (James); Ian Patrick Williams (Stubs); Paul O'Neill (Himself); Thomas Dekker (Bobby); Clive Rosengren (Waiter)
RECURRING CAST Richard Herd (Wilhelm)

115. "The Hot Tub"
(October 19, 1995)

SUMMARY Kramer gets a hot tub. Elaine has writer's block. A runner participating in the New York City Marathon is staying with Elaine. George acts annoyed so that he looks busy at work.

DIRECTOR Andy Ackerman
TELEPLAY Gregg Kavet and Andy Robin
GUEST CAST Jeremiah Birkett (Jean-Paul); Leon Russom (Clayton); Ernie Lively (Zeke); Charles Cyphers (Gardner); Kate Mulligan (Sheri); Susan Isaacs (Woman); Thom Barry (Manager); Jeff Miller (Event Guard)
RECURRING CAST Richard Herd (Wilhelm)

116. "The Soup Nazi"
(November 2, 1995)

SUMMARY Everyone wants soup from the Soup Nazi, who has very strict ordering procedures. George and Elaine are bothered by how affectionate Jerry is with his new girlfriend. Elaine buys an armoire, which is stolen while Kramer is supposed to be watching it. He replaces it with one given to him by the Soup Nazi, which contains his soup recipes. Elaine makes an ordering error in front of the Soup Nazi and is banned for a year. George confronts Jerry and reminds him about their pact.
CATCHPHRASE "No soup for you!"
OF SPECIAL NOTE The Soup Nazi is based on Al Yeganeh, the owner of Soup Kitchen International in Manhattan.

DIRECTOR Andy Ackerman
TELEPLAY Spike Feresten
GUEST CAST Alexandra Wentworth (Sheila); Larry Thomas (Soup Nazi); John Paragon (Ray); Yul Vazquez (Bob); Thom Barry (Super); Vince Melocchi (Furniture Guy); Ana Gasteyer (Woman); Cedric Duplechain (Customer); Mike Michaud (Customer)
RECURRING CAST Steve Hytner (Bania); Wayne Knight (Newman); Heidi Swedberg (Susan)

117. "The Secret Code"
(November 9, 1995)

SUMMARY George won't tell anyone his ATM code, including Susan. Jerry's foot keeps falling asleep, making Leapin' Larry, a one-legged man, think Jerry is making fun of him. Kramer tries to help the fire department.

Elaine is interested in a boring guy just because he forgets her. George ends up telling Peterman's dying mother his ATM code.

DIRECTOR Andy Ackerman
TELEPLAY Alec Berg and Jeff Schaffer
GUEST CAST Wayne Tippit (Captain); Lewis Arquette (Leapin' Larry); Fred Stoller (Fred Yerkes); Ellen Albertini Dow (Momma); David St. James (Doctor); Michael Luckerman (Man)
RECURRING CAST John O'Hurley (J. Peterman); Heidi Swedberg (Susan)

118. "The Pool Guy"
(November 16, 1995)

SUMMARY Jerry gets rid of an annoying pool attendant who wants to be his friend. George is upset about his worlds colliding when Elaine and Susan appear to become friends. Kramer's new phone number is similar to a film information line and he gets the line's calls, so he begins giving out the information.

DIRECTOR Andy Ackerman
TELEPLAY David Mandel
GUEST CAST Carlos Jacott (Ramon); Billy Williams (Usher); Alec Mapa (Paul); Dom Magwili (Dustin)
RECURRING CAST Wayne Knight (Newman); Heidi Swedberg (Susan)

119. "The Sponge"
(December 7, 1995)

SUMMARY Elaine has to be picky about her partners after she learns her preferred method of birth control is in short supply. George reveals some secrets about Jerry to Susan. Kramer walks for AIDS but causes an incident when he refuses to wear the red ribbon. Jerry finds the number of a girl he wants to contact on Kramer's AIDS-walk sponsor list.
REVEALED Jerry changes the labels in his jeans so people think he's a size smaller than he really is.
SEINFELD-ESE Spongeworthy—A man worth using one of Elaine's few remaining contraceptive sponges.

DIRECTOR Andy Ackerman
TELEPLAY Peter Mehlman
GUEST CAST Jennifer Guthrie (Lena); Scott Patterson (Billy); John Paragon (Cedric); Yul Vazquez (Bob); David Byrd (Roger); Ileen Getz (Organizer);

Steven Hack (Walker #1); Wren T. Brown (Walker #2); P. B. Hutton (Walker #3); Susan Moore (Monica)
RECURRING CAST Heidi Swedberg (Susan)

120. "The Gum"
(December 14, 1995)

SUMMARY Kramer opens an old movie theater and befriends Lloyd, a childhood friend of George's who had a nervous breakdown. Elaine tries not to lead Lloyd on, because she feels partly responsible for the breakdown, then loses a button on her blouse and exposes herself to Lloyd and Kramer. George's car catches fire, and another old friend thinks he's mentally ill.

OF SPECIAL NOTE Larry David makes a cameo appearance as the guy who sells George a pack of gum.

DIRECOR Andy Ackerman
TELEPLAY Tom Gammill and Max Pross
GUEST CAST Matt Mc Coy (Lloyd); Mary Jo Keenen (Deena); Eric Christmas (Haarwood); Sandy Ward (Pop Lazzari); Ruth Cohen (Cashier); Lionel Mark Smith Vito D'Ambrosio (Cop); Alan Watt (Attendant)

121. "The Rye"
(January 4, 1996)

SUMMARY Elaine is dating a jazz saxophonist who's spongeworthy, but he doesn't really like to do "everything" sexually. Susan's parents meet and have dinner with the Costanzas for the first time. George tries to replace a rye bread that his father took back from Susan's parents after their dinner. Kramer gives Susan's parents a ride in a friend's horse-drawn carriage—after feeding the horse Beef-A-Reeno, which causes the horse to be extremely flatulent. Jerry mugs an old lady for her loaf of marble rye. After finally doing "everything," the saxophonist can't play his instrument any more.

OF SPECIAL NOTE Three of this episode's guest stars—Frances Bay, Warren Frost, and Grace Zabriskie—were alumni of David Lynch's series *Twin Peaks*.

DIRECTOR Andy Ackerman
TELEPLAY Carol Leifer
GUEST CAST Grace Zabriskie (Mrs. Ross); Warren Frost (Mr. (Henry) Ross); Jeff Yagher (John); Frances Bay (Mabel Choate); Leonard Lightfoot

(Clyde); Don Amendolia (Dennis); Kathryn Kates (Counter Woman); Steve Ireland (Music Guy); Dean Fortunato (Manager)

RECURRING CAST Estelle Harris (Estelle Costanza); Jerry Stiller (Frank Costanza); Heidi Swedberg (Susan)

122. "The Caddy"
(January 25, 1996)

SUMMARY George leaves his car at Yankee Stadium, making people think he's working extra long hours. Kramer befriends a caddy. Elaine meets an old friend who never wears a bra, and Elaine gets her one for her birthday. When the friend wears the bra as a top, Kramer and Jerry have an accident with George's car. George and Susan go up north to her parents' rebuilt cabin.

DIRECTOR Andy Ackerman
TELEPLAY Gregg Kavet and Andy Robin
GUEST CAST Brenda Strong (Sue Ellen); Armin Shimerman (Stan); Arthur Rosenburg (Judge); Cynthia Madvig (Woman #1); Marilyn Tokuda (Woman #2)
RECURRING CAST Estelle Harris (Estelle Costanza); Richard Herd (Wilhelm); Phil Morros (Jackie Chiles); John O'Hurley (J. Peterman); Heidi Swedberg (Susan)

123. "The Seven"
(February 6, 1996)

SUMMARY George tells Susan he wants to name his first child Seven. Jerry dates a girl who always wears the same dress. Elaine buys a little-girls' bike. After she strains her neck trying to get the bike down from the wall in her apartment, she promises the bike to Kramer if he can fix her neck. Kramer works out an arrangement with Jerry to keep track of what he takes from Jerry's kitchen.

DIRECTOR Andy Ackerman
TELEPLAY Alec Berg and Jeff Schaffer
GUEST CAST Ken Hudson Campbell (Ken); Shannon Holt (Carrie); Lisa Deanne (Christie); Charles Emmett (Orderly); David Richards (Maitre d'); Matthew McCurley (Kid); Josh Abramson (Man #1)
RECURRING CAST Wayne Knight (Newman); Heidi Swedberg (Susan)

124. "The Cadillac (Part I)"
(February 8, 1996)

SUMMARY Jerry visits his parents in Florida and surprises them by buying them a new Cadillac. Kramer is worried his friendship with Jerry will change now that he knows what Jerry earns. Jack Klompus accuses Morty of embezzling funds to pay for his new Cadillac. George is set up with Oscar-winning actress Marisa Tomei. The cable company is looking for Kramer.

OF SPECIAL NOTE Episodes 124 and 125 were originally aired as a one-hour special.

DIRECTOR Andy Ackerman
TELEPLAY Larry David and Jerry Seinfeld
GUEST CAST Walter Olkewicz (Nick); Annabelle Gurwitch (Katy); Bill Macy (Herb); Jesse White (Ralph); Marisa Tomei (Herself)
RECURRING CAST Sandy Baron (Jack Klompus); Barney Martin (Morty Seinfeld); Liz Sheridan (Helen Seinfeld); Heidi Swedberg (Susan)

125. "The Cadillac (Part II)"
(Febraury 8, 1996)

SUMMARY George's obsession with Marisa makes Susan suspicious. Elaine calls Jerry in Florida and tells him she wants to come and join him now that she knows what he earns. George's meeting with Marisa doesn't go as well as planned and Susan thinks he he's having an affair with Elaine. Morty's only chance to avoid impeachment from the retirement village board lies with the woman Jerry mugged for the marble rye.

DIRECTOR Andy Ackerman
TELEPLAY Larry David and Jerry Seinfeld
GUEST CAST Marisa Tomei (Herself); Walter Olkewicz (Nick the Cable Guy); Ann Guilbert (Evelyn); Frances Bay (Mabel Choate); Bill Macy (Herb); Jesse White (Ralph); Annie Korzen (Doris Klompus); Daniel Zacapa (Power Guy (John)); Golde Starger (Bldg. A); Janice Davis (Bldg. B); Art Frankle (Bldg. C)
RECURRING CAST Sandy Baron (Jack Klompus); Barney Martin (Morty Seinfeld); Liz Sheridan (Helen Seinfeld); Heidi Swedberg (Susan)

126. "The Shower Head"
(Febraury 15, 1996)

SUMMARY After visiting Jerry in New York, his parents won't go back to Florida because George convinced his parents to move there. Elaine tests positive for opium after eating poppy seeds. Low-flow shower heads are installed in the building, leaving everyone with flat hair; Newman finds a source for black market replacements. Jerry makes a joke at the expense of Uncle Leo on *The Tonight Show* with Jay Leno.

DIRECTOR Andy Ackerman

TELEPLAY Peter Mehlman and Marjorie Gross

GUEST CAST Jay Leno (Himself); Ron West (Dr. Strugatz); Tim deZarn (Salesman); Michelle Bonilla (Waitress); Angelo Di Mascio Jr. (Man)

RECURRING CAST Estelle Harris (Estelle Costanza); Wayne Knight (Newman); Len Lesser (Uncle Leo); Barney Martin (Morty Seinfeld); John O'Hurley (J. Peterman); Liz Sheridan (Helen Seinfeld); Jerry Stiller (Frank Costanza)

127. "The Doll"
(February 22, 1996)

SUMMARY Susan has a doll that resembles George's mother, which makes him unable to perform sexually. Susan's old college roommate gives Jerry a package, which he loses. Frank turns George's room into a pool hall, and the Maestro and Kramer play in their underwear. Elaine tries to get an autograph of the third of the Three Tenors. Elaine tells Frank about a man she saw in Tuscany who looks just like him; Frank thinks it may be the cousin who stayed behind. Jerry has no material for his next gig.

DIRECTOR Andy Ackerman

TELEPLAY Tom Gammill and Max Pross

GUEST CAST Mark Metcalf (Maestro); Kathy Griffin (Sally); Mary Jo Keenen (Deena); Monica Allison (Stewardess); Larry Braman (Stage Manager); John Lizzi (Other Guy)

RECURRING CAST Estelle Harris (Estelle Costanza); Jerry Stiller (Frank Costanza); Heidi Swedberg (Susan)

128. "The Friar's Club"
(March 7, 1996)

SUMMARY George fixes Jerry up with Susan's best friend. Jerry has to borrow a jacket at the Friar's Club, which he forgets to return; he thinks the Gypsies stole it. Kramer tries to sleep only twenty minutes at a time. Elaine thinks a coworker is pretending to be deaf to get out of work. George's wedding is delayed until June.

OF SPECIAL NOTE This episode has also been referred to as "The Gypsies."

DIRECTOR Andy Ackerman

TELEPLAY David Mandel

GUEST CAST Rob Schneider (Bob); Pat Cooper (Himself); Samantha Smith (II) (Hallie); Lisa Kushell (Connie); Robert Martin Robinson (Maître d'); Norman Large (Detective); Peggy Lane (Waitress); The Flying Karamazov Brothers (The Flying Sandos Brothers)

RECURRING CAST Phil Morris (Jackie Chiles); John O'Hurley (J. Peterman); Heidi Swedberg (Susan)

129. "The Wig Master"
(April 4, 1996)

SUMMARY A salesman trying to sell Jerry a jacket asks Elaine out, which insults Jerry. George has an unwanted houseguest, the wig master (a person in charge of the wigs in a theatrical production) for the touring company of *Joseph and the Amazing Technicolor Dreamcoat*. While having drinks at a cafe, a guy comes on to the wig master and Jerry is insulted. George and Kramer park their cars in a cheap lot and their cars are used by hookers to turn tricks. Kramer is allowed to borrow the backup "Dreamcoat," and police mistake him for a pimp.

TELEPLAY Spike Feresten

GUEST CAST Patrick Bristow (Ethan); Harry Van Gorkum (Craig); Gina Mastrogiacomo (Prostitute); Kim Chase (Charmaine); Chaim Jeraffi (Jiffy Park Guy); Michael James McDonald (Jesse); Pamela Dillman (Salesperson); Zack Phifer (Bob); Shashi Bhatia (Flower Girl); Norman Brenner (Ian)

RECURRING CAST Heidi Swedberg (Susan)

130. "The Calzone"
(April 25, 1996)

SUMMARY George becomes Steinbrenner's pet when he shares an eggplant calzone with him. Jerry is dating a woman who gets anything she wants. George doesn't get "credit" for his tip at the calzone shop. Elaine is going out with someone who uses a dating loophole. Kramer will only wear warm clothes right out of the dryer.

DIRECTOR Andy Ackerman

TELEPLAY Alec Berg and Jeff Schaffer

GUEST CAST John D'Aquino (Todd); Peter Allas (Counter Guy); Danette Tays (Nicki); Greg Collins (Policeman); Jane A. Johnston (Todd's Mother)

RECURRING CAST Wayne Knight (Newman)

131. "The Bottle Deposit (Part I)"
(May 2, 1996)

SUMMARY George gets an assignment but doesn't know what it is. Elaine spends a fortune buying JFK's golf clubs for J. Peterman at an auction, then leaves them in the back of Jerry's car. Jerry's mechanic steals his car. Kramer and Newman use a mail truck to take bottles to Michigan, where they can double their deposit money.

OF SPECIAL NOTE Episodes 131 and 132 originally aired as a one-hour broadcast.

DIRECTOR Andy Ackerman
TELEPLAY Gregg Kavet and Andy Robin
GUEST CAST Brad Garrett (Tony); Brenda Strong (Sue Ellen); Patrick Kerr (Clerk); Harvey Jason (Auctioneer); Larry Polson (Homeless Guy)
RECURRING CAST Richard Herd (Wilhelm); Wayne Knight (Newman); John O'Hurley (Peterman)

132. "The Bottle Deposit (Part II)"
(May 2, 1996)

SUMMARY Wilhelm is delighted with the job George did on the project; however, George still has no idea what he did or how he did it. Kramer spots Jerry's stolen car in Ohio, so he and Newman tail it. The mechanic throws the clubs and bag at Kramer's truck and gets away. Steinbrenner calls George into his office about the project report and has him committed.

DIRECTOR Andy Ackerman
TELEPLAY Gregg Kavet and Andy Robin
GUEST CAST Brad Garrett (Tony); Mary Jo Keenen (Deena); Rance Howard (Farmer); Nicholas Mele (Detective); Karen Lynn Scott (Farmer's Daughter); Sandy Ward (Pop); Dan O'Connor (Young Cop); Bonnie McNeil (Woman)
RECURRING CAST Richard Herd (Wilhelm); Wayne Knight (Newman); John O'Hurley (Peterman)

133. "The Wait Out"
(May 9, 1996)

SUMMARY Jerry and Elaine are waiting for a married couple to separate, so they'll be fair dating game again. Kramer's new jeans are so tight that he can't get them off. Elaine has a new hairstyle. Her driving makes Jerry sick. Susan is upset with George, and he hopes she'll break up with him.

DIRECTOR Andy Ackerman

TELEPLAY Peter Mehlman; story: Peter Mehlman and Matt Selman

GUEST CAST Cary Elwes (David); Debra Messing (Beth); Allan Havey (Policeman); Diana Castle (Mrs. Zanfino); Todd Bosley (Joey); J. C. Hertzler (Mr. Berger); Nicole Tocantins (Barbara)

RECURRING CAST Heidi Swedberg (Susan); Danny Woodburn (Mickey Abbott)

134. "The Invitations"
(May 16, 1996)

SUMMARY George tries to figure out ways to get out of getting married. Kramer calls Susan by the wrong name, and she cuts him and Elaine out of the wedding. Jerry, nervous about his single future without George, gets engaged to someone just like him, then has second thoughts. Susan dies after licking all the cheap envelopes for the wedding invitations George bought. Free at last, George makes another attempt at Marisa Tomei.

DIRECTOR Andy Ackerman

TELEPLAY Larry David

GUEST CAST Janeane Garofalo (Jeannie Steinman); Stephen Root (Mr. Lager); Victor Raider-Wexler (Doctor); John Riggi (Teller); Sue Goodman (Clerk); Julie Clark (Waitress); Fred Goehner (Delivery Guy); Marisa Tomei (Herself)

RECURRING CAST Heidi Swedberg (Susan)

SEASON EIGHT

This was the first season without Larry David's input.

135. "The Foundation"
(September 19, 1996)

SUMMARY Susan's parents want to keep her memory alive, so they start a foundation in her honor with George on the board. Jerry studies the perfect breakup story. Kramer learns karate. Elaine gets appointed president of J. Peterman's company after he has a breakdown. Jerry runs into

Dolores from "The Junior Mint," and she suggests that they get together again. George discovers how much he lost when he lost Susan.

OF SPECIAL NOTE This episode was dedicated to Marjorie Gross, who died of ovarian cancer earlier in the year.

DIRECTOR Andy Ackerman
TELEPLAY Alec Berg and Jeff Schaffer
GUEST CAST Janeane Garofalo (Jeannie Steinman); Bruce Davison (Wyck); Grace Zabriskie (Mrs. Ross); Warren Frost (Mr. (Henry) Ross); Joe Urla (Dugan); Susan Walters (Dolores Mulva); Todd Bosley (Joey); Diana Castle (Mrs. Zanfino); Stuart Quan (Sensei); Herb Mitchell (Businessman #1); Robert Louis Kempf (Businessman #2); Lawrence A. Mandley (Larry); Lauren Bowles (Waitress #1); Peggy Lane (Waitress #2); Paige Tamada (Clara); Robert Padnick (Willie); Ruth Cohen (Ruthie)
RECURRING CAST John O'Hurley (Peterman)

136. "The Soul Mate"
   (September 26, 1996)

SUMMARY Kramer has feelings Jerry's girlfriend Pam and goes to Newman for advice. George thinks the foundation suspects him of killing Susan. Elaine doesn't want to have a baby even though her friends insist she should. Newman bribes Jerry in hopes of finding out more about his obsession with Elaine, whose new boyfriend gets a vasectomy to show her how committed he is to not having children. When Jerry and Kramer find out Pam isn't interested in having children either, they line up for their own vasectomies.

OF SPECIAL NOTE This episode was dedicated to Victor Wayne Harris, an assistant prop master, who died in August 1996 of complications from a stroke.

DIRECTOR Andy Ackerman
TELEPLAY Peter Mehlman
GUEST CAST Bruce Davison (Wyck); Tim DeKay (Kevin); Lisa Mende (Carol); Kim Myers (Pam); Rende Rae Norman (Ms. Baines); Tommy Hicks (Mr. Cross); Jill Talley (Gail); Jill Holden (Lisa)
RECURRING CAST Wayne Knight (Newman)

137. "The Bizarro Jerry"
   (October 3, 1996)

SUMMARY Elaine's new friends are the opposites of George, Kramer, and Jerry. Jerry dates a beautiful girl with big, masculine hands. Kramer uses a bathroom in an office building, then just begins working there. George passes a picture of Jerry's girlfriend off as one of his dead financée, Susan, so he can get into the Forbidden City, where high-priced models hang out. With Kramer working, George inside the walls, and Elaine hanging out with Kevin, Jerry begins to feel alone.

DIRECTOR Andy Ackerman
TELEPLAY David Mandel
GUEST CAST Tim DeKay (Kevin); Kristin Bauer (Gillian); Pat Kilbane (Bizarro Kramer—Feldman); Kyle T. Hefner (Bizarro George—Gene); Justina Vail (Amanda); J. Patrick McCormack (Leland); Harry Murphy (Office Manager); Dana Patrick (Model #1); Shireen Crutchfield (Model #2); Robin Nance (Model #3); Mark S. Larson (Bizarro Newman—Vargas); James Lesure (Office Worker); Jason Beck (Bouncer)

138. "The Little Kicks"
(October 10, 1996)

SUMMARY Elaine reluctantly lets George attend a party she is throwing at work. George's bad-boy image makes him more attractive. Jerry is forced to bootleg movies by a friend of Kramer's. Elaine's coworkers lose respect for her after she dances at the party, but her dance becomes a big hit on the streets of New York.
TRIVIA It was reported that Julia Louis-Dreyfus was imitating *Saturday Night Live* producer Lorne Michael's dance moves.

DIRECTOR Andy Ackerman
TELEPLAY Spike Feresten
GUEST CAST Neil Giuntoli (Brody); Rebecca McFarland (Anna); Joseph Urla (Dugan); Tim O'Hare (Vendor)
RECURRING CAST Jerry Stiller (Frank Costanza)

139. "The Package"
(October 17, 1996)

SUMMARY Kramer tries to get Jerry a refund for his broken stereo by mailing it insured. Elaine has a rash but can't find a doctor because her medical records say she is difficult. George discovers the woman at the photo store is looking at his pictures. Jerry refuses delivery of a package with no return address. Newman grills Jerry on suspicion of mail fraud.

DIRECTOR Andy Ackerman
TELEPLAY Jennifer Crittenden

GUEST CAST Richard Roat (Dr. Berg); Fort Atkinson (Dr. Stern); David Purdham (Dr. Resnick); Heather Campbell (Sheila); Ramon Franco (Mailman); Bari K. Willerford (Ron); Shuko Akune (Receptionist); F. William Parker (Country Doctor); Lynn A. Henderson (Clerk); Bill Gratton (Postal Official); Susan Leslie (Nurse)

RECURRING CAST Wayne Knight (Newman); Len Lesser (Uncle Leo)

140. "The Fatigues"
(October 31, 1996)

SUMMARY Elaine promotes the mailroom psycho instead of firing him. Jerry's girlfriend has a mentor who dates Bania. Kramer needs Frank to help him cook for 150 people on Jewish Singles Night. George discovers that blind people can get any book on tape, so he plans to fail an eye test. Jerry's girlfriend sees Bania's act and loses respect for her mentor. Frank Costanza's cooking skills are reborn, until he sees someone choking.

DIRECTOR Andy Ackerman
TELEPLAY Gregg Kavet and Andy Robin
GUEST CAST Joseph Urla (Dugan); Ned Bellamy (Eddie); A. J. Langer (Abby); Katie Layman (Cynthia); Eddie Allen (Doctor); Gwen McGee (Janine); Lynn Manning (Blind Man)
RECURRING CAST Estelle Harris (Estelle Costanza); Richard Herd (Wilhelm); Steve Hytner (Bania); Jerry Stiller (Frank Costanza)

141. "The Checks"
(November 7, 1996)

SUMMARY Elaine's new boyfriend, Brett, is obsessed with designer furniture and the song "Desperado." Jerry gets hundreds of twelve-cent royalty checks from an appearance he made on Japanese television. George can't get recruited by a cult. Kramer helps out Japanese tourists. Brett delivers a large chest of drawers to Kramer and thinks that Jerry might be jealous. George gets the cleaners to do the offices at Yankee Stadium, where they find a new recruit.

DIRECTOR Andy Ackerman
TELEPLAY Steve O'Donnell, Tom Gammill, and Max Pross
GUEST CAST James Patrick Stuart (Brett); Gedde Watanabe (Mr. Oh); Sab Shimono (Executive #1); John Bowman (Teddy); Jock Plotnick (Crew Leader); George Wallace (Doctor); Toshi Toda (Mr. Tanaka); Goh Misawa (Mr. Yamaguchi); Tony V. (Clicky); Akane Nelson (Executive #2); Cherie Hankal (Nurse)
RECURRING CAST Richard Herd (Wilhelm)

142. "The Chicken Roaster"
(November 14, 1996)

SUMMARY Elaine overuses her expense account at work. Kramer and Jerry switch apartments and begin to take on each other's personalities. Jerry gets a college buddy fired after the buddy spends time with Jerry and misses a meeting. Newman gets Kramer hooked on Kenny Roger's Roasters chicken. Elaine goes to Burma in search of Peterman to get her expenses authorized.

DIRECTOR Andy Ackerman
TELEPLAY Alec Berg and Jeff Schaffer
GUEST CAST Mark Roberts (Seth); Kymberly Kalil (Heather); Michael D. Roberts (Ipswich); Wesley Leong (Clerk); Christopher Aguilar (Burmese Boy)
RECURRING CAST Wayne Knight (Newman); John O'Hurley (J. Peterson)

143. "The Abstinence"
(November 21, 1996)

SUMMARY George's girlfriend has mononucleosis, so he can't have sex with her for six weeks, and he suddenly becomes smart. Elaine is dating someone who is "almost" a doctor. Jerry gets bumped from career day at his junior high, and it affects his career. After getting kicked out of Monk's, Kramer opens a smokers' lounge at his apartment. He also sees his lawyer about a case against the tobacco company, claiming smoking has destroyed his looks.

DIRECTOR Andy Ackerman
TELEPLAY Steve Koren
GUEST CAST Debra Jo Rupp (Katie); Brenda Strong (Sue Ellen); Bob Odenkirk (Ben); Meagen Fay (Mrs. Burns); Tamara Bick (Louise); Alex Trebek (Voice of Himself); Derek Jeter (Himself); Bernie Williams (Himself); Lawrence A. Mandley (Larry the Cook); Fern Fitzgerald (Ms. Wilkie); Noelle Balfour (Waitress); Kyle Gass (Smoker); Judy Kerr (Woman); David Letterman (Himself)
RECURRING CAST Phil Morris (Jackie Chiles)

144. "The *Andrea Doria*"
(December 19, 1996)

SUMMARY Elaine dates a guy who is bad at breaking up. Kramer goes to a veterinarian to get rid of his cough. Jerry and Kramer discover Newman has been hiding bags of mail. George competes with a survivor of the *Andrea Doria* for an apartment; neither gets it. Elaine's blind date breaks up with her and tells she has a big head. Kramer begins to act like a dog and bites Newman's ankle.

SEINFELD-ESE Bad breaker-upper—a guy who doesn't know how to end a relationship without making the woman furious.

DIRECTOR Andy Ackerman
TELEPLAY Spike Feresten
GUEST CAST Tom Gallop (Alan); Ray Stricklyn (Clarence); Diana Bellamy (Mrs. Ricardi); Rick Hall (Vet); Carl Banks (Policeman #1); Barry Cutler (Policeman #2); Kev O'Neil (Waiter); Ossie Mair (Driver); Fred Pinkard (Old Man); Rene Weisser (Ex-Girlfriend); Brian Blondell (Dog Guy); Theresa Mulligan (Woman); Florinel Fatulescu (Stand Owner)
RECURRING CAST Estelle Harris (Estelle Costanza); Wayne Knight (Newman); Jerry Stiller (Frank Costanza)

145. "The Little Jerry"
(January 9, 1997)

SUMMARY Jerry bounces a check at the market. Everyone finds out, including his parents, who want to cover the check for him. Kramer gets a pet rooster and names him Jerry Seinfeld. Elaine dates a man who shaves his head. George visits a woman's prison and starts dating a prisoner, who later breaks out.

DIRECTOR Andy Ackerman
TELEPLAY Jennifer Crittenden
GUEST CAST John Michael Higgins (Kurt); Miguel Sandoval (Marcelino); Andrea Bendewald (Celia); Kathryn Joosten (Betsy); Paul Perri (Detective Banner); Al White (Detective Udewitz); Ray Proscia (Guard)
RECURRING CAST Barney Martin (Morty Seinfeld); Liz Sheridan (Helen Seinfeld)

146. "The Money"
(January 16, 1997)

SUMMARY Jerry has to rebuy the Cadillac for his parents after they sell it to Jack Klompus for $6,000 in order to give Jerry some money to help him out. George finds out his parents are loaded. Kramer needs to get some sleep after sex. Elaine hires Morty to work at J. Peterman. Kramer moves in with the Costanzas, who tell George that they are all moving to Florida.

DIRECTOR Andy Ackerman

TELEPLAY Peter Mehlman

GUEST CAST Sarah Silverman (Emily); Leon W. Grant (Counterperson)

RECURRING CAST Sandy Baron (Jack Klompus); Estelle Harris (Estelle Costanza); Barney Martin (Morty Seinfeld); John O'Hurley (J. Peterman); Liz Sheridan (Helen Seinfeld); Jerry Stiller (Frank Costanza)

147. "The Comeback"
(January 30, 1997)

SUMMARY George can't think of a comeback after getting zinged at a meeting. Elaine connects with a video store employee. Kramer wants a living will, with Elaine as the executrix. Jerry buys a racket from a tennis shop pro, who turns out to be a hack player. Kramer goes into a coma after being hit with tennis balls.

OF SPECIAL NOTE Originally Ben Stein was cast to play George's office adversary, but it was decided to make that character younger, so the new part of Shellbach was written for Stein.

DIRECTOR David Owen Trainor

TELEPLAY Gregg Kavet and Andy Robin

GUEST CAST Mark Harelik (Milos); Ben Stein (Shellbach); Joel Polis (Reilly); Ivana Milavich (Patty); Danny Strong (Vincent); Richard Livingston (Bill); Charles Kahlenberg (Fred); Stan Sellers (McAdam); Peggy Mannix (Woman); Fatima Love (Secretary); Nancy Linehan Charles (Woman Executive); Jeff Hatz (Manager—Gene)

148. "The Van Buren Boys"
(February 6, 1997)

SUMMARY Jerry's girlfriend Ellen seems perfect to him in every way, but everyone else seems to have a problem with her. George interviews candidates for the foundation's first scholarship. Peterman buys stories from Kramer's life to use in his own autobiography, which Elaine will ghostwrite. Jerry flies his parents in to get their impression of Ellen.

TRIVIA The character name "Steven Koren" is the name of one of Seinfeld's writers.

DIRECTOR Andy Ackerman

TELEPLAY Darin Henry

GUEST CAST Bruce Davison (Wyck); Christine Taylor (Ellen); Jed Rhein (Steven Koren); Tony Colitti (Leader); David Moscow (Lomez Jr.); Yunoka Doyle (Lydia); Dublin James (Maurice); Justine Slater (Melissa); Michelle Maika (Kim); Steve Hofvendahl (Man)

RECURRING CAST Barney Martin (Morty Seinfeld); John O'Hurley (J. Peterman); Liz Sheridan (Helen Seinfeld)

149. "The Susie"
(February 13, 1997)

SUMMARY Kramer decides that daylight savings time isn't coming fast enough, so he sets his watch ahead an hour. Peggy, a coworker of Elaine's, calls her Susie, so Elaine pretends to be two different people. George gets dumped. Kramer bets with Jerry's money and then thinks Jerry roughed up the bookie. Elaine and Jerry, in his car, decide it would be best to eliminate Susie. Elaine delivers the eulogy at Susie's funeral. Peterman puts her in charge of a foundation in Susie's honor.

DIRECTOR Andy Ackerman
TELEPLAY David Mandel
GUEST CAST Lee Arenberg (Mike); Shannon Kenny (Allison); Megan Cole (Peggy); Jane Edith Wilson (Woman)
RECURRING CAST Richard Herd (Wilhelm); John O'Hurley (J. Peterman)

150. "The Pothole"
(Febraury 20, 1997)

SUMMARY George tries to recover his lost key chain. Elaine tries to get Chinese food delivered. Jerry goes to extreme measures to avoid germs when he's with his new girlfriend after she uses a toothbrush he accidentally dropped in the toilet. Kramer adopts a mile of highway.

DIRECTOR Andy Ackerman
TELEPLAY Steve O'Donnell and Dan O'Keefe
GUEST CAST Kristin Davis (Jenna); Jack McGee (Ralph); George Kee Cheung (Owner); Seraiah Carol (Mrs. Allister); Radmar Agana Jao (Delivery Boy); Walter Addison (Man)
RECURRING CAST Wayne Knight (Newman)

151. "The English Patient"
(March 13, 1997)

SUMMARY Jerry is going to Florida to help his parents move, so Kramer asks him to pick up some Cuban cigars from his supplier. Elaine's dislike of

The English Patient makes her unpopular and causes her boyfriend to break up with her. Peterman loved the movie, so Elaine is forced to go to the Tunisian desert and live in a cave if she wants to save her job. An eighty-year-old challenges Jerry to a weightlifting competition.

CATCHPHRASE It's go time!

DIRECTOR Andy Ackerman

TELEPLAY Steve Koren

GUEST CAST Lloyd Bridges (Izzy); Chelsea Noble (Danielle); O'Neal Compton (Earl Haffler); Lisa Mende (Carol); Gene Dynarski (Izzy Jr.); Marco Rodriguez (Guillermo); Joseph Urla (Dugan); Jill Talley (Gail); Jill Holden (Lisa); Todd Jeffries (Blaine); Earl Schuman (Izzy Sr.); Edgar Small (Sid Luckman); Lauren Bowles (Waitress); Juan Garcia (Jaime); Jeff Miller (Neil)

RECURRING CAST Barney Martin (Morty Seinfeld); John O'Hurley (J. Peterman); Liz Sheridan (Helen Seinfeld)

152. "The Nap"
(April 10, 1997)

SUMMARY George starts taking naps under his desk. Jerry gets his kitchen redone. Kramer starts going for swims in the East River. Elaine meets someone who is concerned about her back; when he sends her a new mattress, she gets the wrong idea, then throws her back out trying to get rid of the mattress. Kramer's river gets too crowded, and George finds a new place to nap.

DIRECTOR Andy Ackerman

TELEPLAY Gregg Kavet and Andy Robin

GUEST CAST Stephen Lee (Conrad); Vince Grant (Hal); Angelo Tiffe (Delivery Man); Jonell Kennedy (Secretary); Mik Scriba (Bomb Squad Guy); Terry Rhoads (Father); Sid Newman (Old Man); Kevin Keckeisen (Brian); Kyle Sullivan (Son)

RECURRING CAST Richard Herd (Wilhelm)

153. "The Yada Yada"
(April 24, 1997)

SUMMARY George's new girlfriend uses the phrase "yada, yada, yada" to gloss over details. Jerry gets offended when Dr. Whatley, his dentist, converts to Judaism and then starts telling Jewish jokes. Elaine hurts her friends' chance of adopting a child. Kramer and Mickey can't decide who gets which girl on a double date. After hearing Jerry's complaints about Dr. Whatley, Kramer accuses Jerry of being an anti-dentite.

CATCHPHRASE Yada, yada yada.

DIRECTOR Andy Ackerman

TELEPLAY Peter Mehlman and Jill Franklyn

GUEST CAST Robert Wagner (Dr. Abbott); Jill St. John (Mrs. Abbott); Debra Messing (Beth); Suzanne Cryer (Marcy); Stephen Caffrey (Arnie); Henry Woronicz (Father Curtis); Monica Lacey (Julie); Ali Marsh (Karen); David Chandler (Brian); Virginia Watson (Nun); Walter Franks (Waiter); Jerry Maren (Dad)

RECURRING CAST Bryan Cranston (Tim Whatley); Danny Woodburn (Mickey Abbott)

154. "The Millennium"
(May 1, 1997)

SUMMARY Elaine gets bad service at a clothing store, so she begins shopping at a similar, different one. Jerry notices that he is on his girlfriend's speed dial and becomes obsessed with being number one on it. Kramer's millennium party clashes with Newman's. George tries to get fired. Jerry gets caught in the middle of a speed-dial war between his girlfriend and stepmother.

DIRECTOR Andy Ackerman

TELEPLAY Jennifer Crittenden

GUEST CAST Lauren Graham (Valerie); Louan Gideon (Mrs. Hamilton); Victoria Mahoney (Gladys); Michael Laskin (Minkler); Bruce Jarchow (Mooney); Maria Cina (Saleswoman); Steve Koren (Himself)

RECURRING CAST Richard Herd (Wilhelm); Wayne Knight (Newman)

155. "The Muffin Tops"
(May 8, 1997)

SUMMARY George watches a bag for a tourist who never comes back, so he starts wearing some of the clothes. Elaine tells Kramer that the stories he sold to Peterman were put into the book. Kramer goes to the book signing, claiming he is the real Peterman. Elaine goes into business selling just the tops of muffins. George pretends he is a tourist to get a girl. Jerry takes shaving a bit too far and ends up shaving his entire chest.

OF SPECIAL NOTE This episode incorporates one of Seinfeld's personal quirks of eating just the muffin tops and leaving the bottoms.

"Tyler Chicken" was supposed to be "Tyson Chicken" at one point but was changed to avoid any legal entanglements.

DIRECTOR Andy Ackerman
TELEPLAY Spike Feresten
GUEST CAST Rena Sofer (Mary Anne); Melinda Clarke (Alex); Chaim Jeraffi (Jiffy Dump Guy); Sonya Eddy (Rebecca); Barry Kramer (Bag Guy); Elayn Taylor (Book Fan); Paige Moss (Girl); Viola Kates Simpson (Old Woman); Jack Riley (Rider); Bunny Summers (Rider); Earl Carroll (Rider); Norman Brenner (Rider); Reuven Bar (Foreign Guy); Vince Donvito (Passerby); Chris Burmester (Passerby); Deck McKenzie (Man); Victoria Fischer (Bartender); Keith Sellon-Wright (Guy)
RECURRING CAST Richard Fancy (Lippman); Wayne Knight (Newman); John O'Hurley (J. Peterman)

156. "The Summer of George"
(May 15, 1997)

SUMMARY When he realizes his severance package from the Yankees will last three months, George decides to plan a special summer for himself. Both Jerry and Kramer are going to the Tony Awards—Jerry as a guest, Kramer as a seat-filler. Elaine gets catty with a coworker. Kramer accepts a Tony Award and then is told he has to earn it by firing Raquel Welch from a play. Jerry and George team up to date a high-energy woman. George slips on an invitation and ends up in the hospital, the same one where Susan died.

DIRECTOR Andy Ackerman
TELEPLAY Alec Berg and Jeff Schaffer
GUEST CAST Raquel Welch (Herself); Molly Shannon (Sam); Amanda Peet (Lanette); Joe Urla (Dugan); Victor Raider-Wexler (Doctor); Peter Dennis (Lew); Tucker Smallwood (Malcolm); Wayne Wilderson (Walter); Blake Gibbons (Lyle); Adrian Sparks (Man); Jane A. Johnston (Woman); Lauren Bowles (Waitress); Sue Goodman (Clerk); Neil Flynn (Cop #1); Tom Michael Bailey (Cop #2); Denise Bessette (Therapist); Dave Mandel (Himself)
RECURRING CAST John O'Hurley (Peterman)

SEASON NINE

This was the series' final season.

157. "The Butter Shave"
(September 25, 1997)

SUMMARY Jerry might get another chance at NBC. George is hired for a job because the employer thinks he's handicapped. Kramer starts putting butter on his face after shaving but learns a painful lesson when he goes out in the sun. Elaine and Puddy take a trip. Jerry resents Bania riding on his comic coattails.

OF SPECIAL NOTE This episode was in memory of Brandon Tartikoff, a former NBC executive who was one of the show's bigger supporters in its early, less-than-popular days.

DIRECTOR Andy Ackerman

TELEPLAY Alec Berg and Jeff Schaffer and David Mandel

GUEST CAST Gordon Jump (Mr. Thomassoulo); Kristin Davis (Jenna); Everett Greenbaum (McMaines); Connie Sawyer (Old Woman); Matthew Fonda (NBC Executive); Chris Parnell (NBC Executive); Frank Van Keeken (Vegetable Lasagna); Shannon Whirry (Cute Girl); Nancy Balbirer (Woman); Erica Y. Becoat (Stewardess); Torsten Voges (Cab Driver); George Georgiadis (Cab Driver); Brian Callaway (Passenger)

RECURRING CAST Steve Hyntnet (Bania); Wayne Knight (Newman); Patrick Warburton (David Puddy)

158. "The Voice"
(October 2, 1997)

SUMMARY George refuses to leave his job after it's discovered he's not handicapped. Elaine tries to break up with Puddy but can't—even though she keeps losing money to Jerry betting she can. Jerry's girlfriend's stomach makes strange sounds during the night. Kramer hires an intern from NYU to help him develop some of his ideas.

DIRECTOR Andy Ackerman

TELEPLAY Alec Berg, Jeff Schaffer, and David Mandel

GUEST CAST Gordon Jump (Mr. Thomassoulo); Sara Rose Peterson (Claire); Jarrad Paul (Darin); Ella Joyce (Dean Jones); Nancy Balbirer (Alice); Brian J. Williams (Glenn); Cindy Lu (Worker)

RECURRING CAST Patrick Warburton (David Puddy)

159. "The Serenity Now"
(October 9, 1997)

SUMMARY Jerry suddenly starts feeling a range of emotions. George goes to work for his father selling computers. Elaine seeks help from a rabbi to see if she can reduce her "shiksappeal" with the Lippman men, who want to denounce their religion. The release of emotions from George has an impact on emotional Jerry.

DIRECTOR Andy Ackerman
TELEPLAY Steve Koren
GUEST CAST Lori Loughlin (Patty); Ross Malinger (Adam); Matt McCoy (Lloyd Braun); Bruce Mahler (Rabbi Glickman)
RECURRING CAST Richard Fancy (Lippman); Estelle Harris (Estelle Costanza); Jerry Stiller (Frank Costanza)

160. "The Blood"
(October 16, 1997)

SUMMARY Jerry's parents are concerned about his lack of exercise. Elaine tries to prove she's a responsible person by agreeing to baby-sit a friend's difficult child. George decides he needs to incorporate television and food into his sex life. After a blood bank raises its blood-storage rates, Kramer retrieves the blood he donated. Jerry starts a purification program to improve his diet.

DIRECTOR Andy Ackerman
TELEPLAY Dan O'Keefe
GUEST CAST Kellie Waymire (Vivian); Audrey Kissel (Tara); Colton James (Jimmy); Gene Dynarski (Izzy Jr.); Yvonne Farrow (Employee); Lloyd Bridges (Izzy)
RECURRING CAST Wayne Knight (Newman); Barney Martin (Morty Seinfeld); Liz Sheridan (Helen Seinfeld)

161. "The Junk Mail"
(October 30, 1997)

SUMMARY Jerry gets paid with a van instead of cash for a gig. George's parents rekindle their romance at his expense. Kramer plans his revenge on a company that has sent him an overabundance of catalogs in the past month. Elaine, back with Puddy, meets the man of her dreams.

DIRECTOR Andy Ackerman

TELEPLAY Spike Feresten

GUEST CAST Laurie Taylor-Williams (Rhisa); Toby Huss (Jack); Dana Gould (Frankie); Richard Kuhlman (Man); Montrose Hagins (Old Woman— Betty); Peggy Blow (Mail Clerk); Clement E. Blake (Dirt Person #1); D. A. Johnson (Dirt Person #2); Wilford Brimley (Postmaster General Henry Atkins)

RECURRING CAST Estelle Harris (Estelle Costanza); Wayne Knight (Newman); Jerry Stiller (Frank Costanza); Patrick Warburton (David Puddy)

162. "The Merv Griffin Show"
(November 6, 1997)

SUMMARY Kramer discovers the set of the old *Merv Griffin Show* in a dumpster and brings it home, then starts conducting interviews with anyone who comes into his apartment. George's girlfriend Miranda is disgusted when George runs over some pigeons with his car. Jerry's girlfriend won't let him play with her collection of old toys. Elaine's new coworker is a sidler.

SEINFELD-ESE Sidler—a person who sneaks up near you and you don't know he's there.

DIRECTOR Andy Ackerman

TELEPLAY Bruce Eric Kaplan

GUEST CAST Rick Hall (Vet); Brent Hinkley (Lou); Julia Pennington (Celia); Arabella Field (Miranda); Jim Fowler (Himself); Wayne Wilderson (Walter)

RECURRING CAST Estelle Harris (Estelle Costanza, voice-over); Wayne Knight (Newman); John O'Hurley (J. Peterman); Jerry Stiller (Frank Costanza, voice-over)

163. "The Slicer"
(November 13, 1997)

SUMMARY Elaine's neighbor forgot to turn off her alarm clock before leaving on a trip to Europe. George tries to prevent his new boss from recognizing him as the man who threw his son's boom box into the ocean. Dissatisfied with the meat he is getting in his sandwiches, Kramer gets his own meat slicer. Elaine tries to use the slicer to fix her high heels. Jerry dates a lifesaving dermatologist.

DIRECTOR Andy Ackerman

TELEPLAY Gregg Kavet and Andy Robin; story: Gregg Kavet, Andy Robin, and Darin Henry

GUEST CAST Marcia Cross (Sara); Daniel Von Bargen (Kruger); Larry B. Scott (Arthur Milano); David Moreland (Mr. Parry)

164. "The Betrayal"
(November 20, 1997)

SUMMARY Jerry, George, and Elaine go to India for a wedding. Jerry sleeps with the woman George is currently seeing. Kramer is angry at Newman because he didn't use his birthday wish to save Kramer from FDR.

OF SPECIAL NOTE The scenes in this episode are shown from the "ending" to the "beginning." The Pinter character is an obvious reference to playwright Harold Pinter, in whose love-triangle drama *Betrayal* presents its story backwards through time.

DIRECTOR Andy Ackerman
TELEPLAY David Mandel and Peter Mehlman
GUEST CAST Brenda Strong (Sue Ellen); Michael McShane (FDR—Franklin Delano Romanosky); Justine Miceli (Nina); Bart Braverman (Zubin); Shaun Toub (Pinter); Noor Shic (Usha); Jocelyne Kelly (Model); Brian Kaiser (Postman); Shelley Malil (Usher); Bill Lee Brown (Partygoer)
RECURRING CAST Wayne Knight (Newman); Heidi Swedberg (Susan)

165. "The Apology"
(December 11, 1997)

SUMMARY Jerry learns that there is such a thing as "bad naked." George becomes obsessed with getting an apology from a now-sober friend who once embarrassed him at a party over the "neck-hole" incident. Kramer starts living full time in his shower. Elaine is offended when a coworker acts as if she's contaminated but doesn't mind other people's germs. George ends up at a Rage-oholics Anonymous (RA) meeting. Puddy admits being a germophobe.

DIRECTOR Andy Ackerman
TELEPLAY Jennifer Crittenden
GUEST CAST James Spader (Jason [Hanke?]); Megan Cole (Peggy); Kathleen McClellan (Melissa); Jack Hackett (Alan); Michael Fishman (Gregg); David Dunard (Leader); Wayne Wilderson (Walter); Brian Levinson (Andy); Eric Simonson (Friend)
RECURRING CAST John O'Hurley (J. Peterman); Patrick Warburton (David Puddy)

166. "The Strike"
(December 18, 1997)

SUMMARY George, Elaine, and Jerry attend Tim Whatley's Hanukkah party. George dreads Festivus, a holiday his father created many years ago. Elaine tries to retrieve her coupon for a free submarine sandwich. Kramer goes back to work at the bagel place, which has been on strike for the past twelve years. Jerry starts dating a girl whose appearance seems to change.

DIRECTOR Andy Ackerman

TELEPLAY Dan O'Keefe, Alec Berg, and Jeff Schaffer

GUEST CAST Daniel Von Bargen (Kruger); Karen Fineman (Gwen); Dave Florek (Harry); Kevin Hamilton MacDonald (Denim Vest); Tracy Letts (Counterguy); Amit Itelman (Employee); Stacey Herring (Sandy); Colin Malone (Sleazy Guy); Jerry Dixon (Customer)

RECURRING CAST Bryan Cranston (Tim Whatley); Estelle Harris (Estelle Costanza); Jerry Stiller (Frank Costanza)

167. "The Dealership"
(January 8, 1998)

SUMMARY Elaine breaks up with Puddy, who's been promoted to salesman, before Jerry can get a deal on a new car. George tries to find his stolen Twix candy bar. Kramer tests drives a car. Jerry snaps at being asked one too many times for a "high five."

OF SPECIAL NOTE This is one of the few episodes in which none of the action takes place in Jerry's apartment.
  The Sunday after this episode aired, Seinfeld won the People's Choice Award for Favorite Comedy Series.

DIRECTOR Andy Ackerman

TELEPLAY Steve Koren

GUEST CAST Daniel Hagen (Rick); Joel McCrary (Don); Michael Kagan (Willie); Dee Freeman (Service Assistant); Rif Hutton (Salesman); Howard Mann (Willie Sr.); Steve Susskind (Customer #1); Loretta Fox (Customer #2); Catherine Schreiber (Saleswoman)

RECURRING CAST Patrick Warburton (David Puddy)

168. "The Reverse Peephole"
(January 15, 1998)

SUMMARY Kramer and Newman reverse their apartment-door peepholes. Puddy starts wearing a "man fur." Jerry stops carrying a wallet in favor of something that is "not a purse." George's wallet gives him a sore back.

CATCHPHRASE It's not a purse, it's European.

OF SPECIAL NOTE The voice of Superman on Jerry Seinfeld's American Express commercial that debuted in January 1998 is none other than Patrick Warburton, who plays David Puddy. Also, Lois Lane is Audrey Kissel, who played George's girlfriend Tara in episode 160, "The Blood."

DIRECTOR Andy Ackerman

TELEPLAY Spike Feresten

GUEST CAST Jon Polito (Silvio); Pat Finn (Joe Mayo); Jennette Robbins (Keri); Fitz Houston (Cop); Joe Basile (Delivery Guy); Lauren Bowles (Waitress)

RECURRING CAST Wayne Knight (Newman); Patrick Warburton (David Puddy)

169. "The Cartoon"
(January 29, 1998)

SUMMARY Elaine tries to prove a *New Yorker* cartoon isn't funny. Kramer, miffed at being told he doesn't know when to keep his mouth shut, stops talking. A comic Jerry thinks stinks becomes a big hit with her *Jerry Seinfeld Is the Devil* one-woman show. George dates a woman who looks like Jerry.

OF SPECIAL NOTE Kathy Griffin's *(Suddenly Susan)* stand-up routine includes a bit about how rude Jerry Seinfeld was to her when she first appeared on the series in episode 127, "The Doll."

DIRECTOR Andy Ackerman

TELEPLAY Bruce Eric Kaplan

GUEST CAST Kathy Griffin (Sally Weaver); Tracy Nelson (Janet); Joe Urla (Dugan); Paul Benedict (Mr. Elinoff); Bart McCarthy (Cab Driver)

RECURRING CAST Wayne Knight (Newman); John O'Hurley (J. Peterman)

170. "The Strong Box"
(February 5, 1998)

SUMMARY Kramer puts all his valuables in a strongbox for safekeeping but can't find the perfect hiding place. George's girlfriend refuses to break up with him. Jerry insults his next-door neighbor by mistaking him for a stranger and not opening their building's door for him. Elaine wonders why her new boyfriend is so mysterious, until she discovers he's poor—and married.

OF SPECIAL NOTE Jerry uses his computer in this episode for only the second time in the course of the series. The first time was in episode 76, "The Stall."

DIRECTOR Andy Ackerman
TELEPLAY Dan O'Keefe
GUEST CAST Illeana Douglas (Loretta); Alex Kapp (Maura); Louis Mustillo (Phil); Nicholas Paul Walker (Glenn); Mary Scheer (Ms. Smoth); Bonnie McNeil (Alison); Rosie Malek-Yonan (Wife)

171. "The Wizard"
(February 26, 1998)

SUMMARY Jerry buys his dad a $200 Wizard organizer for a birthday present, which he only uses to calculate tips. Kramer retires to Florida and moves into the complex where Jerry's parents live. George lies and tells the parents of his dead fiancée that he has a house in the Hamptons. Elaine thinks she's in an interracial relationship.
OF SPECIAL NOTE The *Boca Breeze* newspaper shown in the episode, also contained an item on Larry David's hole in one, reporting how he hurt his elbow and will never play golf again.

DIRECTOR Andy Ackerman
TELEPLAY Steve Lookner
GUEST CAST Grace Zabriskie (Mrs. Ross); Warren Frost (Mr. [Henry] Ross); Samuel Bliss Cooper (Darryl); Edgar Small (Sid Luckman); Vic Helford (Tom); Michael McShane (FDR—Franklin Delano Romanosky); Bahni Turpin (Waitress #1); Constance Zimmer (Waitress #2); Jeanette Miller (Old Woman); Murray Rubin (Rubin)
RECURRING CAST Liz Sheridan (Helen Seinfeld); Barney Martin (Morty Seinfeld)

172. "The Burning"
(March 19, 1998)

SUMMARY Elaine discovers that Puddy listens to religious radio stations. George tries to always leave a room on a high note. Kramer and Mickey get jobs feigning ailments for medical students. Jerry doesn't recognize his girlfriend Sophie when she calls and says, "It's me." Sophie verifies you can get venereal disease from a tractor seat.
OF SPECIAL NOTE This episode was dedicated "In Memory of Our Friend Lloyd Bridges." Bridges appeared as "It's go time!" Izzy in episodes 151, "The English Patient," and 160, "The Blood."

DIRECTOR Andy Ackerman

TELEPLAY Jennifer Crittenden

GUEST CAST Daniel Von Bargen (Kruger); Cindy Ambuehl (Sophie); Henry Woronicz (Father Curtis); Ursaline Bryant (Dr. Wexler); Daniel Dae Kim (Student #1); Alex Craig Mann (Student #2); Brian Posehn (Artie); Alec Holland (Coworker #1); Suli McCullough (Coworker #2)

RECURRING CAST Patrick Warburton (David Puddy); Dany Woodburn (Mickey)

173. "The Bookstore"
(April 9, 1998)

SUMMARY George is forced to buy an expensive book after he reads it while using a bookstore bathroom. Jerry catches Uncle Leo shoplifting and accidentally gets him arrested. Kramer and Newman hire homeless people for their new rickshaw business. Elaine gets drunk at the office party and makes out with a guy.

DIRECTOR Andy Ackerman

TELEPLAY Spike Feresten; story: Spike Feresten, Darin Henry, and Marc Jaffe

GUEST CAST Jonathan Penner (Zach); Ted Rooney (Crichton); John Gries (Rusty); Sonya Eddy (Rebecca DeMornay); Merrin Dungey (Cashier); Kevin Ruf (Security Guard); Heather Morgan (Server); Lauren Bowles (Waitress); Mark Daniel Cade (Walter); Sloppy Joe (Hobo Joe)

RECURRING CAST Wayne Knight (Newman); Len Lesser (Uncle Leo); Barney Martin (Morty Seinfeld); John O'Hurley (J. Peterman); Liz Sheridan (Helen Seinfeld)

174. "The Frogger"
(April 23, 1998)

SUMMARY Jerry and George are going to their high school hangout for one last slice of pizza. While there, George tries to buy a Frogger machine in order to preserve his decades-old high score. Jerry's new girlfriend is a sentence-finisher. Elaine takes a stand against meaningless office parties, then starts to miss the cake.

SEINFELD-ESE Sentence-finisher—someone who finishes your sentences for you.

DIRECTOR Andy Ackerman

TELEPLAY Gregg Kavet and Andy Robin; story: Gregg Kavet, Andy Robin, Steve Koren, Dan O'Keefe

GUEST CAST Julia Campbell (Lisi); Peter Stormare (Slippery Pete); Reuven Bar (Shlomo); Sam Shamshak (Sal); Wayne Wilderson (Walter); Mark Daniel Cade (Other Walter); Jack Esformes (Mike); Melissa Denton (Kobe); Oliver Muirhead (Lubeck); Drake Bell (Kenny)
RECURRING CAST John O'Hurley (J. Peterman)

175. "The Maid"
(April 30, 1998)

SUMMARY Jerry starts sleeping with his cleaning lady and she stops cleaning his apartment, even though he's still paying her. When Elaine requests a new phone number, she gets the new 646 area code with it. George wants a cool nickname but instead gets nerdy ones. Kramer's girlfriend moves downtown.

DIRECTOR Andy Ackerman
TELEPLAY Alec Berg, David Mandel, and Jeff Schaffer; story: Alec Berg, David Mandel, Jeff Schaffer, Kit Boss, Peter Mehlman
GUEST CAST Daniel Von Bargen (Kruger); Angela Featherstone (Cindy); Anthony Crivello (Maxwell); Markus Flanagan (Charles); Sam Whipple (Phone Guy #1); Kyle Colerider-Krugh (Phone Guy #2); Steve Franken (Brendan); Davenia McFadden (Coco); Damon Jones (Watkins); Chip Chinery (Co-Worker #1); Colin McClean (Coworker #2); Anthony Mangano (Fireman)

176. "The Puerto Rican Day"
(May 7, 1998)

SUMMARY Because of the Puerto Rican Day Parade, Jerry, Elaine, Kramer, and George get stuck in traffic on the way home from a Mets game. Elaine is desperate to make it home in time to watch 60 Minutes, her weekend wind-down program. Jerry and another driver get into a feud. George tries to make a movie audience laugh but is upstaged, and stalked, by a laser pointer. Kramer infuriates the Puerto Rican community when he accidentally sets their flag on fire.
OF SPECIAL NOTE NBC was forced to issue an apology to the Puerto Rican community, many members of which were offended by the use of the flag as a comic prop in the episode.

DIRECTOR Andy Ackerman
TELEPLAY Alec Berg, Jennifer Crittenden, Spike Feresten, Bruce Eric Kaplan, Gregg Kavet, Steve Koren, David Mandel, Dan O'Keefe, Andy Robin, and Jeff Schaffer

GUEST CAST Mario Joyner (Lamar); Dayton Callie (Cabbie); James Karen (Mr. Canterman); Helen Carey (Mrs. Christine Nyhart); Yul Vasquez (Bob); John Paragon (Cedric); Jenica Bergere (Leslie); Monica Allison (Gail); Marcelo Tubert (Father); Armando Molina (Amigo); Tom Agna (Gary); Tom Dahlgren (Priest); Bert Rosario (Man); Raoul N. Rizik (Parade Goer); Scott Conte (Sketch Guy); Mimi Cozzens (Mrs. Canterman); Alison Martin (Lucy); Marc Hirschfeld (Ellis); Chip Heller (Policeman)

177. "The Clip Episode"
(May 14, 1998)

SUMMARY Jerry looks back at nine years of memorable moments, ending with a series of bloopers.

OF SPECIAL NOTE This episode was forty-five minutes long.

DIRECTOR Andy Ackerman
TELEPLAY Darin Henry

178. "The Finale (Part 1)"
(May 14, 1998)

SUMMARY The new president at NBC gives Jerry and George a thirteen-episode deal on Jerry's old pilot. The gang decides to celebrate by going to Paris on the NBC corporate jet, only to find themselves stranded in a small Massachusetts town.

OF SPECIAL NOTE Episodes 178 and 179 originally aired as a one-hour special; counted separately in syndication.

DIRECTOR Andy Ackerman
TELEPLAY Larry David
GUEST CAST Peter Blood (Jay Crespi); David Byrd (Pharmacist); Steve Carlson (Captain Maddox); David Dunard (Guard); Donna Evans (Woman); Geoffrey C. Ewing (Bailiff); Warren Frost (Mr. [Henry] Ross); Keith Hernandez (Himself); Scott Jaeck (Officer Vogel); Wendle Josepher (Susie); Robert Katims (Mr. Deensfrei); Scott Klace (Guard); Bruce Mahler (Rabbi Glickman); Ed O'Ross (Det. Blake); Kevin Page (Stu Chermak); James Pickens Jr. (Det. Hudson); John Pinette (Howie); Victor Raider-Wexler (Dr. Wexler); James Rebhorn (DA Hoyt); Peter Riegert (Kimbrough); Geraldo Rivera (Himself); McNally Sagal (Carol); Gay Thomas (O'Neal); Myra Turley (Foreman); Jane Wells (Herself); Grace Zabriskie (Mrs. Ross); Van Epperson (Passerby); Jeff Johnson (Criminal); Sean Moran (Man); Dianne Turley Travis (Receptionist); Jim Zulevic (Bernie)

RECURRING CAST Estelle Harris (Estelle Costanza); Steve Hytner (Bania); Wayne Knight (Newman); Len Lesser (Uncle Leo); Barney Martin (Morty Seinfeld); Phil Morris (Jackie Chiles); John O'Hurley (J. Peterman); Liz Sheridan (Helen Seinfeld); Jerry Stiller (Frank Costanza); Patrick Warburton (David Puddy); Danny Woodburn (Mickey Abbott)

179. "The Finale (Part 2)"
(May 14, 1998)

SUMMARY Jerry, George, Kramer, and Elaine go on trial for breaking the new Good Samaritan law when they fail to help an obese man who was being robbed. During the trial, a succession of character witnesses recounts the groups' less-than-charitable acts of the past. The trial is presided over by Judge Art Vandelay, who gives them a sentence of one year behind bars. Jerry closes the series with a prison-themed monologue.

DIRECTOR Andy Ackerman
TELEPLAY Larry David
GUEST CAST Stanley Anderson (Judge Vandelay); Frances Bay (Mrs. Choate); Peter Blood (Jay Crespi); David Byrd (Pharmacist); Tony Carlin (Coworker); Steve Carlson (Captain Maddox); Melanie Chartoff (Robin); Brian Doyle-Murray (Mel Sanger); David Dunard (Guard); Geoffrey C. Ewing (Bailiff); Warren Frost (Mr. (Henry) Ross); Brian George (Babu Bhatt); Philip Baker Hall (Mr. Bookman); Teri Hatcher (Sidra); John Hayman (Bubble Boy); Keith Hernandez (Himself); Carlos Jacott (Pool Guy); Scott Jaeck (Officer Vogel); Wendle Josepher (Susie); Robert Katims (Mr. Deensfrei); Scott Klace (Guard); Janes Leeves (Marla); Bruce Mahler (Rabbi Glickman); Wendel Meldrum (Low-Talker); Sheree North (Babs); Ed O'Ross (Det. Blake); Kevin Page (Stu Chermak); James Pickens Jr. (Det. Hudson); John Pinette (Howie); Victor Raider-Wexler (Dr. Wexler); James Rebhorn (DA Hoyt); Geraldo Rivera (Himself); McNally Sagal (Carol); Miguel Sandoval (Marcelino); Reni Santoni (Poppie); Gay Thomas (O'Neal); Larry Thomas (Soup Nazi); Myra Turley (Foreman); Jane Wells (Herself); Grace Zabriskie (Mrs. Ross); Van Epperson (Passerby); Dianne Turley Travis (Receptionist); Jim Zulevic (Bernie)
RECURRING CAST Ian Ambercombie (Mr. Pitt); Richard Fancy (Lippman); Estelle Harris (Estelle Costanza); Richard Herd (Wilhelm); Steve Hytner (Bania); Wayne Knight (Newman); Len Lesser (Uncle Leo); Barney Martin (Morty Seinfeld); Phil Morris (Jackie Chiles); John O'Hurley (J. Peterman); Liz Sheridan (Helen Seinfeld); Jerry Stiller (Frank Costanza); Patrick Warburton (David Puddy); Danny Woodburn (Mickey Abbott)

INDEX